Introduction to Moral Theology

CATHOLIC MORAL THOUGHT

General Editor: Romanus Cessario, O.P.

Introduction to Moral Theology

Revised Edition

Romanus Cessario, O.P.

The Catholic University of America Press

Washington, D.C.

The paper used in this publication meets the minimum requirements
of American National Standards for Information Science—
Permanence of Paper for Printed Library Materials, ANSI z39.48-
1984.

∞

Library of congress cataloging-in-publication data
Cessario, Romanus.
Introduction to moral theology / Romanus Cessario, O.P. —
Revised edition.
pages cm. — (Catholic moral thought)
Includes bibliographical references and index.
ISBN 978-0-8132-2131-1 (pbk. : alk. paper)
1. Christian ethics.   2. Catholic Church—Doctrines.   I. Title.
BJ1249.C29 2013
241'.042—dc23   2013018060

For
Bernard Francis Cardinal Law
Archbishop of Boston
on the occasion of his seventieth birthday

Contents

Preface to the Revised Edition

The revised edition of *Introduction to Moral Theology* owes much to the assiduous work of Reverend Monsignor Laurence W. McGrath, former librarian at Saint John's Seminary, Brighton, Massachusetts. This distinguished Boston cleric has devoted the better part of his long priesthood to the intellectual formation of Catholic seminarians. I also acknowledge the generous and fraternal assistance of Cajetan Cuddy, O.P., who patiently assisted in making the revisions.

Since the publication of *Introduction to Moral Theology* in 2001, the Catholic University of America Press's Catholic Moral Thought Series has completed the first phase of its program.[1] The series now includes individual volumes for the core curriculum stipulated by the ecclesiastical authorities: "fundamental moral theology, medical-moral ethics, sexual morality, and social ethics."[2] As we approach the twentieth anniversary of the issuance of *Veritatis splendor*, seminarians and other students of Catholic theology now enjoy access to a comprehensive presentation of Catholic moral thought that accords with the principles set down in Blessed Pope John Paul II's historic encyclical that treats "certain fundamental questions of the Church's teaching."

This first revised edition appears during the "Year of Faith" that Pope Benedict XVI announced to mark the fiftieth anniversary of the opening of the Second Vatican Council (1962–65) and the thirtieth anniversary of the publication of the *Catechism of the Catholic Church* (1983). In his Apostolic Letter announcing the Year of Faith, Pope Benedict stated that "the teaching of the Catechism on the moral life acquires its full meaning if

---

1. Some public reactions to the 2001 edition may be found in the following discussion and reviews: "Book Symposium" in *Nova et Vetera* (English) 2 (2004): 169–210 and John M. Grondelski, *Homiletic & Pastoral Review* (October 2002): 75–76; Thomas Hibbs, *The Thomist* 66 (2002): 629–32; Michael Dauphinais, *Nova et Vetera* (English) 1 (2003): 222–24; Christopher Thompson, *Pro Ecclesia* 12 (2003): 501–2; Carlo Leget, *Bijdragen* 64 (2003): 230.

2. United States Conference of Catholic Bishops, *Program of Priestly Formation*, 5th ed. (2006), no. 204.

placed in relationship with faith, liturgy and prayer."[3] And on the Feast of the Most Holy Trinity, Pope Francis reminded us that love, the theological virtue that abides beyond faith and beyond hope, stands at the center of our Christian faith and life: " 'God is love.' His is not a sentimental, emotional kind of love but the love of the Father who is the origin of all life, the love of the Son who dies on the Cross and is raised, the love of the Spirit who renews human beings and the world." The Catholic Moral Thought series aims to present Catholic moral teaching so as to encourage in everyone full participation in these Christian mysteries that Pope Francis summarizes.

---

3. Apostolic Letter, "Motu Proprio Data," *Porta Fidei* of the Supreme Pontiff Benedict XVI for the Indiction of the Year of Faith, no. 11.

Acknowledgments

"To live is Christ" (Phil 1:21). This book represents the fruit of two decades of teaching moral theology in Catholic settings. I acknowledge especially the support and invaluable assistance given, most recently, by the Reverend Monsignors Richard G. Lennon, Rector, and Laurence W. McGrath, Librarian, at Saint John's Seminary (Brighton, Massachusetts). Sister Susan Heinemann, O.P., Monastery of Our Lady of Grace (North Guilford, Connecticut) transformed the text into a useful instrument by her meticulous indexing. My gratitude to her extends also to those other Dominican nuns who have been a source of special encouragement. The initiative for this volume and the series it initiates came from Dr. David J. McGonagle at the Catholic University of America Press. His co-workers, the Mmes. Susan Needham and Elizabeth Benevides, have exhibited a spirit of dedication that transcends what professional responsibility imposes. This volume is dedicated to His Eminence, Bernard Cardinal Law, Archbishop of Boston, who has helped so many people throughout the world learn the meaning of "to live is Christ," especially by his promotion of the *Catechism of the Catholic Church*. The ninth anniversary of its publication this year coincides with the Cardinal's seventieth birthday. *Ad multos annos.*

Brighton, Massachusetts
19 March 2001
Feast of Saint Joseph, Patron of the Universal Church

Introduction

The present volume introduces a series of textbooks which aims to provide upper division and graduate students with a well-rounded and readable account of the principal branches of moral theology according to the way that the discipline has actually developed and is now practiced within the Roman Catholic tradition.[1]

Each volume in the Catholic Moral Thought Series is designed to provide students with a comprehensive presentation of both the principles of Christian conduct and the specific teachings and precepts for fulfilling the requirements of the Christian life. The authoritative statements of the Roman Catholic Church supply the normative principles for determining what constitutes these basic elements of moral theology. Although the several authors who contribute to the series have been trained in various approaches to and outlooks on Christian ethics and moral theology, they each agree that it is impossible to develop successfully a moral theology without first holding by divine and Catholic faith to the once and for all divine revelation that the Church of Christ safeguards for every generation. Soundly based, then, in the teaching of the Church, the volumes of the series will set out in depth, in a manner and style suitable for scholars, students, and general readers, the basic principles of Catholic moral thought and the application of those principles within areas of ethical concern that are of paramount importance today.

For theological reasoning to illuminate honestly and explicate adequately the general principles of ethical decision-making requires that moral theologians remain faithful to their ecclesial vocation. What is handed over in divine revelation not only provides the first principles for

1. Though each volume in the Catholic Moral Thought Series treats a specific area of moral theology, the volumes complement one another. References to the present text will be found in subsequent volumes of the series so that the reader will possess an easy way to cross reference topics and undertake a more developed and unified research. Each volume refers readers to the secondary literature so that both student and teacher can pursue in a fuller way those specialized topics that would be impossible to summarize within the scope of the present project.

developing a moral theology, it also and antecedently commits one to a particular view of the Church. "For the believer," explains Cardinal Joseph Ratzinger, "the Church is not a sociological subject created by human agreement, but a truly new subject called into being by the Word and in the Holy Spirit."[2] Theologians enjoy the responsibility of helping the Church safeguard the deposit of faith *(depositum fidei)*, so that the bonds of unity in the apostolic faith will continue to grow extensively and develop coherently. The authors who contribute to this series seek to fulfill this mission for the benefit of those who will use the volumes of Catholic Moral Thought, normally but not necessarily under the tutelage of a person trained in theology.

In order to introduce this series, I want first to say something about the current climate, at once cultural and ideological, that attends any consideration of moral theology today; secondly I will describe the series generically; and finally I will offer a summary-analysis of the present volume.

I

It has been observed that the Catholic moral theologian is obliged to carry out in the midst of a largely alien cultural environment the responsibility confided to him or her by the Church. Because of the shaping forces active in contemporary culture, insisting on the perennial validity of norms for human conduct, especially those precepts that, because of their necessary relation to fostering the good of the human person, allow for no exception, has generated a challenging project. Even secular authors recognize both the dominant cultural attitudes and the risks inherent in allowing them to remain unchallenged. For instance, Alan Wolfe has observed that while most Americans want to decide for themselves what is right, good, and meaningful, this kind of autonomy risks weakening the institutions that make civil life possible.[3] When one accedes to the abandonment of metaphysical study that the ultimate human questions impose on the human spirit, he pays the price.

2. See his *"Deus locutus est nobis in Filio:* Some Reflections on Subjectivity, Christology, and the Church," in *Proclaiming the Truth of Jesus Christ. Papers from the Vallombrosa Meeting* (Washington, D.C.: United States Catholic Conference, 2000), p. 23.

3. Alan Wolfe, "The Pursuit of Autonomy," *The New York Times Magazine,* May 7, 2000, pp. 53–56: "No strong God. No strong rules. No strong superiors, moral or otherwise.... Most Americans want to decide for themselves what is right, good, and meaningful."

One conclusion that has emerged among some theologians active in the post-conciliar period is that Enlightenment views about autonomy are difficult, if not impossible, to reconcile with the demands of Christian discipleship. Furthermore, it is little appreciated to what extent peculiarly modern versions of individual liberty are able to thwart the power inherent in moral action to unite human beings in achieving common goals that embody the goods of excellence. The Gospel announces that human communion achieves its summit in a divinely initiated communion of charity. This means that the deleterious effects of an alleged conflict between enjoying freedom and pursing the good threaten directly what the Christian believer holds most dear, namely, life in Christ. As the device for the Vatican newspaper, *L'Osservatore Romano*, reminds us, the Church of Christ is committed to ensuring that "to each his own" will not prevail ("*unicuique suum non praevalebunt*").

Exaggerated conceptions of human freedom, when allowed to govern a Christian's spiritual life, undermine even those moral actions strengthened by the virtue of charity. When reliance on God is removed from the practice of the moral life, the theological virtues are impeded, as the *Catechism* says, from providing "the foundation of Christian moral activity" (1813). The confusion that arises from competing claims about what constitutes human freedom and what perfects human nature intrudes into every area of the Christian life.[4] Because of this situation, the need for sound instruction in each branch of moral theology acquires a new urgency.

The great advantage that an authentically Christian moral theology affords the believer derives principally from the fact that moral teaching is located within a larger picture of saving doctrine. As the very ordering of the *Catechism of the Catholic Church* suggests, determining and living the truth about human action supposes two other features of Christian faith and practice. The Christian moral life follows upon belief in the articles of faith articulated in the Christian creed and participation in the sacraments of faith celebrated in the Christian Church. The unity of the mystery of God, represented by Christ who teaches us about both the Father in heaven and the right norms for human conduct, ultimately ensures that people come to recognize that freedom of every kind—personal, do-

---

4. *Veritatis splendor*, nos. 35ff., explicitly acknowledges this development: "The modern concern for the claims of autonomy has not failed to exercise an influence also in the sphere of Catholic moral theology" (no. 35).

mestic, political, ecclesial—remains but an instrumental good. We know, moreover, that it is the Church herself that overcomes the seemingly insurmountable confines of human subjectivity by putting the human person in contact with the ground of reality which exists prior to the human creature.[5] Because moral truth conforms to God's very own wisdom, it remains a hallmark of Catholic moral instruction that it never adopts the shrill tones of high-minded moralizing. Following the example of Christ, then, the Catholic moralist welcomes the contemporary scene, for it presents a challenge that enlightens even as it burdens.

II

The books that compose this series illuminate the moral life as it unfolds within the parameters set by Catholic moral teaching. If the individual volumes exhibit different, though complementary, theological styles, the explanation lies in the fact that the authors agree on the principles that ensure an adequate moral methodology. They recognize, furthermore, that the density of Catholic doctrine allows for different modes of exposition, provided that the integrity of the truth, as judged by those who enjoy the authority to protect that truth, remains intact. To put it differently, it is agreed that one can foster communion of thought without insisting on a dull and repetitious uniformity, provided that the diversity of theological expression does not compromise the integrity of the Gospel's teaching.[6] Variety flourishes within true catholic communion.

Because we are persuaded of the intrinsic fruitfulness of authentic theological investigation, the authors who contribute to this series eschew a rigidly stylized account of moral theology. In particular, the series does not intend to replicate the style found in the manuals of standard theology that dominated during the four-hundred-year period before the Second Vatican Council. To address, moreover, the moral problems that the Church faces at the start of the twenty-first century from within the methodological confines of a narrowly moralistic framework still proves fruitless, even though appeals for a repristination of post-Tridentine casuistry are heard from some quarters. In the documents of the Church, we

5. See Ratzinger, "Some Reflections on Subjectivity," p. 23.

6. This point is developed in the 1990 "Instruction on the Ecclesial Vocation of the Theologian" from the Congregation for the Doctrine of the Faith, esp. chap. IV, "The Magisterium and Theology."

cannot find any warrant for new forms of casuistry. The 1993 encyclical letter *Veritatis splendor* presented Catholic theologians with a vision for moral theology that fulfilled the criteria that the New Testament itself supplies for judging the authentic transmission of divine truth: "And [Jesus] said to them, 'Therefore every scribe who has been trained for the kingdom of heaven is like a householder who brings out of his treasure what is new and what is old'" (Mt 13:52). But the encyclical made no effort to restore the complicated moral-juridical structures of the casuists. It is illusory, in any event, to envisage a return to post-Tridentine casuistry, since the relationships between the Church and the secular political orders that enabled the Church's efforts in the area of morals during the baroque and early modern periods no longer exist.

The series illustrates that one can practice a sound moral theology by employing fully and honestly the classical sources that from the beginning have nourished the discipline, and at the same time honor the Magisterium as a guide on contemporary problems and issues. The important work of Father Servais Pinckaers illuminates the historical background to and the key methodological elements of what can be styled a Second Vatican Council moral theology; it will come as no surprise that the sketch for such a moral theology resembles what we find in the New Testament, the early Church Fathers, notably Saint Augustine, and the Medieval scholastics, especially Saint Thomas Aquinas.[7] The authors who contribute to the Catholic Moral Thought Series observe what Pope John Paul II wrote in *Fides et ratio* (no. 68):

In the New Testament, human life is much less governed by prescription than in the Old Testament. Life in the Spirit leads believers to a freedom and responsibility which surpass the law. Yet the Gospel and the apostolic writings still set forth both general principles of Christian conduct and specific teachings and precepts. In order to apply these to the particular circumstances of individual and communal life, Christians must be able fully to engage their conscience and the power of their reason.

The volumes that are included in this series aim to assist careful and assiduous readers to carry out this engagement, which, it should be recalled, forms an exercise intimately connected to their salvation.

---

7. See especially his *The Sources of Christian Ethics*, trans. Sr. Mary Thomas Noble, O.P. (Washington, D.C.: The Catholic University of America Press, 1995).

III

This first volume begins the series by presenting an account of fundamental principles that must govern any study of Catholic moral theology.[8] The promulgation in 1993 of John Paul II's encyclical letter *Veritatis splendor*, which represents the first time that the Magisterium set forth in detail the fundamental elements of the Church's moral teaching, provided strong impetus for not only the publication of this volume but also the inauguration of the series. Earlier, the promulgation of the *Catechism of the Catholic Church* also made clear the need for an integral presentation of the Church's basic moral teaching. *Introduction to Moral Theology* affords its benevolent reader the opportunity to return to these two foundational documents of the post-conciliar Magisterium of Pope John Paul II, which serve, as it were, as two companion volumes that should be consulted frequently while undertaking this introductory study.

Another source for the moral theology found in these pages comes from a figure in the Church's theological tradition whose contribution has achieved a permanent place in Catholic theology. The realist conception of moral theology that controls these pages finds its inspiration and first major elaboration in the work of St. Thomas Aquinas. His "enduring originality" in expounding the fundamental harmony between the knowledge of faith and the knowledge of philosophy has been repeatedly confirmed by the Church.[9] One does not easily insert the moral realism that Aquinas developed in the course of his theological appropriation of the treasures of ancient philosophy into the categories that we find em-

8. Sometimes English usage, as illustrated in the translation of Pinckaers' *Les sources de la morale chretienne*, makes it preferable to speak about Christian or theological ethics instead of moral theology. Of course, it is important to underline that Catholic moral theology is not a sectarian enterprise that interests only Catholic believers. However, European-trained scholars sometimes consider the difference between moral theology and Christian ethics more than just a question of nomenclature to the extent that the word "ethics" signals commitment to a philosophical model different from that on which Roman Catholic moral theology has traditionally relied. In the United States, however, this allusion is largely absent, and so the present volume of moral theology serves also as a primer in what American usage designates Christian or theological ethics. Thus, my *The Moral Virtues and Theological Ethics* (Notre Dame, Ind.: The University of Notre Dame Press, 1991).

9. For the most recent confirmation of this evaluation, see *Fides et ratio*, no. 43. Jude P. Dougherty offers a brief but comprehensive introduction to the tradition in his article "Thomism," in *Encyclopedia of Applied Ethics*, vol. 4 (Academic Press, 1998), pp. 365–72.

ployed by many schools of contemporary philosophical ethics. For instance, the moral realism of Aquinas remains something entirely different from the moral realism espoused by G. E. Moore and British intuitionists, and it certainly does not in any way resemble the emotive theory of morals that sought to break out of the epistemological impasse created by Moore and his followers. On the contrary, Aquinas's realism flows from what Pope John Paul II has described as "the fundamental role of truth in the moral field."[10]

The kind of moral realism that distinguishes the Roman Catholic tradition recognizes that "moral theology requires a sound philosophical vision of human nature and society as well as of the general principles of ethical decision making."[11] This means that realist moral theology proceeds on the basis of convictions about the human being, about the world, and about being that depend on objective truth as its foundation. Aquinas expresses these convictions with a consistent metaphysical rigor that distinguishes him from theologians who rely exclusively on other disciplines such as history, literature, various forms of idealism, or analytical philosophy as their preferred vehicles for theological discourse.

Many persons consider Aquinas's theology to be oddly out of tune with contemporary outlooks and preferences; they judge in particular that his moral theology remains so inextricably bound up with suppositions about the concrete structure of the human person that it is impossible to relate his claims to questions that occupy moral philosophers and theologians.[12] Today, these same persons frequently find it difficult to reconcile Aquinas's convictions about a God-given natural order of things with the cultural preference for freedom to create a new and better world independent of God. The present volume, however, proceeds on the assumption that the plan of divine Providence is both wise and loving, and that submission of all things to God results not in their destruction but in their flourishing.

10. See *Fides et ratio*, no. 98. The Pope goes on to assert: "In order to fulfill its mission, moral theology must turn to a philosophical ethics which looks to the truth of the good, to an ethics which is neither subjectivist nor utilitarian." For a study of this theme in the writings of the Karol Wojtyla/John Paul II, see Jaroslaw Kupczak, O.P., *Destined for Liberty* (Washington, D.C.: The Catholic University of America Press, 2000).

11. *Fides et ratio*, no. 68.

12. It is impossible to address these methodological questions within the objectives imposed by this series. For an initial discussion, see Alasdair MacIntyre, *Dependent Rational Animals. Why Human Beings Need the Virtues* (Chicago and La Salle, Ill.: Open Court, 1998).

Other critics wonder why Aquinas does not more frequently and directly appeal in the course of his moral theology to the person and the work of Christ. There are several important reasons why Aquinas structured his moral theology in the way that he did, but suffice it to remark that to the extent that his moral theology aims to place the human person into the concrete rhythms of God's wisdom and love, Thomist moral theology exhibits in fact an eminently Christological dimension. On the cross at Calvary, Christ embodies the supremely religious man. His death and all the mysteries of Christ's life make it possible for the human race to practice that obedience to the divine will that restores and perfects the whole of creation.

The volume is divided into five chapters. Chapter One discusses three topics that serve to situate within a broad theological context what is said in the remaining chapters. The chapter begins with an overview of theology that governs what in the following chapters develops. Specifically, it argues that theology is not the religious equivalent of a philosophical discipline. On the contrary, a truly theological discipline can proceed only as a dependent or subordinate study. Theology exists only because God has communicated to the human race knowledge about himself and about divine things, and because God endowed the human creature with the capacity to reflect on this revealed truth. From this perspective it becomes clear that theology does not so much seek to discover new truths as to ponder more deeply the truths that have been already revealed. For this reason, theology may be described as a *cogitatio fidei,* a thinking about the faith. This *cogitatio* occurs within the believer once the natural activities of knowledge and love are informed by the truths of divine faith. As a result, every believer in some measure becomes either a contemplative, or a theologian, or, what is best, both.

Chapter One also considers the pre-ethical foundations of moral action. Philosophical anthropology can teach us a great deal about the human person, but moral theology must proceed on the basis of the biblical revelation that the human person is created in the image of God. The doctrine of *imago Dei,* developed from the Genesis account of the creation of man in the image of God, supplies the theological anthropology that governs and shapes the following discussion of human action and purpose. Moral theology begins by taking seriously the givens of the Catholic faith: "This one true God, by his goodness and almighty power, not with the intention of increasing his happiness, nor indeed of obtaining happiness, but in order to manifest his perfection by the good things which he bestows on what he creates, by an absolutely free plan, together from the beginning of time brought into being from nothing the twofold created order, that is the spiritual and the bodily...."[13] Creation grounds the meaning of the divine image that man enjoys, even though this free and rational creature remains open to a destiny that separates him from all other living things on earth. *Gaudium et spes* 24 refers to the only creature God has loved for himself.

Realist moral theology views the human person as set between God and God. This means that God remains not only the Creator of each human being but also the final perfective End for each man. While it is important to know in whose image the human creature has been created, it is more important to grasp the high destiny that belongs to the human person by reason of a gracious call to everlasting communion with the Persons of the Blessed Trinity. There is a startling truth that emerges from the fact that each person on earth is called to enjoy a life that exceeds the reach of his or her native human energies. Dr. Steven Long has developed an appealing metaphor to describe the critical distinction between what is found in us by nature and what can come to be in us through the gift of salvific grace:

The similitude of the stained-glass window illuminated by the sun's rays well bespeaks the character of the doctrine of the obediential potency as applied to the relation of nature and grace. The stained-glass window, were it cognizant, could not 'know what it was missing' were it never to irradiate its brighter colors under the influence of the sun. It would be a window, still, and function as part of a structure—though it would, in a given respect, not be fulfilled. It would be what it is, not fail to be part of the whole structure of which it would form an integral part, nor lack its own participation in the good of the whole as a specific perfection. Yet its nature stands properly revealed only under the extrinsic causality of the sun's illumination: seeing it so illumined, we know what stained glass truly is for.[14]

Moral theology is more about completion than it is about choice. So at

---

13. See the Constitution on Divine Revelation of the First Vatican Council, *Dei Filius*, 1 (DS 3002) cited in *CCC*, no. 293. Here and throughout this volume, quotations of documents of the councils are taken from *Decrees of the Ecumenical Councils*, ed. Norman P. Tanner, S.J., vol. 2, *Trent to Vatican II* (Sheed & Ward/Georgetown University Press, 1990).

14. "On the Possibility of a Purely Natural End for Man," *The Thomist* 64 (2000): 211–37 at 236.

the very start of the discussion of human action, this volume anticipates the final end or completion of the human person, which is both a fulfillment of human nature as such and a fulfillment of the new nature that the Christian receives in Baptism.

Chapter Two develops in more detail the theme of moral realism, especially by explaining the place that natural law retains in Roman Catholic moral theology. Perhaps no concept is more misunderstood throughout the period immediately following the Second Vatican Council than natural law.[15] Every attempt has been made to interpret the natural law in a way that leaves this participation of the rational creature in the eternal law without any relation to the God-given objective truth found in creation. What had been often forgotten in these discussions, however, is that natural law in Roman Catholic moral theology should not be treated in complete isolation from other theological topics.[16] If one takes seriously the relationship of natural law to God himself, more specifically, to what is called the "eternal law," then it becomes very clear that natural law associates the human creature and his actions in a distinct way with the divine origin and exemplar of right human conduct. When one agrees that the foundations of all moral truth abide in God himself and reflect his wisdom, then moral realism appears in a new and fascinating theological light. Nothing is more real for the human creature than to seek conformity with the truth that exists in God. So much does divine truth govern the rule of morality that even bad actions committed out of invincible ignorance thwart the good of the human person and in some way diminish the dignity of the person who performs them.

15. Discussed, for instance, in my "Why Aquinas Locates Natural Law within the *Sacra Doctrina*," at the Conference on St. Thomas Aquinas and the Natural Law Tradition, Sacred Heart Major Seminary & Ave Maria School of Law, Detroit, Michigan, 2–4 June 2000.

16. See *Veritatis splendor*, no. 45: "Even if moral-theological reflection usually distinguishes between the positive or revealed law of God and the natural law, and, within the economy of salvation, between the "old" and the "new" law, it must not be forgotten that these and other useful distinctions always refer to that law whose author is the one and the same God and which is always meant for man. The different ways in which God, acting in history, cares for the world and for mankind are not mutually exclusive; on the contrary, they support each other and intersect. They have their origin and goal in the eternal, wise and loving counsel whereby God predestines men and women 'to be conformed to the image of his Son' (Rom 8:29). God's plan poses no threat to man's genuine freedom; on the contrary, the acceptance of God's plan is the only way to affirm that freedom."

Chapter Three examines the origin and structure of specific instances of virtuous behavior. Natural law represents a dynamic concept; since the nature of every living being is to act in accord with its nature, it is impossible to consider a pure or abstract human nature. The human person by nature is destined for committing actions. To put it differently, the image of God found in each human creature could never remain inert or actionless without traducing its native intelligence and freedom. To enjoy a human nature means to possess the principles of human action. The wellspring of human activity is found in the voluntary, which, when impeded by opposing factors, inhibits the human person from acting in a fully moral way. Roman Catholic moral theology acknowledges that certain factors can inhibit the movement of authentic freedom in a human person and so result in a diminishment of culpability. Because they impede the full realization of human moral action, these factors are called the "enemies" of the voluntary. An account of these factors is indispensable to a full analysis of concrete human action, which must observe the obvious circumstances of everyday life, especially when persons do things that are difficult to reconcile with the choices of deliberate freedom. At the same time, realist moral theology does not make a judgment of culpability the only consideration in its evaluation of a human action. Virtue perfects not only an action but also the character of the actor who performs the action.

Chapter Three provides an extended analysis of the execution of virtuous actions through the instrumentality of the virtue of prudence. As an intellectual virtue, prudence requires formation through knowledge. Only informed prudence ensures that we commit actions that conform to the good of the human person. Counsel too forms an indispensable part of the prudent person's life. Among the various sources of ethical wisdom that are available to the Christian believer, the guidance offered through the Magisterium holds a privileged place because of the divine warrant that it enjoys. Some contemporary moral theologians have adopted a skittish attitude toward the Magisterium, whereas others concede that what the Church teaches sets up an ideal, but do not agree that the ideal can be easily, if ever, reached. This volume adopts neither viewpoint. Instead it aims to show how the Magisterium helps everyone discover the truth about being human. This claim is not surprising since the God who created man is the same God upon whom the Magisterium depends.

A brief excursus appended to this chapter explains the theory of divine and human causality that substantiates the prudential account of human action contained in Chapter Three.

Veritatis splendor (see nos. 71ff.) acknowledges that moral theology in the Roman Catholic tradition is impossible without a proper understanding of teleology, and at the same time, the encyclical cautions against various forms of teleologisms that distort the relationship of man's freedom with the authentic good. Chapter Four considers how one may determine what constitutes a good human act. In particular, the chapter treats the "form" of the moral good, or what makes something a perfective end for the human person. It is the actual embracing of these good moral ends that perfects the human person. Warrant for this discussion comes from the present-day practice of the Church as much as from the historical contributions of St. Thomas Aquinas. The documents of the Church have retained the classical doctrine of objects, ends, and circumstances as the three considerations that govern analysis of the moral act. "A morally good act requires the goodness of the object, of the end, and of the circumstances together" (*CCC*, no. 1755). It is imperative to identify the right interrelationship of these factors in order to ensure a correct judgment about human behavior. Chapter Four concludes with a discussion of teleology, virtue, and heavenly beatitude as well as some mistakes that, unfortunately, remain too common about reaching it.

Chapter Five completes the introduction to moral theology by considering the Christian believer as a moral agent within a life of Christian community and commitment. What are the spiritual endowments that make it possible for him or her to lead a Christian life? Three specific graces are held up for consideration: the Christian virtues, the gifts of the Holy Spirit, and the grace of true freedom lived in a rhythm of conversion and reconciliation. The Christian virtues develop in a person as the result of the action of God's grace. They are part of the gifts that each one receives at Baptism, and which enable the believer to grow into the likeness of Christ. They may be designated as the virtues of the imitation of Christ, provided it is recalled that these virtues come not as a result of human striving or initiative, but as free gifts of divine grace that shape human freedom, setting it more and more upon its Godly perfection.

God is never outdone in generosity. Besides the virtues, the Christian believer also receives special gifts of the Holy Spirit that aid the virtues. These gifts correspond to the particular needs that persons experience in the course of facing the difficulties of human life: complex situations require the gift of counsel, exaggerated threats to our well-being require fortitude, the high demands of justice lived in community, not to mention the complexity that fulfilling the law of justice introduces, require piety, and the difficult and sometimes strong circumstances of sense attractions require fear of the Lord. The gifts provide for the complexities of human life without sacrificing the fullness of moral truth that is embodied in the virtues. Instead of compromise with divine truth, the gifts of the Holy Spirit ensure a perfect fulfillment of the law.

The final section of Chapter Five offers an account of human freedom that represents an established theological reading of the New Testament. The treatment depends especially on the Pauline doctrine that Christian freedom enters into human life as a gift of divine grace. Because of the weakness that original sin introduces into the world, the realization of this freedom is impossible apart from the offer of forgiveness and reconciliation. The volume closes by pointing to the sacramental life of the Church which remains the concrete and historical context within which the authors of this series wish to situate the requirements of the moral life.

A short Appendix reviews some of the features of classical casuistry, which governed the practice of moral theology from about the middle of the sixteenth century until the 1960s, roughly from the Council of Trent (1545–1563) until the close of the Second Vatican Council in 1965.

Introduction to Moral Theology

CHAPTER ONE

The Starting Point for Christian Moral Theology

Introduction to Moral Theology proceeds on the view that the best introduction to a theological understanding of the moral life proclaimed in the name of Christ by the Catholic Church is one rooted in the moral realism developed, among others, by Saint Thomas Aquinas.[1] This text presents moral theology as integrally united with dogmatic and spiritual theology, as the systematically ordered study of the journey of a human person, made in the image and likeness of God, back to the Father. It is held that the moral realism identified with the Thomist tradition and found in the ethical writings of Pope John Paul II not only represents what is best in the Catholic moral tradition, but also provides the most promising way to overcome the confusions and some of the vacuity characteristic of much of Christian ethics today. In particular, the following pages point out emphatically the resemblances between the moral realism of Aquinas and the encyclical letter *Veritatis splendor*. Creation and eschatology inform the broad vision within which practitioners of moral realism situate their ethical investigations. In order properly to treat ethical issues, however, it is first necessary to provide a view of theology, of the human person, and of the human person's final end.

Sacra Doctrina and Moral Theology

In order better to serve the nearby papal administration, the Dominican authorities shortly before the feast of the Exaltation of the Holy Cross in 1261 sent Friar Thomas Aquinas to the Italian city of Orvieto,

1. In this present study, "moral realism" refers to the classical notion of metaphysical realism in the tradition of St. Thomas as represented, for example, by the work of Joseph de Finance, *Etre et agir dans la philosophie de saint Thomas* (Paris: Beauchesne, 1945). While distinct from the more restricted, specialized discussions amongst contemporary

where he took up residence and teaching responsibilities in the local Dominican convent.[2] At that time, Pope Urban IV was especially concerned to restore full ecclesial union between the Roman See and the separated churches of the East.[3] Because the development of common theological understandings between the Latins and the Greeks would further this objective, the study of oriental theology held a high place on the agenda of theologians in the service of the papal curia.[4] But for many of these scholars, including Thomas Aquinas, this sort of work meant that they had to employ Latin translations of Greek philosophical and theological texts.[5] While the efforts of the thirteenth-century popes failed to heal the schism which had begun symbolically in 1054 under the Constantinople Patriarch Michael Cerularius, the Latin Church nevertheless gained some

---

philosophical and religious ethicists, this tradition of realism nonetheless remains pertinent to them. For such discussions, see, for example, Franklin I. Gamwell, "Moral Realism and Religion," *Journal of Religion* 73 (1993): 475–95, criticizing anti-realist theories of truth such as S. W. Blackburn, "Moral Realism," in *Morality and Moral Reasoning*, ed. John Casey (London: Methuen, 1971), pp. 101–24.

2. Jean-Pierre Torrell, O.P., *Initiation à saint Thomas d'Aquin, Sa personne et son oeuvre* (Paris: Éditions du Cerf, 1993), pp. 171–206, discusses this period in Aquinas's career and the principal writings. English edition: *Saint Thomas Aquinas. Vol. 1, The Person and His Work*, trans. Robert Royal (Washington, D.C.: The Catholic University of America Press, 1996), pp. 117 ff.

3. For a study of papal efforts in the thirteenth century toward healing the schism with the Churches of the East, see Martin Jugie, *Le schisme byzantin* (Paris: Lethielleux, 1941), pp. 246–70.

4. Aquinas, for example, responded by composing his *Contra errores Graecorum, ad Urbanum IV Pontificem Maximum* to a papal request for an expert opinion concerning a questionable compilation of texts from the Greek Fathers on the *filioque* and other doctrines disputed by the Churches of the East. Aquinas's work was well received by some in the Byzantine tradition: "Oh Thomas," wrote a fifteenth-century patriarch of Constantinople, "if you had only been born in the East rather than in the West! What an Orthodox you would have been! For then you would have been as sound in your thought about the procession of the Holy Spirit as you are when you speak so well about all the other [doctrines]." These words of George Scholarius, Gennadius II, (c.1405–c.1472) are cited in Jaroslav Pelikan, *Confessor between East and West: A Portrait of Ukranian Cardinal Josyf Slipyj.* (Grand Rapids, Mich.: Eerdmans, 1990), p. 116.

5. If we accept the analysis of Erasmus of Rotterdam (c. 1469–1536), Aquinas was shaped by the educational outlooks of his period. See Erasmus's *Annotationes in Novum Testamentum* (1515), Basileae, fol. 228v: "Et quid aliud potuisset Thomas, alioqui vir bono ingenio, qui ea temporum natus est, in quibus bonae litterae omnes et Latinae et Graecae et Hebraicae tamquam sepultae et emortuae ignotae jacebant…."

advantage from the research and translations which Pope Urban IV had initiated and supported.[6]

A Scheme: *Exitus-Reditus*

The intellectual development of Thomas Aquinas particularly benefitted from his exposure to the texts of classical Greek authors. In fact, as a result of the translations provided in all likelihood by his Dominican confrère William of Moerbeke, Aquinas for the first time came into immediate contact with early Greek religious and philosophical literature.[7] There are reasons to suppose that Aquinas uncovered the Neoplatonist theme of the *exitus-reditus* while studying certain works of the Athenian syncretist Proclus (410–485).[8] This construct, which envisions a movement composed of both downward "procession" and upward "return," proves useful in at least three different areas of philosophical and theo-

6. See Kurt Koch, "Recent Ecumenical Progress and Future Prospects," *Origins* 41 (November 24, 2011): 96: "The great schism … is usually associated with the year 1054, which is of course to be understood more symbolically than historically."

7. The German Dominican Ignatius Eschmann explains: "It seems that in the first part of [Aquinas's] Italian sojourn, in the years of Urban IV, Thomas, in a way, discovered Greek theology, the part it played in theology, and the consequences which would ensue, if it were neglected, as indeed it was neglected, in a theology that was nourished by Latin thought." The text is cited without reference in James A. Weisheipl, *Friar Thomas D'Aquino. His Life, Thought, and Works* (Washington, D.C.: The Catholic University of America Press, 1983), p. 173. Several older studies discuss the influence of Greek thought on the intellectual development of Thomas Aquinas; for example, I. Backes, *Die Christologie des hl. Thomas von Aquin und die griechischen Kirchenväter* (Paderborn: Schöningh, 1931). Also, Gottfried Geenen, O.P., "The Council of Chalcedon in the Theology of Saint Thomas," in *From an Abundant Spring* (New York: P. J. Kenedy & Sons, 1952), pp. 172–217. R.-A. Gauthier closely reexamined the collaboration between Thomas Aquinas and William of Moerbeke and arrived at a modest estimate of their mutual dependence. For a summary of this research, see Torrell, pp. 253–59 (ET, pp. 174–78).

8. Considered the greatest scholastic of antiquity, the fifth-century author Proclus possessed a wide knowledge concerning the philosophies of Plato and Aristotle and of his Neoplatonic predecessors which he combined with an enthusiasm for all sorts of religious beliefs. Weisheipl considers Aquinas's exposure to Proclus a critical moment in the former's intellectual development: "The most important work William translated while living with Thomas at Viterbo was the *Elementatio theologica* of Proclus. It was completed on May 18, 1268. Through this translation Thomas came to realize the true Platonic source of *Liber de causis*, which he commented on later" (p. 235). On the other hand, R.-A. Gauthier, "Quelques questions à propos du commentaire de S. Thomas sur le *De anima*," *Angelicum* 51 (1974): 419–72, has argued that Aquinas was actually in Rome during this period.

logical inquiry. *Exitus-reditus* can be used, first, to account for the production and final end of all reality; second, to support a logic of affirmation and negation about the highest realities; third, to describe a process in the human person of spiritual purification and union with the divine.[9] In each of these three areas of enquiry Aquinas significantly adapts the received *exitus-reditus* model to fit the specific requirements of authentic Christian theology.[10]

First, the *exitus-reditus* illuminates the doctrine of creation. As a theological realist, Aquinas of course recognizes the need to supply a corrective for the undifferentiated emanationism that this model could suggest as much as it postulates a going-out from God and a coming-back to God. Since he uses the model to illustrate a specifically Christian doctrine of creation, Aquinas situates the *exitus-reditus* theme within a causal scheme of explanation that acknowledges the finitude of creatures and safeguards the transcendence of God.[11] Thus he preserves the fundamental Christian view about God's agency in the world which the early Roman theologian Hippolytus summarizes in the following way: "The divine will in moving all things is itself without motion."[12] This distinction foreshadows the much later, and more philosophically sophisticated, appeal, at least among Thomists, to the diverse relationships between essence and existence which exist in God and the creature as a way of explaining the divine transcendence in theological discourse.[13]

9. The works of Pseudo-Dionysius the Areopagite (ca. 500), especially *De mystica theologia*, offer a prime example of how a Neoplatonic author employs the *"exitus-reditus"* theme in order to provide a formal unity to questions of philosophical theology. For further discussion, see Paul Rorem, *Pseudo-Dionysius. A Commentary on the Texts and an Introduction to Their Influence.* (New York: Oxford University Press, 1993), pp. 183–236.

10. André Hayen, *Saint Thomas d'Aquin et la vie de l'Église*, Essais philosophiques 6 (Louvain: Publications Universitaires, 1952), p. 88, argues that the general thrust of Aquinas's modification betrays his preference for final over efficient causality. The contemporary Thomist scholar Msgr. Inos Biffi has written an introduction to a recent Italian translation of Hayen's essay, *San Tommaso e la vita della Chiesa oggi* (Milan: Jaca Books, 1993).

11. Kenneth L. Schmitz, in his 1982 Aquinas Lecture *The Gift: Creation* (Milwaukee: Marquette University Press, 1982), p. 18, nicely summarizes this point: "Creation is not a transference of being or substance to the creature at the expense of the creator, for the creator gives without diminishing his own being. It is a work *(opus)* without toil *(labor)*."

12. *Contra Noetum*, c. 10 (PG 10, col. 818). In his *De fide orthodoxa*, Book I, c. 3 (PG 94, col. 796), John Damascene affirms the immutability of the creator and the mutability of creatures. (Translations of Patristic sources are by ICEL in *The Liturgy of the Hours*, 4 vols. [New York: Catholic Book Pub. Co., 1975].)

13. For an incisive treatment of this, see Ambroise Gardeil, *Le donné révélé et la*

Second, as regards theological language (a logic of affirmation and negation), Aquinas adapts the *exitus-reditus* model to take full account of the definitive character of the revelation made in Jesus Christ. Because the Christian faith bases itself on the revealed word of God, the Church implicitly trusts the capacity of human words adequately to communicate divine truth. The Second Vatican Council (1962–1965) expressly states: "By this revelation the truth, both about God and about the salvation of humankind, inwardly dawns on us in Christ, who is in himself both the mediator and the fullness of revelation."[14] The historical fact of the Incarnation illustrates the ability of created reality to manifest or carry a divine meaning in the world. As a divine Person who comes forth from the Father, Christ substantiates and verifies the created words which truly express, without exhausting, the meaning of God's truth. The Church of Christ now possesses the authority and the obligation to safeguard these truths about doctrine and morals, even though human language remains unable to communicate fully the divine mysteries to the believer. This incommensurateness invites the believer neither to speculate idly about God nor to abandon any thought of him; rather, the darkness of faith urges one to yearn for a communion with God that surpasses the ordinary modes of human understanding. It forms part of the divine plan to grant these graces to Christ's members.

Third, since it supposes that human existence takes on a new meaning when interpreted as a journeying back to God, the *exitus-reditus* model bears immediately on issues in moral theology. Because the human person is set between God as both Origin and Goal, the moral theologian needs to point out the way that leads to God. Though congenial to the modern spirit of evolutionary development, the metaphor of a journey alone does not suffice to communicate fully what Aquinas understands by the moral life as a way back to God. An adequate presentation of Christian moral theology also requires that some account be given of what constitutes the proper steps along the way. Aquinas discovers the dramatic conflicts of human existence in prudential decision and free choice. He also insists that rendering an accurate account of what makes up the everyday good and complete human life ranks among the highest obligations of the mor-

---

théologie (Paris: Éditions du Cerf, 1932), p. 313: "Pas une ligne de la *Somme* qui ait été écrite indépendamment de cette vérité fondamentale: En Dieu l'essence et l'existence sont un: dans l'être créé l'essence et l'existence ne s'impliquent pas."

14. The Dogmatic Constitution on Revelation, *Dei verbum*, chap. 1, no. 2.

al theologian. Pope John Paul II takes up this theme in *Veritatis splendor:* "Moral theology is a reflection concerned with 'morality,' with the good and the evil of human acts and of the person who performs them.... It acknowledges that the origin and end of moral action are found in the One who 'alone is good' and who, by giving himself to man in Christ, offers him the happiness of divine life."[15]

To sum up: Christian moral theology invites one to hold certain views about the place that the created order holds in moral reasoning, about the nature of theological doctrine, and about the ultimate destiny that belongs to each human person. When expounding these views, sound moral theology always points to Christ. The doctrine of the Incarnation stipulates that the individual human nature of the incarnate Logos remains the visible agent of divine action in the world. In the hypostatic union, Christ's human nature provides a real, living principle for his human activity. When he acts, Christ restores creation to the pattern of its divinely established constitution. When he teaches, Christ himself illustrates that human language can communicate divine truth. When he dies on the cross, Christ restores the human race to its supernatural destiny and provides for each human being the means to obtain it.

Christian theology is synonymous with Christian realism. As the sacrament of God's presence in the world, the Church came into being when the Word became flesh in the womb of the blessed Virgin Mary. As the Spotless Bride washed clean by the blood of Christ, the Church returns to God in the Lord's resurrection and ascension. If it would fulfill its charter to serve as an authentic instrument of God's truth about salvation, Christian ethical discourse must remain rooted in the Incarnation of the Word. This means that moral theologians are required, first, to recognize that doctrines properly formulated in propositions are capable of communicating authentic knowledge about the divine mysteries; secondly, to acknowledge that since human reason is able to discover theological sense in created realities, human nature is to be accorded its full standing in discussions about the harmonies between nature and grace; and thirdly, to point out the relationship between those charity-infused

---

15. Encyclical Letter *Veritatis Splendor* addressed by the Supreme Pontiff Pope John Paul II to all the Bishops of the Catholic Church Regarding Certain Fundamental Questions of the Church's Moral Teaching (Vatican City: Libreria Editrice Vaticana, 1993), no. 29. All citations from the encyclical are taken from the official Vatican edition.

good actions performed here and now and the beatitude that both awaits in heaven and yet now satisfies those who love the members of Christ's Body and, in so doing, him (see Mt 25:40).

It happened that Aquinas's exposure to oriental theology took place during the same decade, the 1260s, when he began work on his comprehensive *Summa theologiae*. If one accepts the hypothesis that Aquinas gained an original insight from his reading of authors such as Proclus, M.-D Chenu's supposition that the principal divisions of the *Summa theologiae* reflect an adaptation of the *exitus-reditus* theme to the distinctive requirements of revealed doctrine seems plausible.[16] Father Chenu asserts that in the prologue to the body of the *Summa theologiae*, one uncovers the hermeneutical key both to the work's guiding objective as well as to its chief sections. There Aquinas describes his theological project as follows:

So because ... the fundamental aim of divine teaching *(sacra doctrina)* is to make God known, not only as he is in himself, but as the beginning and end of all things and of reasoning creatures especially, we now intend to set forth this divine teaching by treating, first, of God, second, of the journey to God of reasoning creatures, third, of Christ, who, as man, remains our road to God.[17]

16. See M.-D. Chenu, O.P., *Towards Understanding St. Thomas*, trans. A.-M. Landry, O.P., and D. Hughes, O.P. (Chicago: Henry Regnery Company, 1964), pp. 309ff. The proposal was first set forth in his "Le plan de la Somme théologique de saint Thomas," *Revue Thomiste* 47 (1939): 93–107. Thomas F. O'Meara, O.P., "Grace as a Theological Structure in the *Summa theologiae* of Thomas Aquinas," *Recherches de théologie ancienne et médiévale* 55 (1988): 130–53, claims that M.-D. Chenu is the first one to propose a "philosophico-theological form" for the *Summa theologiae*. O'Meara further asserts that subsequent critics pursued the search for the key to the structural unity of the *Summa theologiae* "[b]ecause of Chenu's work" (p. 131). In particular, O'Meara cites theologians such as A. Hayen, E. Persson, G. Lafont, E. Schillebeeckx, M. Seckler, and O. Pesch.

17. Thomas Aquinas, *Summa theologiae* Ia, q. 2, prologue: "Quia igitur principalis intentio hujus sacrae doctrinae est Dei cognitionem tradere, et non solum secundum quod in se est secundum quod est principium rerum et finis earum et specialiter rationalis creaturae, ..., ad hujus doctrinae expositionem intendentes, primo tractabimus de Deo, secundo de motu rationalis creaturae in Deum, tertio de Christo, qui secundum quod homo via est nobis tendendi in Deum." [References to the *Summa theologiae* follow the accepted practice, namely, the part of the work, e.g., Ia-IIae for the *prima secundae;* the question, e.g., q. 3; the article, e.g., a. 4; the specific part of an article where required, e.g., ad 2, for the reply to the second objection. Unless otherwise noted, translations are those found in the English text of the multivolume Blackfriars edition published at intervals in the 1960s and 1970s by Eyre & Spottiswoode in London and McGraw-Hill Book Company in New York. References to individual volumes of the Blackfriars *Summa* include the volume's editor, title, and number. References to the other works of Aquinas

We learn from this outline that Aquinas places moral theology, his analysis "of the journey to God of reasoning creatures," between an account of the Trinitarian God, who though infinitely perfect and happy in himself created humankind to share in his happiness, and an account of the redemptive mission of the incarnate Son, who, through the action of the Holy Spirit, calls every man and woman to participate in divine beatitude. His conception, it should be noted, affords no support to those who want to distinguish strongly between theocentric and Christocentric moral theology. In continuity with his teacher, Albert the Great, Aquinas offers an account of the moral life that both reflects and conforms to Christ's own prayer for his disciples: "And this is eternal life, that they know thee the only true God, and Jesus Christ whom thou hast sent" (Jn 17:3).[18]

Integrality of Divine Teaching

Since the present volume deals with the general principles of moral theology, the following chapters mainly treat topics that fall under Aquinas's second heading in the text above, namely, the human person's journey back to God. It is important to recall, however, that Aquinas consciously elaborates the basic elements of his moral theology as an integral part of the entire "divine teaching."[19] The placement of moral theology within the *sacra doctrina* accomplishes more than giving a religious tone to what otherwise would be an unadorned, bare-boned moral discourse. Rather Aquinas's method aims to situate every question related to our achieving perfect happiness within a full theological context, with the result that only pedagogical considerations warrant distinguishing between moral and dogmatic theology. In his commentary on the Apostles' Creed, Aquinas puts succinctly the superintending article of faith that directs his elaboration of moral theology: "only God satisfies us."[20]

---

specify the title of the work along with the usual way of citing it, and, when required, the English translation.]

18. For background information on the Christological emphases present in the early mainline Dominican tradition, see Edward P. Mahoney, "Albert the Great on Christ and Hierarchy," in *Christ among the Medieval Dominicans. Representations of Christ in the Texts and Images of the Order of Preachers*, ed. Kent Emery, Jr., and Joseph Wawrykow (Notre Dame, Ind.: University of Notre Dame Press, 1998), pp. 364–92.

Here, as throughout the book unless otherwise noted, English quotation of Scripture is from the Revised Standard Version, Catholic Edition.

19. The analysis of the general principles of moral theology belongs to the "first part of the second part" of the *Summa theologiae*; in Latin, the *prima secundae*.

20. See *Collationes super Credo in Deum* I: "Deus enim solus satiat."

So much does an explicitly evangelical purpose control Aquinas's method in the *Summa theologiae*, that one author contends that Aquinas's original purpose in composing this handbook "for beginners" developed out of his recognition of the need for a primer that would assist young Dominicans to prepare for confessional practice. And while there already existed in his day a number of *vademecums* and other confessional aids, none of these compositions, as far as is known, consciously located moral theology within the broader perspectives of the *sacra doctrina*.[21] In the *Summa theologiae*, Aquinas tells us that he will proceed "according to the order of learning,"[22] but this experiment in teaching the *sacra doctrina* presupposes an order of being and intelligibility based on the reconciliation that God has achieved through Christ; "that is, in Christ God was reconciling the world to himself, not counting their trespasses against them" (2 Cor 5:19). The Second Vatican Council expresses a complementary truth when it affirms that "all have been created in the image of God who 'made from one every nation of humankind to live on the whole face of the earth' (Acts 17:26), and all have been called to one and the same end, God himself."[23] It is characteristic of Catholic theology, and a condition of the integrality of divine teaching, to welcome metaphysics as a friendly companion, and to shun theories that assume a dialectical opposition between the orders of creation and redemption.

Being and Truth of *Sacra Doctrina*

Aquinas's theological method is built on the foundational truth that the principles of the being and of the truth of anything are the same.[24] So before one approaches Aquinas's moral theology (which constitutes his effort to express the truth about human behavior), it is wise to consider the being and truth of two overarching areas of theological enquiry. The first area inquires about the nature of divine teaching itself, which we refer to as *sacra doctrina*, while the second area (which is considered below,

21. See Leonard Boyle, O.P., "The Setting of the *Summa theologiae* of Saint Thomas," Etienne Gilson Lecture Series, no. 5 (Toronto: Pontifical Institute of Mediaeval Studies, 1982).

22. See *Summa theologiae* Ia, Foreword: "secundum ordinem disciplinae."

23. Second Vatican Council's Pastoral Constitution on the Church in the Modern World, *Gaudium et spes*, no. 24: "Omnes enim creati ad imaginem Dei, qui fecit 'ex uno omne genus hominum inhabitare super universam faciem terrae' (Ac 17, 26), ad unum eumdemque finem, id est ad Deum ipsum, vocantur."

24. See his *Sentencia super Posteriora Analytica*, Bk. 1, lect. 4.

in the second section [2] of this chapter) elaborates the biblical doctrine that God created the reasoning creature after his own image and likeness (Gn 1:27), which we refer to as the doctrine of the *imago Dei*.

As a *sermo de Deo*, a word about God, Christian theology embodies an intelligent reflection on the living word of God as revealed through the instrumentality of Jesus Christ.[25] Since theology employs human language to speak meaningfully about God and things as they are related to God, the theologian is required to choose language carefully. But as important as correct language is for theological discourse, theology's task does not end once the correct grammar of faith and proper rules for doctrine have been agreed upon. All theological discourse remains ordered to real truth, and so it appropriately embraces everything that God has revealed about himself and about the created universe. As part of the fulfillment of the divine plan for our salvation, the Holy Spirit confirms the whole of Christ's ministry. The communication of divine truth, then, does not involve just any word, but a "word breathing forth love."[26] Aquinas always interprets the *sacra doctrina* as a Trinitarian event, a teaching that originates in the very inner life of God. Jesus himself testifies concerning the starting point of *sacra doctrina*: "Now they know that everything you have given me is from you; for the words that you gave to me I have given to them, and they have received them and know in truth that I came from you; and they have believed that you sent me" (Jn 17:7–8). Christ's words and deeds, confirmed by the power of the Holy Spirit, provide the norm for all Christian theology because Christ himself is the eternal Word of the Father.

Preambles to Faith

Revealed truth comes forth from God, not only as a free gift of grace that likewise causes the required assent constitutive of the act of belief, but also as a lavish outpouring or effusion of doctrine about those things which pertain to our salvation. Of course, some knowable truths which

---

25. For a classical view of the development of theology as an intelligent reflection on God's revelation, see Francisco Muniz, O.P., *The Work of Theology*, trans. John P. Reid, O.P. (Washington, D.C.: Thomist Press, 1953). Cornelius Ernst, O.P., aims to develop the classical view along lines more familiar to contemporary philosophy in "Metaphor and Ontology in *Sacra Doctrina*," *The Thomist* 38 (1974): 403–25.

26. See *Summa theologiae* Ia, q. 43, a. 5, ad 2: "The Son is the Word; not, however, just any word, but the Word breathing Love."

bear on human well-being, such as what is taught in biochemistry or nuclear physics, do not concern revealed truth. But there are naturally knowable truths, both in doctrine and morals, that serve as preambles to the grace of Christian belief. In an early essay, the Flemish Dominican theologian Edward Schillebeeckx even argued that "if man does not make definite contact with God at one point that is not grace (in the theological sense of the word), then the God who reveals himself cannot address man meaningfully."[27] This epistemological conviction partially explains why the Church traditionally includes among the tasks of the theologian the explication of the *praeambula fidei*. Since certain persons believe revealed truths even though human reason can, under certain circumstances, arrive at the same truths by its own proper resources, we can think of these *praeambula fidei* as the locus where faith embraces reason.[28]

It is useful to recall a distinction that the scholastic theologians had posited between what is supernatural in itself (*supernaturale quoad substantiam*) and what is supernatural in the way that it is communicated (*supernaturale quoad modum*).[29] The first category of truths embraces those things that we know only because they have been communicated to the human race through divine revelation, whereas the second category includes those truths which in themselves remain knowable to human reason, but which, for purposes of the divine pedagogy, have also been revealed in the Church of faith and sacraments. The distinction still holds. The Munich philosopher Robert Spaemann has observed that, contrary to a now widespread prejudice, the existence of God, the immortality of the human soul, and the divine judgment which determines our eternal destiny are not merely dogmas of Christian faith or of religions of biblical origins, but they are age-old insights of philosophy.[30] Pope John Paul glosses

---

27. See his *Revelation and Theology*, vol. 1, trans. N. D. Smith (New York: Sheed & Ward, 1967), p. 154. The author also cites examples: "Hence the solemn declaration by the Church that the existence of God can in principle be naturally known (DS 3004, 3026) and that the human soul is immortal (DS 1440)" (p. 155).

28. It is true, however, that the only text where Aquinas uses the term *praeambula fidei* describes this embrace from the side of faith: "ea quae sunt praeambula fidei, quae necesse est in fide scire ..." (*Expositio super librum Boethii De trinitate*, q. 2, a. 3). For further discussion, see my *Christian Faith and the Theological Life* (Washington, D.C.: The Catholic University Press of America, 1996), esp. pp. 79–81, 115, 117–20.

29. For further discussion, see *Christian Faith and the Theological Life*, p. 80, note 80.

30. Robert Spaemann, "On the Anthropology of the Encyclical *Evangelium vitae*," forthcoming in a volume published in the series of the Pontifical Academy for Life (Rome).

this assertion when he writes in *Evangelium vitae:* "Revelation progressively allows the first notion of immortal life planted by the Creator in the human heart to be grasped with ever greater clarity" (no. 31). It is imperative to recall that when the Church instructs about the good of human life, she enunciates truths that are not foreign and strange to human beings. The promise given us by the Church is that grace perfects nature.

Analogy

Aquinas demonstrates in his own work that sound theological argument requires recourse to a Christian form of analogy. "Something is predicated analogically," he explains, "when many things are made equal in an intention of something common, but when that common intention does not have the being of one *ratio* in all the things of which it is predicated."[31] For our present purposes in moral theology, it is sufficient to recall that analogy is concerned with judgments, not with isolated concepts. It is a characteristically Thomist insistence that judgments are able to attain the existence of the other even though this existence transcends our concepts, even in ordinary experience. Thus analogy is primarily concerned with the claim that Christian believers, when they talk about God, are really talking about God, that is, that they attain in some way his reality. Conceptualization functions only within this sort of dynamic realism.[32]

One of the tasks of theology is to explicate what the Church proposes for our belief. Hence in its broadest sense, analogy justifiably holds a place in theology on account of the dogmatic truth that our Lord Jesus Christ is, according to the fifth-century Council of Chalcedon, "one and the same" (*hena kai ton auton*) God and man.[33] Whenever she formulates a truth that forms part of the deposit of faith, the Church asserts that what is signified by the subject is identical in reality with what is signified by the predicate, that is, "one and the same."[34] The articles of faith, formulated in the Creed or by the Church, observe this rule, which imposes on the *articuli fidei* the full philosophical weight of the verb "to be." For exam-

31. See Aquinas's *Scriptum super libros Sententiarum*, Bk. 1, d. 19, q. 5, a. 2, ad 1.

32. For a fuller treatment of this important feature of realist theological method, see Colman E. O'Neill, O.P., "Analogy, Dialectic and Inter-Confessional Theology," *The Thomist* 47 (1983): 43–65.

33. See the Council of Chalcedon (451), "Definition of Faith," (*DS* 301).

34. For a fuller discussion of this principle in reply to claims that theological language remains simply part of a conceptual world, see Colman E. O'Neill, O.P., "The Rule Theory of Doctrine and Propositional Truth," *The Thomist* 49 (1985): 417–42, esp. 438ff.

ple, to proclaim that the Blessed Virgin Mary is immaculately conceived is to make a true judgment about her person and grace, not to devise a metaphor about something else. In 1889, the Russian theologian Vladimir Solovieff (1853–1900) expressly linked the hypostatic union of human and divine in Christ to the Church's status as being a real instrument and visible image of divine power. And from this comparison he concluded that "in the Christian Church, there exists a materially fixed point, an external and visible center of action: the apostolic See of Rome, that miraculous icon of universal Christianity." The doctrine of papal infallibility, which supposes the special assistance of the Holy Spirit to the Vicar of Christ in matters of faith and morals, develops the logical implications of this gift of God's own truth to the Church.

Sacra Doctrina and Grace

There are discernible similarities in the way that Aquinas gives an account of creation and the way that he describes the transmission of the *sacra doctrina*. For Aquinas's conception of the *sacra doctrina* resembles the effusion of being which originates in the blessed Trinity as the source of every created thing. Just as the creative act has its starting point in the uncreated God, though it terminates in a multiplicity of created beings, so the *sacra doctrina* begins with God, but results in manifold expressions of divine truth in the world. Instruction about the moral life flows from this effusive divine goodness. From God and the blessed to the angels to the prophets to Christ and his apostles to the bishops and teachers and preachers of the Church, Aquinas claims both a formal community in those who are taught and one universal causal order of principal to instrumental or ministerial teachers. In order to account for the unique place which the incarnate Word holds in the economy of salvation, we have to adjust the above-mentioned pattern somewhat, so that Christ himself stands at the center of this revelatory process. And because of his divine personhood, it is Christ who also teaches the angels. The Second Vatican Council took up this theme when it affirmed that Christ, the last Adam, "fully discloses man to himself and unfolds his noble calling by revealing the mystery of the Father and the Father's love."[35]

35. This text found in *Gaudium et spes*, no. 22, *De Christo novo homine*, serves to remind us that while theology remains firstly and foremostly a word about God, the only Word that God has ever spoken is his Son, who in our time was born of the Virgin Mary, and so can disclose perfectly what it means to be human: "Christus, novissimus Adam, in

While the event of God's self-disclosure in Christ historically employs the mediation of the scriptural revelation, the explicitation of *sacra doctrina* falls into the professional hands of theologians, who, among other duties, are asked to uncover the authentic intent of the biblical author. This explains why the Renaissance theologian Thomas de Vio Cardinal Cajetan (1469–1534) defines the *sacra doctrina* as "all knowledge taught us by God's grace."[36] Theology concerns the transmission of living truth, not abstract deductions about divine life. Cajetan's description of what constitutes theological truth recalls Christ's own promise: "It is written in the prophets, 'And they shall all be taught by God.' Everyone who has heard and learned from the Father comes to me" (Jn 6:45). It is entirely wrongheaded to imagine that Aquinas in the *Summa theologiae* devises a thinly Christianized account of what remains substantially pagan moral theory, whether of the Stoic, Aristotelian, or Neoplatonic variety. On the contrary, at the beginning of his treatise, Aquinas himself makes it very clear that the *"principia revelata,"* the revealed starting points of his doctrine, remain the substance of divine grace, the actions of infused charity, and the end of eternal life.[37] The *sacra doctrina* is not to be conflated with the canonical Scriptures, which serve as a medium of its communication. Of course, the Church's certainty as to what God reveals rests on the witness of Scripture and of Tradition, which together with the Scriptures forms a single deposit of the Word of God. Thus "by God's wise design, tradition, scripture, and the Church's teaching function contribute effectively to the salvation of souls."[38] Theologians are expected to conform not only their work but their lives as well to these expressions of divine truth.

---

ipsa revelatione mysterii Patris eiusque amoris, hominem ipsi homini plene manifestat eique altissimam eius vocationem patefacit." For a fuller discussion of the grace and nature distinction as it is employed by Aquinas, see my "What the Angels See at Twilight," *Communio* 26 (1999): 583–94.

36. See his *Commentary* on the *Summa theologiae, Iam,* q. 1, a. 1.

37. See *Summa theologiae* Ia, q. 1, a. 2 where Aquinas defends the scientific character of theology on the grounds that it derives from God's very own knowledge of himself which he shares with the blessed.

38. Dogmatic Constitution on Divine Revelation, *Dei verbum,* no. 10. For a recent and comprehensive theological study of the place that *sacra doctrina* holds in the life of the Church, see Lawrence J. Donohoo, O.P., "The Nature and Grace of *Sacra Doctrina* in St. Thomas's *Super Boetium De Trinitate," The Thomist* 63 (1999): 343–401. For commentary on recent documents from the Holy See that explain the weight of Magisterial teaching, see Tarcisio Bertone, S.D.B., "The Magisterium of the Church and the *Professio Fidei,"* in *Proclaiming the Truth of Jesus Christ,* pp. 31–48.

Moral Theology within a *Sacra Doctrina*

As a practical science ordained to guide human actions, moral theology supplies authoritative direction for the *reditus*, the return journey of the human creature to God.[39] But for anyone to achieve the high destiny that God has established for the intelligent, reasoning creature, he or she must receive and appropriate all the truths that embody the plan of Christian salvation. Dependent on the entire body of theological instruction for its bearings, moral theology offers a comprehensive divine teaching about good human conduct. *Veritatis splendor* in fact describes moral theology specifically "as a scientific reflection on the *Gospel as the gift and commandment of new life*, a reflection on the life which 'professes the truth in love' (cf. Eph 4:15) and on the Church's life of holiness, in which there shines forth the truth about the good brought to its perfection."[40]

In the first encyclical to treat certain fundamental questions of the Church's moral teaching, we find appeal made to that sharing in the divine life that comes to us as a complete gift from the blessed Trinity; to the pattern of the created order and the reasoning creature's place within it; to the fact and consequences of divine governance active in the world; to the distinction between the old dispensation given by Moses and the new law of grace revealed in the Incarnation; to the dynamics of the specifically Christian virtues of faith, hope, and love; to the special states of life within the Church; and, finally, to the seven sacraments of the Christian Church. These theological coordinates locate moral theology within its proper place in Christian instruction and enable it to provide the Christian people not only with a teaching about their common end and *salus*, but also about the means available to them to achieve it. The fulfillment of the divine plan for our salvation remains the dominant *raison d'être* for the *sacra doctrina*, and this explains why Saint Thomas never addresses questions of moral theology outside of the fuller context of "all knowledge taught us by God's grace."[41]

39. Still, Aquinas affirms that the *sacra doctrina* remains "mainly concerned with the divine things that are, rather than with things men do; it deals with human acts only insofar as they prepare us for that achieved knowledge of God in which our eternal bliss reposes." See *Summa theologiae* Ia, q. 1, a. 4.

40. *Veritatis splendor*, no. 109.

41. Victor White, O.P., "Holy Teaching, the Idea of Theology according to St. Thomas Aquinas," Aquinas Papers 33 (London: Blackfriars Publications, 1958), makes a strong case for interpreting the *sacra doctrina* mainly as an instrument of the divine

Four Features of Realist Moral Theology

From these general remarks about how the Thomist tradition describes moral theology, there are four further considerations about the nature of moral theology that emerge. First, because it derives from a single source, *sacra doctrina* composes a unity. As the elaborated expression of *sacra doctrina*, theology too remains formally one science; only purposes of academic organization or pedagogy require drawing a distinction between moral and dogmatic theology.⁴² Because of the unity of theology, the theologian, in order better to develop a theological argument for moral truth, is able to appeal to and even start with explanations about, for instance, the inner life of the blessed Trinity, the work of Christ the Savior, and the grace of the blessed Virgin Mary. Above all, however, the moral theologian should pay special attention to the mystery of the Trinitarian indwelling active in those who have done the will of God throughout the ages. We can glimpse the splendor of the blessed Trinity in the saints because they enjoy proper relations of knowledge and love with each of the three divine Persons. In their own way, holy persons as much as sound doctrines reveal moral truth.

Second, moral theology is a science of faith. Although the exact relationship between philosophical ethics and moral theology remains a topic for discussion, a complete and adequate moral theology develops only in harmonious union with a living faith. This means that God's truthfulness alone, as mediated through the witnesses of Scripture and Tra-

---

pedagogy. Even before the beginning of the Second Vatican Council, he could write: "Our present-day understanding of the psychological function of symbols and beliefs may help us to understand how eminently practical and inherently salutary are such seemingly 'speculative' treatises as those of the Trinity, the Incarnation, the Eucharist. In any case, St. Thomas here [in *Summa theologiae* Ia, q. 1, a. 4] expressly repudiates such a division in the *sacra doctrina* as we find in Greek philosophy between 'speculative' metaphysics or physics and 'practical' ethics; and we may leave to others to reconcile with this their sharp distinction between 'dogmatic' and 'moral' theology as best they can" (p. 14).

42. In his *Theologia* (Philadelphia: Fortress Press, 1983), Edward Farley provides an important historical analysis of the fragmentation of theological studies. Significantly, he observes that "practical" theology tends most easily to break away and develop into an autonomous science. We recognize this phenomenon today in the various attempts to attenuate moral theology with the methods and conclusions drawn from or used in other forms of scientific investigation, such as sociological, psychological, or cultural anthropological.

dition and safeguarded by the Magisterium, guarantees the authenticity, that is, the true supernatural character, of a revealed teaching about morals. What else can explain the claim that the Church makes about her own teaching mission? "In proclaiming the commandments of God and the charity of Christ, the Church's Magisterium also teaches the faithful specific particular precepts and requires that they consider them in conscience as morally binding."[43] Strong emphasis on the role of the Magisterium in setting forth moral truth does not gainsay the role of human reason in deliberating about moral truth. On the contrary, the Magisterium invites sound moral reasoning.[44] Even when moral theology employs arguments or reaches material conclusions that resemble those of rational ethics, it still looks back, as it were, at the blessed truth that God shares with the saints and the angels. The specificity of Christian ethics derives from its dependence on the *sacra doctrina*.

As an elaboration of divine truth, Christian moral theology does not depend slavishly on the inductive method as commonly employed in statistical research about human conduct.[45] The general rule that Aquinas sets down concerning human reason and divine truth holds true in morals: the *sacra doctrina* borrows from philosophy not because God needs to learn about us, but because we need to have God's Word expressed in the forms open to human comprehension.[46] Divine truth, not approximations and conjectures, sets the authentic measure for human conduct. This assertion does not mean that the life sciences or human sciences contribute nothing to our knowledge of the human person; the claim rather considers the case of human reasoning failing to achieve moral truth because of undue subjectivist or utilitarian influences.[47] Suspicion about the reliability of collective efforts to determine moral truth is likewise raised by the privation of original sin and its effect on the way men and women make judgments about moral truth. St. Paul, it is true, affirms that "where sin

---

43. *Veritatis splendor*, no. 110.   44. See *Fides et ratio*, no. 68.

45. "The affirmation of moral principles is not within the competence of formal empirical methods. While not denying the validity of such methods, but at the same time not restricting its view point to them, moral theology, faithful to the supernatural sense of the faith, takes into account first and foremost *the spiritual dimension of the human heart and its vocation to divine love*" (*Veritatis splendor*, no. 112; italics in original).

46. See *Summa theologiae* Ia, q. 1, a. 5, ad 2.

47. In *Fides et ratio*, no. 98, the Pope adverts to such a circumstance: "Faced with contemporary challenges in the social, economic, political and scientific fields, the ethical conscience of people is disoriented."

increased, grace abounded all the more" (Rom 5:20); but this affirmation about the divine generosity does not support the view that such statistically frequent forms of human behavior as oppressing the weak and marginalized, killing the unborn, engaging deliberately in masturbatory sex, and committing injustices in speech constitute legitimate expressions of moral goodness which conduce to eternal life. To live by Christian faith, points us in other directions.

Because it claims a privileged source of authenticity, Christian morality is not therefore restricted to those already persuaded for whatever reason to accept its truthfulness. Christian moral theology is not a sectarian enterprise. As *Veritatis splendor* again reminds us, the Christian commitment to natural law emphasizes the essential subordination of reason and human law to the Wisdom of God and to his law.[48] And because human nature exhibits a recognizable stability, universal statements about moral activity can be incorporated into a coherent body of knowledge. It belongs, however, to the practitioner of moral theology to give an account as to how these general principles are to be translated into more proximate principles that govern everyday activity. The end is the total good, especially the good for human beings or integral human perfection. Human actions achieve their moral meaning only in relationship to the end of human life: "Only the act in conformity with the good can be a path that leads to life."[49] In the concrete circumstances of life, to pursue virtuous action means that the human person embraces a particular good that contributes to human fulfillment. No account of natural law is complete without an analysis of the virtues. Again, the true ends of human life give particular actions their specific quality as either good or bad, and this determination applies to all members of the species, which is why *Veritatis splendor* speaks about the good of the human person, not the good of Catholics.

Aquinas and the realist tradition that follows him teach that Christian morals lead to a personal state of blessedness that transcends the reductively ethical world of human decisions and strivings. Even the natural desire for God expresses itself in a way that is pertinent for the moral life in each person.[50] "For inscribed in their hearts by God, human be-

48. *Veritatis splendor*, no. 44.

49. *Veritatis splendor*, no. 72.

50. This theme is developed extensively in Pinckaers, *The Sources of Christian Ethics.* Jean Porter, *The Recovery of Virtue: The Relevance of Aquinas for Christian Ethics* (Louisville, Ky.: Westminster/John Knox Press, 1990) offers her own interpretation of Aquinas's texts.

ings have a law whose observance is their dignity and in accordance with which they are to be judged."[51] In the final analysis, the biblical revelation concerning God's love for his children and the biblical ordinance that each human being love God above all things control the way that a science of faith sets forth its moral instruction.

Third, realist moral theology is concerned first of all to explain the good ends of human flourishing, and not to expound whatever ecclesiastical pronouncements instruct about them. Since he understood this axiom, "The Church teaches something because it is true; it is not true because the Church teaches it," Aquinas accepted the Church's Magisterium in morals as an unerringly faithful expression of what leads to the true end of human life. But the juridical order does not establish the principal frame of reference for his moral teaching. Thomism dwells in a larger moral universe. For example, because human reason is able to discover what suits the in-built entelechies of human nature, the Christian moral theologian can confidently expound on the teleological dimension of the moral life without undue appeal to legal sanctions and punishments. Behind this optimism that eschews moral badgering stands an unshakeable confidence in the Christian teaching, suggested in Greek philosophy, that the end draws. To express this point differently, while it remains true that the Church is committed to the language of the Commandments, the realist moral theologian seeks to describe what is contained in the Decalogue through the more descriptive language of the virtues, which constitute so many ways of expressing the good of the human person. Among other benefits, this practice advances the credibility of sound Christian moral instruction, and it avoids the unhappy consequences that result from a too-exclusive reliance on extrinsic authority.

Aquinas found Aristotle's ethical categories congenial for a theological expression of the moral life. But this conviction about the reasonableness of the Christian moral life antedates the medieval appropriation of Aristotelian ethical theory. Even the early apologist Clement of Alexandria accepted the rational character of virtue as expressed within the context of Stoic moral theory: "For virtue itself is a state of soul rendered harmonious by reason in respect to the whole life."[52] Translated into Chris-

---

51. *Gaudium et spes*, no. 16: "Nam homo legem in corde suo a Deo inscriptam habet, cui parere ipsa dignitas eius est et secundum quam ipse iudicabitur."

52. Clement of Alexandria, *Paedagogus*, Bk. 1, chap. 13.

tian language, "to act for the sake of the ultimate end for its own sake" means loving in a fully Christian and ecclesial way.[53] As the New Testament makes plain, the true finalization of the rational creature lies in loving God and embracing the neighbor in God's love. Charity underlies the noblest vision of the moral life; the French author A.-M. Carré even identifies its movement with the very bestowal of human existence.[54] A moral theology that predominantly bases itself on the jurisprudential order neither offers nor supports such an uplifted conception of the moral life.

End rather than precept dominates the dynamic of morality from a realist's point of view. God and the things that direct us to God specify the kind of life that the Christian should embrace. Realist Christian moral theology exploits the dynamism of a real final causality active in every human being. Since divine grace establishes a personal bond of love between the human creature and God, it makes sense to speak about God as an end.[55] Just as one cannot define fishing without a fish, so it is impossible to imagine the Christian moral life apart from the human person's movement toward beatific union with God. The person who moves unhesitatingly toward this goal possesses divine wisdom. "That person," says Aquinas, "who considers maturely and without qualification the first and final cause of the entire universe, namely God, is to be called supremely wise; hence wisdom appears in St. Augustine as knowledge of divine things."[56] Within the Church of Christ, this gift of wisdom is attributed to the workings of the Holy Spirit.

Fourth, all accounts of moral realism remain incomplete without proper attention to the revelation that the Holy Spirit furnishes a distinctive kind of assistance for the moral life. This promise is distinctively Christian. The Apostles, explains St. John Chrysostom, "did not come down from the mountain carrying, like Moses, tablets of stone in their hands; but they came down carrying the Holy Spirit in their hearts ...

53. See *Veritatis splendor*, no. 1. For these remarks, I follow T. C. O'Brien's introductory essay in *Effects of Sin, Stain and Guilt*, Blackfriars *Summa*, vol. 27 (1974), pp. xiii–xviii.

54. Ambroise-Marie Carré, *Le Christ de Saint Thomas d'Aquin* (Paris: Revue des jeunes, 1944), p. 14.

55. For an account of Aquinas's moral theology that stresses this point, see Paul J. Wadell, *The Primacy of Love. An Introduction to the Ethics of Thomas Aquinas* (New York: Paulist Press, 1991).

56. *Summa theologiae* Ia, q. 1, a. 6. For further discussion, see J. Cahill, O.P., "The Sapiential Character of Moral Theology," *Irish Theological Quarterly* 27 (1960): 132–45.

having become by his grace a living law, a living book."[57] The full meaning of the interiority of the new law of grace emerges only within the context of the Holy Spirit as a source of movement and inspiration. These movements are called the gifts of the Holy Spirit.

Knowledge by connaturality distinguishes the gifts of the Holy Spirit from the virtues. Following a theological tradition that dates from the period of patristic theology, Aquinas recognizes that the Christian believer can regard the moral life from a double perspective. On the one hand, a person can learn about the Christian moral life from moral argument; on the other hand, the Christian can seize moral truth from personal experience. Aquinas describes this second mode of knowing as the way of connaturality. While the virtues produce their own conformity with the good ends of human life, the gifts introduce a higher kind of connaturality, one that makes it possible for the Christian believer to respond to divine inspirations.[58] The Second Vatican Council expresses the purpose of connatural knowledge in similar terms: "By the gift of the Holy Spirit humankind attains in faith to the contemplation and savoring of the mystery of God's design."[59] The gifts of the Holy Spirit complete the realism of the Christian moral life, and they exhibit in those who possess them—or better, are possessed by them—the full dimensions of God's saving doctrine.

The Human Person as *Imago Dei*

Since moral theology concerns the good of the human person, it is necessary to consider the nature of the creature whose good it directs. Mistakes about the human being prompt mistakes in ethics. Catholic moral theology finds some, but not all, philosophical perspectives on the nature of the human person congenial to its purposes. As one involved in a scientific enquiry that shapes human behavior, the moral theologian needs to be informed about the conclusions of anthropology. The Scottish Enlightenment philosopher David Hume (1711–1776) declared the assumption that moral obligations can suitably be derived from the onto-

---

57. *In Matthaeum*, Hom. I, 1 (PG 57, 15). Cited in *Veritatis splendor*, no. 24.

58. See *Summa theologiae* Ia, q. 1, a. 6, ad 3.

59. *Gaudium et spes*, no. 15: "Spiritus sancti dono, homo ad mysterium consilii divini contemplandum et sapiendum fide accedit."

logical structure of the human person an illegitimate transition from the order of "is" to the order of "ought." Others coined the expression "naturalistic fallacy" to describe what they thought constituted the alternative to Hume's carving off morals from metaphysics. The legacy of David Hume, common-sense moralist, skeptical metaphysician (to borrow the title of David Fate Norton's book),[60] affords a good example of how philosophical assumptions in general, but especially anthropological assumptions, can adversely influence the development of moral philosophy and, in turn, the shape of moral theology.

There is an adage commonly repeated in the Thomist schools which affirms that action follows being (*agere sequitur esse*). Realist philosophy envisions a close affinity between the form that a being possesses—its nature, if you will—and the way that a particular being acts. Christian moral realism accordingly adopts an entirely different perspective on the relationship between being and acting from what Humean skepticism would invite. Recall Aquinas's important premise that the principles of the being and of the truth of anything are the same. If we apply this axiom to the human person, it means that, contrary to what one who adopts the Humean outlook might anticipate, the moral theologian is perfectly justified to look for analogous forms in the truth about human behavior and in the being of human nature. In fact, the word "nature" suggests etymologically a description of what a body is born to do. The Latin terms for both nature (*natura*) and birth (*nativitas*) come from the same root, *nasci*, meaning "to be born."

While the philosophical justification for confidence about the analogous structure of nature and action distracts some moral philosophers, moral theologians enjoy an advantage afforded them by their commitment to and dependence on revealed truth.[61] For the faith teaches that the

60. David Fate Norton, *David Hume: Common-Sense Moralist, Skeptical Metaphysician* (Princeton: Princeton University Press, 1982).

61. The philosophic issue, roughly framed, is whether necessity and intelligibility pertain to being and nature, or merely to logic and mathematics. Negatively, it may be noted that Hume's identification of real possibility with mere conceivability begs the very question at issue. Positively, one notes that the ontological principle of contradiction—establishing real distinction between the "is" of being and the merely propositional "is" of privation—apodictically settles the question. Being is not non-being, and this is a necessary ontological principle—a principle of being and nature—at the fount of all human knowledge. But these are matters of philosophic rather than theological rectitude.

same divine omnipotence that establishes the goodness of the moral order also constitutes human nature as a specific kind of being. The divine omnipotence is not an enemy of human freedom. With the guidance of Christian revelation, it is easy to see that "God's plan poses no threat to man's genuine freedom; on the contrary, the acceptance of God's plan is the only way to affirm that freedom."[62] The reference to the divine plan in this text refers both to the work of creation and to the work of divine providence that sustains and guides it. A sound theological anthropology, one that gives full weight to what the Christian faith professes about creation, can produce a settling effect on discussions about the relationship between human nature and human action.

The theological doctrine of the *imago Dei* recapitulates what theologians have said about the origin and nature of the human creature. It also controls theological reflection on the nature of human action and the movement of human freedom. To include instruction in moral theology about the anthropology of the *imago Dei* enjoys a long history among Thomists, as the lectures of the twentieth-century Dominican moralist Ignatius Eschmann demonstrate.[63] But the intuition that God supplies what we need to know about the happy life reaches back to the earliest moments of theological reflection on the moral life. From the time that St. Augustine said of the blessed Trinity, "Blessed the one who knows Thee, even were he to know nothing else," Christian believers have understood that they receive sure knowledge about their destiny and how to reach it from revealed truth rather than in philosophical speculation.[64] God constitutes the objective happiness of every person. Since complete happiness for the human person is found only in the happiness that results from God's own happiness, the moral theologian finds true consolation in the guidance that divine revelation gives for the moral life.[65]

Although theological handbooks usually consider creation under the

---

62. *Veritatis splendor*, no. 45.

63. See his "The Ethics of the Image of God," in *The Ethics of Saint Thomas Aquinas. Two Courses*, ed. Edward A. Synan (Toronto: Pontifical Institute of Mediaeval Studies, 1997), pp. 159–231.

64. *Confessiones* Bk. 5, chap. 4 (PL 32, col. 708).

65. By themselves, the native energies of human nature cannot attain God in a fully complete way; this sort of fulfillment requires the perfection of grace. Thus, among the medieval theologians, Aquinas clearly excludes the possibility that even in the state of original justice, any person would have enjoyed a superior grasp of the divine essence. For further discussion, see *De veritate*, q. 18, a. 1, ad 5.

general heading of dogmatic theology, the moral theologian must especially take account of the theological identity and, therefore, of the privileged destiny that each human person enjoys. As the only creature on earth that God has willed for himself, the human creature holds a central place in the hierarchy of creation. With the angels, man alone can join the intelligent chorus of praise and worship that God welcomes from his entire creation.[66] And as intelligent creatures, our human nature therefore reaches its final perfection "through the wisdom which gently draws the human mind to seek and love what is true and good, and which leads it through visible realities to those which are true and good."[67] Because every person needs to recognize the difference between what conduces to this goal and what deters from it, instruction in morals, especially for the young, ranks among the most important tasks of the Church's catechetical efforts.[68]

Doctrine of the Image

The earliest witnesses of the Christian tradition support the theological postulate that every individual instance of human nature bears the image of God.[69] The version of this theory that Aquinas adopts includes

66. Because intelligent creatures alone are able fully to know and to love God, Aquinas argues that only they are *capax Dei*, i.e., only they possess the capacity for personal union with God. For further argumentation, see *De veritate*, q. 22, a. 2, ad 5.

67. *Gaudium et spes*, no. 15: "Humanae tandem personae intellectualis natura per sapientiam perficitur et perficienda est, quae mentem hominis ad vera bonaque inquirenda ac diligenda suaviter attrahit, et qua imbutus homo per visibilia ad invisibilia adducitur."

68. In addition to the witness of Ignatius Eschmann (see above, note 62), the relationship of the doctrine of the image to moral theology is examined by Michael A. Dauphinais, "Loving the Lord Your God: The *Imago Dei* in Saint Thomas Aquinas," *The Thomist* 63 (1999): 241–67.

69. The Second Vatican Council cites Genesis 1:26 and Wisdom 2:23 as the principal biblical witnesses for this teaching: "For sacred scripture teaches that humankind was created 'in the image of God,' with the capacity to know and love its creator, and was divinely appointed with authority over all earthly creatures, to rule and use them and glorify God" (*Gaudium et spes*, no. 12). For a study of the theological witnesses, see Gunnlaugur A. Jónsson, *The Image of God: Genesis 1:26–28 in a Century of Old Testament Research* (Stockholm: Almqvist & Wiksell, 1988); John Edward Sullivan, *The Image of God: The Doctrine of St. Augustine and Its Influence* (Dubuque, Iowa: Priory Press, 1963); and especially D. Juvenal Merriell, *To the Image of the Trinity: A Study in the Development of Aquinas' Teaching* (Toronto: Pontifical Institute of Mediaeval Studies, 1990). For another account of the doctrine of the image, see my *Christian Faith*, pp. 38–48.

the following main points. According to the classical explanation, the generic aspect of image may be considered under two headings. First and in the most common usage, image belongs to the genus of similitude or likeness; moreover, a true image must not only resemble its original in something characteristic of its species, but also originate from what it images. According to this exact norm, then, only the eternal Son himself manifests the perfect image of God in an absolute similitude of species.

Aquinas draws upon the Fathers, especially St. Augustine, and freely adapts the formal rule for imaging to include an imaging *after* the image of God. Genesis 1:26 supplies the warrant for this development: "Then God said, 'Let us make man in our image, after our likeness....'" Broadening the notion of image to include image as exemplar or model opens the way for Aquinas to discuss how humankind images God.[70] The image of God in the human creature, he proposes, resembles the image of a sovereign on a coin, insofar as what bears the image possesses an entirely different nature from what it images. In the instance of the human creature made after the image of God, the original remains infinitely distant from the image.[71] The tenet that the human person is created after the image of God also signals a certain movement of tending to perfection that forms a constitutive part of human existence. Action follows being.

Image also belongs to the genus of signs. When it functions as a sign, the image makes known or manifests to an intelligent person something other than itself. The image of God in the human creature can exist either as an instrumental sign or as a formal sign. An instrumental sign points beyond itself, as when a road marker on the New Jersey Turnpike tells me that New York is 100 miles down the road. When I see the sign, I gain an image of New York, but I still behold the fields of New Jersey, not the Empire State Building. A formal sign reveals something about what it inheres in, as when a healthy complexion persuades me that I am beholding a healthy person. Every human creature points toward God,

70. In *Summa theologiae* Ia, q. 35, a. 1, ad 1, Aquinas offers this precision: "That is called an image in a literal sense which originates as the likeness of another; that in whose likeness something originates is strictly speaking an exemplar and an image only in an imprecise sense. Yet it is in this sense that Augustine [in *De Trinitate*, Bk. 6, chap. 2] uses the term in stating that the divinity of the holy Trinity is the image after which man is fashioned."

71. For further study of the link which Aquinas makes between the Trinitarian image and image in Christian anthropology, see *Summa theologiae* Ia, q. 35, a. 2, ad 3 and q. 93, a. 1. ad 2.

whereas only the saints reveal the God in whose image they are created.

The principle that an agent produces something like itself (*omne agens agit simile sibi*) applies to the creation of the human person. The reason why human nature bears the image of God is because God created persons with a human nature. Like everything that God does outside of himself, creation in the image of God is a work of Father, Son, and Holy Spirit acting together in the unity of the divine nature. But although creation is the work of the divine nature, the image still reflects its Trinitarian origin.[72] This means that the image of God in us signifies an image both of the divine nature and of the divine Persons.[73] Precisely as image, the image of God properly resides in the intellective power of the soul, that is, in the will as well as in its coordination with the intellect. Furthermore, as discussion about the legitimacy of the *filioque* clause in the Creed indicates, Western theology especially insists that the movement of divine love proceeds from both the Father and the Son. Although God's simplicity allows no real distinctions in the divine nature, we hold that in God truth measures love. What is more important, the relationship of truth to love in God informs the divine imaging that occurs in the human creature, and so shapes the primordial dynamism of human agency. No one can reasonably choose just to love or just to know.

The divine nature abides without potential of any kind; as the Scholastic theologians insist, God is "pure act." The Trinity is not a mode of becoming in God, but of being. God is Father, Son, and Holy Spirit. Because God's being is "to be," the image of God does not most properly consist in the simple intellectual capacities of the soul by themselves, but these capacities as they dynamically actualize intelligent human life. This implies that our full imaging of the blessed Trinity consists in some actualization of our human capacities.[74] If this were not the case, it would make no sense to speak about a call to holiness, and the work of moral

---

72. For the Trinitarian theology implicit in this understanding of the divine activity, see William J. Hill, *The Three-Personed God* (Washington, D.C.: The Catholic University of America Press, 1982).

73. See *Summa theologiae* Ia, q. 93, a. 5, where Aquinas affirms that because humankind is made in the image of God's nature, all three Persons of the blessed Trinity are represented in each one of us.

74. Aquinas teaches that the image of the Trinity is found in our activities of thinking out and formulating an inner word (*conceptum*) from the information we have, and then bursting out from this in the act of love. For further discussion of the stress that the tradition puts on the actuality of immanent action, see *Summa theologiae* Ia, q. 93, a. 7.

theology would loose a great deal of its interest. The more actual the imaging, the more perfect the image. An actual image occurs when the intellectual powers of knowledge and love produce a word, and not just any sort of word, but a word which breaks forth into love *(et ex hoc in amorem prorumpimus)*.[75] It is important to remember that procession within the Trinity occurs only by way of immanent operations. This means that the processions of the Word of God and of the Holy Spirit proceed by way of God's self-knowing and self-loving. In a similar fashion, the image of God in the human creature consists not in any sort of human knowing or loving, but only in those actions not specified by exterior objects. It is customary to describe the image in two ways: as operative either in our acts of self-knowledge and self-love, and this is called the image of representation; or in acts of knowing and loving God, and this is called the image of conformity.

In the image of representation, the soul, in knowing and loving itself, dynamically images the divine self-knowledge constitutive of the Trinity of divine Persons.[76] As Aquinas summarizes it, "man is said to be after God's image in virtue of his intellectual nature."[77] The human intellect and its similitude, its knowledge of self, jointly cause the procession of the term of love, which is a sort of impulse toward the soul loved. For the image of representation, the operative analogy can be expressed thus: human knowing and loving exist in relation to the essence of the soul as divine knowing and loving relate to the divine essence. This structure of human knowing and the *imago Dei* which it produces can be visualized as an image in storage on film. What is more important, the image of representation is found in every human being.

In the image of conformity, the soul, in actually knowing and loving God himself, most perfectly and dynamically images the divine Trinity.[78] In this case, what is imaged exceeds the mere structure of immanent operations whose object is the self; what is imaged achieves the very object the knowledge and love of which constitutes the Trinity of Persons. Con-

---

75. See *Summa theologiae* Ia, q. 93, a. 7. Also, for an elaboration on this aspect of the Trinitarian image, see Ian Hislop, "Man, the Image of the Trinity, according to St. Thomas," *Dominican Studies* 3 (1950): 1–9.

76. *De veritate*, q. 10, aa. 7, 8. For further information, see Aelred Squires, "The Doctrine of the Image in the *De Veritate* of St. Thomas," *Dominican Studies* 4 (1951): 165–77.

77. *Summa theologiae* Ia, q. 93, a. 4: "homo secundum intellectualem naturam ad imaginem Dei esse dicatur."

78. *Summa theologiae* Ia, q. 93, a. 8.

temporary commentary on the image of God even includes reference to the extension or overflow of the divine imaging in the human body. This sort of imaging can be visualized as an image on a television monitor, where the image operates to its maximum capacity; furthermore, through this imaging, Christians, who before Baptism were strangers and aliens (cf. Eph 2:19), are now ushered into the dwelling place of the Trinity. This image is found only in those justified by God's grace.

Natural Image of God

In order to account for the progressive character of Christian life and holiness, professional theologians distinguish among several existential states or moments in which the human person bears the image of God: First, they speak about a natural image of God. In the natural order, that is, without the full bestowal of sanctifying grace that elevates a person to share in the divine friendship, this image achieves only an aptitudinal conformity with the living God. The God thus attained in knowledge is reached not in his very self, but rather according to the soul's own proper mode of being and as the cause of that being. Nor does the creature naturally love God with the all of the fullness which beatific fellowship—whether in grace or in glory—implies, but only under the common aspect of the good and as its principle.[79] While it is true that nature is ordained to love God above all things, certain spiritual authors who repeat this adage seem to ignore that the natural mode of union differs substantially and in kind from that achieved in divine charity.

Since the mid-1960s reflections about the natural image of God in man have not aroused much enthusiasm, even though the Christian tradition teaches that this natural image abides in the person as something more "intimate to the self than the self." Instead, many contemporary theologians choose to start with the supernatural image of God. This is the second realization of *imago*, the image of grace. It is argued, moreover, that since the Church considers it opportune to insist that Christ alone adequately reveals to the world what it means to be fully human, it makes

---

79. For further information, see *Summa theologiae* Ia-IIae, q. 109, a. 3, ad 1: "Charity loves God above all things in a higher way than nature does. For nature loves God above all things, in so far as he is the source and end of natural good ("prout est principium et finis naturalis boni"); but charity loves him above all things in as much as he is the object of blessedness and in as much as man has a certain kind of spiritual fellowship with God."

more sense to begin with the supernatural life.[80] There are nonetheless apologetic reasons for recalling that what is only potentially and aptitudinally an image of the divine Persons by nature, and is so defectively and frustratedly because of human sinfulness, becomes actually an image of God through the conformity of grace. Moral theology is concerned to show how the human person created in the *imago Dei* attains that image of conformity which perdures unto life everlasting. In glory, the *imago Dei* reaches its final and fullest existential state when the soul beholds God face to face. This is the third realization of *imago*, the image of glory. About this moment, St. Paul writes: "He who has prepared us for this very thing is God, who has given us the Spirit as a guarantee" (2 Cor 5:5). Christian theologians are in a better position to encourage people to prepare for this vision when they remind them that, since the natural image of God is never effaced from the human creature, the only alternative to beatific fellowship is that frustration which inexorably accompanies a person's definitive exclusion from glory.

Human Flourishing and *Beatitudo*

Ancient philosophers, such as Plato and Aristotle, and modern philosophers, such as Thomas Hobbes (1588–1679) and David Hume (1711–1776), offer different accounts of what constitutes the fulfillment of desire in the moral life. The Greek thinkers advance the view that, in order to qualify as fully human, human activity should reveal an intelligent purpose; according to this view, the fulfillment of all human desire lies in achieving a perfection that abides outside of the acting subject. The Enlightenment moralists, on the contrary, emphasize the subjective side of desire as the paramount concern for morals, so that reasonable activity, by definition, seeks to bring about the maximum state of personal satisfaction within a subject.

---

80. For example, see the frequently cited text of *Gaudium et spes*, no. 22, "The truth is that only in the mystery of the incarnate Word does the mystery of man take on light," which has set the agenda for a number of important theological projects in the postconciliar period. For a consideration of the centrality of this insight for fathoming the meaning of St. Thomas's doctrine of obediential potency, see Steven A. Long's "On the Possibility of a Purely Natural End for Man," *The Thomist* 64 (2000): 211–37, especially its concluding section, pp. 234–37. In an earlier work, the same author considers this subject for the sake of clarification in philosophic rather than theological anthropology. See his

In an important text from his *Summa contra gentiles,* Aquinas describes the relationship between acting for an intelligible end and acting so as to fulfill the desire of the human person.

Since happiness is the proper good of an intellectual nature, happiness must pertain to an intellectual nature by reason of what is proper to that nature. Now, appetite is not peculiar to intellectual nature; instead, it is present in all things, though it is in different things in different ways. And this diversity arises from the fact that things are differently related to knowledge. For things lacking knowledge entirely have natural appetite only. And things endowed with sensory knowledge have, in addition, sense appetite, under which irascible and concupiscible powers are included. But things possessed of intellectual knowledge also have an appetite proportionate to this knowledge, that is, will. So, the will is not peculiar to intellectual nature by virtue of being an appetite, but only in so far as it depends on intellect. However, the intellect, in itself, is peculiar to an intellectual nature. Therefore, happiness, or felicity, consists substantially and principally in an act of the intellect rather than in an act of the will.[81]

The text introduces the notion of the good-as-meant. Since a moral agent can discover only through an exercise of intelligence whether the objects of any desire comport with the good of the human person, strength of desire in itself does not afford an adequate starting point for directing human action.

Deliberate moral action falls between desire and fulfillment. The human intellect alone can discriminate the authentic goodness of a given end; for this reason, some authors refer to the end of moral action as the "good-as-meant."[82] John Finnis argues that Bernard Lonergan overlooks

---

"Obediential Potency, Human Knowledge, and the Natural Desire for God," *International Philosophical Quarterly* 37 (1997): 45–63.

81. *Summa contra gentiles* III, c. 26, trans. Vernon J. Bourke (Notre Dame, Ind.: University of Notre Dame Press, 1975), p. 104.

82. The human person acts for a *ratio bonitatis,* for what is understood to be good and because it is good. So in Ia-IIae, q. 19, a. 8, Aquinas states that "an act of the will is bad both when it is for bad considered as good and for good considered as bad. In order to be good, however, it must be for a good as meaning good *(sub ratione boni),* viz., it wills what is really good, and for the sake of good." So as to give the full strength to 'ratio' in the phrase 'sub ratione boni,' Thomas Gilby, O.P., *Principles of Morality,* Blackfriars Summa, vol. 18 (1966), p. 70, employs the expression the "good as meant." The good-as-meant, a key concept in Aquinas's moral theory, "is the determinant throughout of virtuous activity, and the lack-of-good-as-meant that of vicious activity. Whatever we do we are

the truly decisive difference between the good as merely experienced and the good as understood or the good-as-meant: "The difference," Finnis says, "is this: between sheerly wanting, and wanting something (to get, to have, to do or to be) *under a description*."[83] From the perspective of moral realism the human person is engaged not only with the description of things but with the real objects themselves, that is, with ultimate and less than ultimate ends, with acting for and against an order to ultimate end. "Acting is morally good when the choices of freedom are *in conformity with man's true good* and thus express the voluntary ordering of the person towards his ultimate end: God himself, the supreme good in whom man finds his full and perfect happiness." Thus, *Veritatis splendor*.[84] Because the human person displays its distinctive rational nature through a synergy of intellecting and willing, free movement toward these ends is marked both by an appetitive or conative aspect and by an intelligible or cognitive aspect.[85] The ends thus sought, and in due course embraced, throughout the course of the moral life remain both known and loved.

It is characteristic of Aquinas to insist that the human mind can achieve the kind of practical understanding that rightly discriminates about those things that are conducive to the good ends of human flourishing. For Aquinas and those who follow him, human behavior remains characteristically intelligent behavior. Moral theories that trim human fulfillment to fit the raw, felt desires of human nature invite subjectivist accounts of human perfection. Theories such as these present human happiness as consisting primarily, if not exclusively, in the satisfaction experienced by the human subject. This sort of reductionism opposes a Christian moral outlook; for human perfection, as *Veritatis splendor* makes clear, always implies the attaining of some good that lies outside of the subject. Only an intelligent ordering of one's life leads to embracing the true human good. In one of the many texts where Aquinas states this fundamental principle of his moral anthropology, he says that "the movement of the will is

---

always in a world of general meanings, historical happenings, and ultimate purpose: accordingly this moral determinant comprises three principles, the specific determinant, which is an act's objective, the individual determinants, which are the circumstances, and the personal determinant, which is intention of its end" (ibid., p. 167).

83. *Fundamentals of Ethics* (Washington, D.C.: Georgetown University Press, 1983), pp. 44–45.

84. *Veritatis splendor*, no. 72.

85. For further discussion, see *Summa theologiae* Ia, q. 80, aa. 1 and 2.

an inclination following upon a form as understood (*formam intellectam*)."[86]

Alasdair MacIntyre has characterized Aquinas's ethical tradition as one which views the moral life in terms of an exercise of craftsmanship.[87] Aquinas, it is true, distinguishes prudence from art on the grounds that the artist employs an extrinsic model in order properly to craft an object, whereas the prudential person commits a perfectly virtuous deed as a result of the internal shaping that *habitus* effects in the person. But since both art and prudence perfect the practical intellect, solid grounds exist for viewing the moral life as a craft inasmuch as the person learns to fashion good deeds with ease, promptness, and joy. In Aquinas's Latin shorthand, "those things which are unto the end"—*ea quae sunt ad finem*—refer to the good ends which collectively establish the stable pattern of a virtuous life. To talk about attaining or reaching or embracing "things" as ends should cause no alarm, since in the context of Christian moral theory, the "things" whose attainment really matters are persons, and, of course, ultimately the three divine Persons of the blessed Trinity.[88]

Final Beatitude

Roman Catholic moral theology particularly concerns itself with what alone constitutes perfect happiness for all men and women, the ultimate good of the person.[89] Perhaps no words in Christian literature better express this conviction than those of St. Augustine in the *Confessions:* "You have made us for yourself, O Lord, and our hearts are restless until they rest in thee." As a theological term, "beatitude" designates specifically Christian happiness, viz., the realization of our human desire to see God.[90] Moral theology first considers beatitude in itself, what Aquinas

86. See his discussion of choice, both angelic and human, in *Quaestiones de quodlibet* 6, q. 2, a. 1, where Aquinas also recalls that the human soul is not completely intellectual, since even its vegetative powers, for instance, participate in intelligence. Cf. Chapter Three, note 5.

87. Alasdair MacIntyre, *Three Rival Versions of Moral Enquiry: Encyclopaedia, Genealogy, and Tradition* (Notre Dame, Ind.: University of Notre Dame Press, 1990), esp. chap. 3, where the author contrasts Aquinas's way of pursuing moral enquiry with that of the "encyclopedic" mentality and of the Nietzschien "genealogical" ethos.

88. See *Summa theologiae* Ia, q. 26 for Aquinas's discussion on God's own happiness, which, significantly in the present context, is the question that introduces the tract on the Trinity.

89. See *Veritatis splendor*, no. 13.

90. For a thorough explanation of the relationship between natural fulfillment and the call to beatific vision, see Benedict M. Ashley, O.P., "What Is the End of the Human

calls objective beatitude: God as he is the highest Goodness. "Just as God possesses existence," writes Aquinas, "though he does not come into existence, so does he possess happiness without deserving [*mereatur*] it."[91] For the greater honor and glory of God, as Saint Ignatius Loyola reminded his first followers, the human person intelligently desires happiness and hopes to obtain its fullness. It is a foundational principle. The theological virtues of hope and charity enable the believer to realize the fulfillment of this end in grace and glory. Philosophers may conclude that one ought to reverence a higher power that transcends the confines of the created order, but only divine grace freely bestowed in Christ enables one to know and love the God of Abraham, Isaac, and Jacob. This reflection attributed to Blaise Pascal still holds true. Furthermore, divine grace is bestowed without regard for a person's human stature. When the dying Christ promises the Good Thief, "Today you will be with me in Paradise" (Lk 23:43), the New Testament makes it abundantly clear that Paradise remains open even to the most miserable among men and women.

Once this fundamental teleological truth is made plain, the theologian can enquire into beatitude from the point of view of the one experiencing it. We sometimes reserve the term "happiness" to signify the subjective state of the one who possesses beatitude. Aquinas of course recognizes that there exists a subjective side to the possession of the ultimate end, as the following text illustrates: "[Our] ultimate end remains uncreated good, namely God, who alone can fill the will of man to the brim because of his infinite goodness. On the other hand, our ultimate end is a creaturely reality in us, for what is it but our coming to God and our joy with God?"[92] The distinction between beatitude itself and our sharing in beatitude forms an important part of how moral realism embodies and serves Christian personalism. As grace signifies both God's favor and its effect in us, so God alone constitutes the happiness that human

---

Person? The Vision of God and Integral Human Fulfillment," in *Moral Truth and Moral Tradition. Essays in Honour of Peter Geach and Elizabeth Anscombe*, ed. Luke Gormally (Dublin: Four Courts Press, 1994), pp. 68–96. Inasmuch as the Beatitudes promise aspects of the good that opens the believer up to eternal life, they lie at the heart of the Christian vocation (see Mt 5:8; 1 Cor 13:12; Heb 12:14; Rv 22:4). See *Veritatis splendor*, no. 16.

91. *Summa theologiae* Ia, q. 26, a. 1, ad 2. Insofar as the divine happiness causes all other lesser forms of beatitude, this text amply demonstrates how much Christian beatitude as a category in ethics transcends the distinction between egoism and altruism.

92. *Summa theologiae* Ia-IIae, q. 3, a. 1.

persons seek. Even in beatific fellowship, the personal fulfillment which Christians rightfully expect always respects the limits of a created human nature.

Personalism and Ends

Christian moral theology promotes authentic personalism to the extent that it takes full account not only of the common requirements of human nature but also of the particular exigencies that distinguish each human person. When human nature is frustrated, it is an illusion to speak of personal fulfillment. Virtuous loving respects persons. A person is at least the co-objective in every act of authentic Christian love; that is, when something less than a person is said to be loved, it is loved for some person, either for oneself or for one's friend. When it is a case of loving some existing reality as the good, just because it is good and as it is, viz., for its own sake, then that objective is always a person. The distinction between the love of friendship and the love of desire leads to a further claim about loving the good. When such a good is real, is in fact a total good, loveable above all else, as it is and for its own sake, then the "it," as both theologian and philosopher should attest, always points to God.[93]

In order to clarify the relationship between an end or object and the individual's embrace of that object, or acting for that end, theologians distinguish three different ways of looking at a person's relationship to an end. First, end signifies the reason why a person would engage in a specific kind of activity—what the Scholastics named the "end-for-the-sake-of-which" (*finis cuius gratia*); second, end signifies that which actually draws a person to embrace an object—the "end-to-which" (*finis cui*); and third, end signifies the means whereby one embraces the good—the "end-by-which" (*finis quo*). One might ask whether a teleological frame of reference allows for performing actions "without reference to any wider aim."[94] As examples of those things which one can simply desire for themselves, we might imagine engagement in or with: "fine music, a life of service, chocolates, children, religious ecstasy, sexual ecstasy ... the list is endless." But this list of examples seems to ignore the fundamental distinction between

---

93. See *Summa theologiae* Ia-IIae, q. 26, a. 4; q. 27, a. 3. For a contemporary study of natural theology, see Pierre-Marie Emonet, *God Seen in the Mirror of the World. An Introduction to the Philosophy of God* (New York: Herder & Herder, 2000).

94. For example, Jean Porter, *Recovery of Virtue*, p. 76.

a *finis cui* and a *finis cuius gratia,* or the difference between something that is sought for itself and something which is sought for the sake of a further end. A person may never virtuously subordinate children and (service to) other people to his or her own goals or purposes (including delight). We can render them their due according to the diverse types of justice, even expect to receive something good from them in theological hope, and above all love them in theological charity. But we can never turn them into an "end-for-the-sake-of-which *(finis cuius gratia).* On the other hand, fine music, chocolates, and ecstasy both sexual and religious (if by the latter one means created thoughts and feelings about God and not union with God himself) always remain instrumental, that is, they can never embody a perfective "end-to-which" *(finis cui)* for the virtuous person.[95]

The human person's joyful possession of the beatific vision locates the consummation of the moral life. There in glory, the person seeks God for his own sake in a union which the divine nature makes possible by establishing a medium in which a poor creature can know and love the infinitely rich God. Christian humanism requires the fulfillment of the law of love and aspires to the plenitude of divine life, which transcends even a comprehensive list of basic human goods.[96] To stress beatitude does not mean that moral theology is bogged down in other-worldliness. Created goods do promote authentic happiness, and the Christian is encouraged to engage them in a distinctive and fulsome way. The Christian Gospel proclaims the original "thick" version of the human good. In order to complete a description of the moral life, the moral theologian must attend to the virtues, the gifts and fruits of the Holy Spirit, and the evangelical Beatitudes—all of which delineate the full dimensions of the Christian life.[97] On the other hand, secular forms of humanism typical-

95. For further explanation of the terminology, see Thomas Gilby, O.P., *Purpose and Happiness,* Blackfriars *Summa,* vol. 16 (1969), "Glossary," pp. 156–60, especially the entries "End" and "Objective."

96. However, one should not confuse the basic goods with a dialectical search for an ultimate end. Perhaps no single author has done more to bring this point to the fore than Germain Grisez: morality is about the integral flourishing of the human person. For the fullest presentation of his views, see Germain Grisez, *The Way of the Lord Jesus,* vol. 1, *Christian Moral Principles,* with the help of Joseph M. Boyle, Jr., Basil Cole, O.P., John Finnis, John A. Geinzer, Robert G. Kennedy, Patrick Lee, William E. May, and Russell Shaw (Chicago: Franciscan Herald Press, 1983). Subsequent volumes provide a complete course in moral theology.

97. Jean Porter, "Desire for God: Ground of the Moral Life in Aquinas," *Theological*

ly adopt "thin" versions of the human good, while also endorsing liberal political views that guarantee maximum freedom of choice. And although one cannot simply develop a natural clone of a complete virtuous life by scraping off what appears distinctively Christian, it is still possible to recognize a "thick" version of human flourishing even in the acquired moral virtues, which lie at the heart of Aquinas's treatise on the moral life. In fact, Aquinas lists scores of specific virtues which shape the human person toward the attainment of human flourishing; in the order of grace these virtues find perfection in charity which, according to Saint Paul (see 1 Cor 13:13), forms the permanent heart of *beatitudo*.

Reality and the good dominate Christian ethics.[98] St. Thomas warns against intrinsically evil acts, but he prefers to describe them in terms of an action which is evil by reason of its object *(malum ex objecto)*, that is, those actions whose objects do not conform to the good of the human person. For the moral realist, the composite of moral objects, concretized in the moral and theological virtues, specify—that is, describe and determine—the contours of a good moral life. In a section on "Fundamental Choice and Specific Kinds of Behavior," *Veritatis splendor* explains that some theologians have argued that none of these categorical goods, which by their nature are partial, could determine the freedom of man as a person in his totality. "The immediate object of such [particular] acts would not be absolute Good (before which the freedom of the person would be expressed on a transcendental level), but particular (also termed 'categorical') goods."[99] The encyclical goes on to suggest that this bifurcated view of the moral good corresponds poorly with the person as a unified moral agent. Moral realism maintains that our happiness in the present life, while we are still on the way to heaven, lies in the complete possession of those virtuous objects that together form the good of the human person. To work effectively, the moral theologian must be in possession of a philosophically sound way to identify the authentic goods of the moral life.

Studies 47 (1986): 48–68, thinks that Aquinas's "overall moral theology is teleological in the sense that it holds that the final purpose of human life gives the moral life its ultimate point, but it is not teleological in the sense that actions and virtues are evaluated by the degree to which they directly foster or hinder the attainment of that final purpose" (65).

98. Josef Pieper's *Reality and the Good* (Chicago: H. Regnery, 1967) provides a sound explanation of this central element of Thomist morals.

99. *Veritatis splendor*, no. 65.

Some Contemporary Issues

We have already observed the influence that David Hume has exercised on modern moral philosophy. He eschews what he considers the groundless view that moral oughts can be discovered on the basis of an analysis of what human nature "is," or deduced from distinctively human properties.[100] For example, on a Humean view, it is wrong to conclude that, since intelligent creatures possess the ability to communicate, human conversation ought to represent the truth. Or to take another example, that, because sexual activity may result in the conception of a new human life, it is wrong to conclude that heterosexual coupling ought to be carried on only within a stable marriage relationship. Hume may in fact have personally held both values, but he simply denied discovering the basis for such norms in a philosophy which takes human nature seriously. If they be good, actions affect an individual human nature only because of the pleasing sentiments that they register in those who perform them.[101] It belongs to philosophers to give an overall evaluation of Hume's moral philosophy; still, it is the case that for nearly two centuries a minimalist position on the relationship between being human and human acting has dominated Anglo-American moral philosophy.[102] If one may be permitted a generalization, this outlook stands in sharp contrast to what

100. One is constrained to note that these conclusions presuppose a prior abstractive reduction of nature to a factive surd, drained of necessity, intelligibility, and teleological structure. As the fruit of prior abstraction that confuses logical and ontological evidence and intelligibility, the identification of real possibility and mere conceivability is (as observed *supra* in note 61) an enormous *petitio principii*; and the real distinction between the "is" of being and the merely propositional "is" of privation witnesses to necessity in being (being *is not* not-being, the "is" of being truly is not the "is" of privation or negation).

101. This at least represents an early formulation by Hume in his 1739 *A Treatise of Human Nature*, ed. L. A. Selby-Bigge (Oxford: Clarendon Press, 1896), Bk. I, chap. iv, 2: "In order to [discover the true origin of morals], ... we shall endeavour to follow a very simple method: we shall analyse that complication of mental qualities, which form what, in common life, we call Personal Merit: we shall consider every attribute of the mind, which renders a man an object either of esteem and affection, or of hatred and contempt, every habit or sentiment or faculty, which, if ascribed to any person, implies either praise or blame, and may enter into any panegyric or satire of his character and manners."

102. For a well-known analysis of Hume's influence on contemporary Anglo-American ethics, see G. E. M. Anscombe's now-classic article, "Modern Moral Philosophy," *Philosophy* 33 (1958), reprinted in *Ethics, Religion and Politics* (Minneapolis: University of Minnesota Press, 1982), pp. 26–42.

was generally accepted in Catholic circles throughout the late medieval and early modern periods, for instance from the death of John Capreolus (1444) to the death of John Poinsot (1644), when the majority of Catholic theologians taught that good moral conduct perfects human nature.

Present-day challenges to moral realism owe much to a received skepticism regarding the truth claims that human nature introduces into moral theory. Egoism and utilitarianism ground their respective ethical views on what causes an individual or the greatest number of individuals the most satisfaction, not what perfects the common nature that individual human beings share. As early as the end of the eighteenth century, Immanuel Kant sought to address the modern tilt toward moral egoism by his categorical imperative, which allows the individual to determine what he would, if he could, dictate to be accepted as a universal precept. But in this clearly deontological plan—for one must act on the basis of a duty to follow the moral imperative—others become disenfranchised members of an illusory moral majority. More significantly, Kant's moral philosophy presupposes and even accentuates Humean agnosticism concerning order and purpose in nature, so that his limited recovery of elements of moral obligation is purchased at the price of an even starker anti-metaphysical reduction: the autonomous human will is left as the highest knowable subject of existence. Needless to say, such an arbitrary foreshortening of the ethical horizon does not conduce either to Christian moral theology or to the more limited objectives of a genuine natural philosophy (either physically or morally).[103] The Thomist tradition of the early modern period exhibits that Aquinas's view of purpose in the *secunda pars* runs much deeper than these rationalist reductionisms.[104]

103. Iris Murdoch in *The Sovereignty of Good* (London: Routledge & Kegan Paul, 1971) describes the irony that she sees in Kant's heritage: "Kant's conclusive exposure of the so-called proofs for the existence of God, his analysis of the limitations of speculative reason, together with his eloquent portrayal of the dignity of rational man, has had results which might possibly dismay him. How recognizable, how familiar to us, is the man so beautifully portrayed in the *Grundlegung*, who confronted even with Christ turns away to consider the judgment of his own conscience and to hear the voice of his own reason. Stripped of the exiguous metaphysical background which Kant was prepared to allow him, this man is with us still, free, independent, lonely, powerful, rational, responsible, brave, the hero of many novels and books of moral philosophy" (p. 80). Her later *Metaphysics as a Guide to Morals* (New York: Allen Lane, Penguin Press, 1993) provides helpful commentary as well.

104. For general information about the history of Thomism, see my *Le thomisme et les thomistes* (Paris: Les Éditions du Cerf, 1999).

While philosophical inquiry alone cannot establish an appropriate and adequate method for theological ethics, philosophers traditionally have provided the basic models used by moral theologians to develop their science.[105] This means that changes in philosophical ethics affect the evolution of Christian moral theology. For example, consider the widely accepted view that "fundamental" moral theology constitutes a sort of meta-discipline whose distinction includes weighing the relative merits of one methodological question or another. Surely this contributes to the confusion that students of moral theology encounter when they begin to confront the thicket of competing claims which seek to direct the successful pursuit of moral theology. Even interpreters of Aquinas have debated about where to locate him on the sometimes Procrustean grids established by moral methodologists.[106] Exaggerated concern over methodology is diversionary. In the early 1980s, one Christian ethicist remarked that if any one had followed the literature on moral philosophy in the major books over the past four decades, it would be clear "that moral philosophers were more interested in the ideas of others about moral philosophy than they were in morality itself."[107] The temptation is a perennial one, and can affect moral theologians as well.

In order to avoid becoming too entangled in problems of methodological taxonomy, we shall consider the two forms of moral argument that appear most frequently in contemporary theological ethics: the teleological model and the deontological model.[108] These two models represent distinct initial emphases in philosophical ethics, proceeding from the difference between the notion of right and the reality of the good.

105. But see John Hill, "The Debate between McCormick and Frankena," *Irish Theological Quarterly* 49 (1982): 121–33, and his interesting observations on what he calls "the intelligibility gap" which exists between moral theologians, represented by Richard McCormick, and moral philosophers, represented by William Frankena.

106. It would be difficult, for instance, to find much sympathy today for the perspective represented by W. A. Wallace, O.P., *The Role of Demonstration in Moral Theology* (Washington, D.C.: The Thomist Press, 1960), even though this work recapitulates some important directions taken in pre-conciliar Thomist moral theology.

107. James M. Gustafson, *Ethics from a Theocentric Perspective*, vol. 1, *Theology and Ethics* (Chicago: University of Chicago Press, 1981), p. 67. Vol. 2, *Ethics and Theology* (Chicago: University of Chicago Press, 1984), includes analysis of specific issues.

108. For one witness, see the discussion by Bruno Schüller, "La moralité de moyen à fin dans une éthique normative de caractère téléologique," *Revue des sciences religieuses* 68 (1980): 205–24, where the author examines the rapport between means and end from within both a teleological and deontological perspective.

Moralists who develop their theories based on distinguishing a proper or right course of action from a wrong or incorrect one are known as deontologists, while those who favor a view of the moral life centering on the embrace[109] of good ends conducive to a state of human fulfillment or flourishing are known as teleologists.[110] Because of the complexity involved in moral theories, it is generally held that no author embodies either species of moral argumentation in its pure form. A brief look at the table of contents of the *Summa theologiae* reveals that this generalization applies even to Aquinas. Though a teleological model dominantly grounds his vision of the Christian moral life, he still grafts deontological branches onto the tree of virtue in order to account for such fundamental rules for Christian behavior as those contained in the Decalogue.

Ends and Obligations

Teleology entered the vocabulary of moral theology only during the late modern period. Because he required a term to distinguish the branch of natural philosophy which treats of final causes from that which treats of efficient causes, Christian Wolff, it seems, devised the term "teleology" as a way to talk about finality in nature. The usually accepted etymological root for the eighteenth-century neologism comes from *telos*, the Greek word for "end." *The Encyclopedia of Religion and Ethics*, edited by James Hastings in 1912, apportions thirty-three columns to the entry on "Teleology," but we find only a single paragraph devoted to how the concept is used in ethics. The author of the article, who significantly subalternates ethics under sociology, presents ethical teleology as the case when "the moral

109. The term "embrace" introduces a new metaphor to describe how a person relates to perfecting goods, but it does correspond to St. Augustine's language, for example, the passage in *Confessiones*, Bk. 13, chap. 9: "pondus meum amor meus; eo feror, quocumque feror," trans. John K. Ryan (New York: Image Books, 1960): "My love is my weight! I am borne about by it, wheresoever I am borne."

110. Lisa Sowle Cahill, "Teleology, Utilitarianism, and Christian Ethics," *Theological Studies* 42 (1981): 601–29, has observed the following about disagreements in Christian ethics: "A major difficulty is that definitions of teleology and deontology rarely are agreed upon and often are promoted tendentiously. That this problem continues can be illustrated quite clearly by the spate of literature prompted by [R.] McCormick and others" (625). She further points out that in Roman Catholic moral theology the misunderstanding especially ensues upon a confusion between ends understood as real objects which perfect moral choices and ends taken as simply another term to describe the consequences of a moral choice.

standard is represented by the idea of good or value."[111] On the basis of this blurry characterization, he concludes that the teleological standpoint is to be distinguished from the abstract and transcendental principles associated with Kantian formalism and that "their value consists not in defining but in their power of promoting the ethical end."[112] Because the term had only entered the vocabulary of ethics in the nineteenth century, Hastings's *Encyclopedia* provides a much briefer entry for "Deontology." The author of this article identifies deontology with the science of ethics. On his account, the term seems to have been used first by Jeremy Bentham, who "had in mind the principles of duty as distinct from those of prudence and interest."

By the last quarter of the twentieth century, we find that ethicists have developed a fuller definition and classification of deontology, which comes from the Greek word for "duty." In its straight forms, a moral deontology appeals to the human person's sense of duty to act in a responsible way. Obligation accordingly affords the main reason for acting, and one can distinguish two ways to specify these obligations: rational principles or positive law. Act-deontologies stress a personal code of responsibility based upon some, usually *a priori*, categories as the principal criteria for guiding moral behavior. On the other hand, rule-deontologies hold that the standard of right and wrong conduct consists of one or more rules properly endorsed by a competent authority. These deontologies both depend on extrinsic warrants for governing moral behavior. The rule can be straightforward and concrete, such as one finds in the Ten Commandments: "You shall not commit adultery" (Dt 5:18), or complex and abstract, such as that proposed by the nineteenth-century English moralist Henry Sidgwick:

It cannot be right for A to treat B in a manner in which it would be wrong for B to treat A, merely on the ground that they are two different individuals, and without there being any difference between the natures or circumstances of the two which can be stated as a reasonable ground for difference of treatment.[113]

111. See William Fulton, "Teleology," in *Encyclopedia of Religion and Ethics*, vol. 12, ed. James Hastings (New York: Charles Scribner's Sons, 1912), p. 228.

112. Ibid.

113. *The Methods of Ethics*, 7th ed. (London: Macmillan and Co., Ltd., 1907), p. 380.

Deontologies fundamentally and principally appeal to our capacity for using our moral imagination; in their contemporary forms, moreover, they almost always oblige the moral agent to engage in some form of calculation.

Both deontology and teleology find their legitimate expressions in Christian moral theology. The Ten Commandments and the directives of the Church provide examples of rules that propose concrete courses of action for us. *Gaudium et spes* even describes a moral conscience which provides the grounds for following an act deontology: "Deep within their conscience individuals discover a law which they do not make themselves but which they are bound to obey, whose voice ever summoning them to love and do what is good and avoid what is evil, rings in their heart when necessary with the command 'Do this, keep away from that.' "[114] In addition, it is possible to find the perspectives and emphases of moral deontologies represented in the works of Catholic spiritual authors and the traditions out of which they write.

Moral realism operates within the framework of a highly refined teleology.[115] I would describe a Christian moral teleology as one which explains and evaluates human behavior on the basis of whether or not a given human action properly and opportunely attains a good which conduces to the complete perfection of the agent. For the moral theologian, "end" then refers to those goods which perfect the human person; broadly speaking, good moral action develops out of a proper love of those goods which constitute human flourishing.[116] Aquinas expresses this truth directly and simply when he inquires whether the emotion of love as a basic element of human psychology does harm to the lover: "The love of a fitting good makes the lover more perfect and better, but love for a good that is unfitting for the lover wounds the lover and makes the lover worse. Hence we are especially perfected and made better through love

114. *Gaudium et spes*, no. 16: "In imo conscientiae legem homo detegit, quam ipse sibi non dat, sed cui obedire debet, et cuius vox, semper ad bonum amandum et faciendum ac malum vitandum eum advocans, ubi oportet auribus cordis sonat: fac hoc, illud devita."

115. For an early study of the relationship and differences between Aristotelian teleology and Aquinas's evangelical eudemonism, see Augustinus Mansion, "L'eudémonisme aristotélicien et la morale Thomiste," *Xenia Thomistica*, vol. 1, ed. Sadoc Szabó (Rome: Typis Polyglottis Vaticanis, 1925), pp. 429–49.

116. For a succinct statement of the moral teleology that informs Catholic moral thought, see *Veritatis splendor*, no. 72.

of God, but are wounded and made worse through love of sin."[117] One author claims that philosophers in their ambition to examine the human powers of the soul often ignore this aspect of Aquinas's existentialism, with the result that not enough emphasis is given to the basic conviction of moral realism, namely, that the good we seek and embrace in love inescapably affects our personal being and goodness.[118]

Metaphysics and Ethics

It is axiomatic that the real goods which perfect the human person exist independently of anyone's actually choosing them as moral goods. It remains, however, a *quaestio disputata* as to whether or not one should regard basic human goods in themselves as good in the strictly moral sense. The Oxford moralist John Finnis argues that the basic human goods remain pre-moral until the moment when practical reasonableness goes to work on them in the living out of the moral life.[119] The American Thomist Ralph McInerny takes strong exception to this opinion on the basis that Finnis's position appears to eviscerate the transcendental goodness resident in the basic human goods, thereby threatening to render unintelligible the Aristotelian notion that the good-as-end draws.[120] This difference

117. *Summa theologiae* Ia-IIae, q. 28, a. 5: "Amor igitur boni convenientis est perfectivus et meliorativus amantis: amor autem boni quod non est conveniens amanti est laesivus et deteriorativus amantis. Unde homo maxime perficitur et melioratur per amorem Dei: laeditur autem et deterioratur per amorem peccati...."

118. For further development of this point in the area of Christian spirituality, see the article by Walter Principe, C.S.B., "Affectivity and the Heart in Thomas Aquinas' Spirituality," in *Spiritualities of the Heart: Approaches to Personal Wholeness*, ed. Annice Callahan, R.S.C.J. (New York: Paulist Press, 1990), pp. 45–63.

119. John Finnis, *Fundamentals of Ethics*, pp. 56ff.

120. Ralph McInerny, *Ethica Thomistica: The Moral Philosophy of Thomas Aquinas* (Washington, D.C.: The Catholic University of America Press, 1982), p. 52, writes: "What Finnis might mean is that the grasp of these basic values is expressed in definitions rather than in precepts and in that sense no practical advice, moral or otherwise, is being given. Only when we judge that we should pursue the basic value or when we judge that such-and-such is a way of attaining or participating in the basic value, stating this in a prescriptive way—only then do we enter the domain of the moral proper. But surely that would not lead one to say that such precepts are pre-moral." In the revised 1997 edition, McInerny removed this text, since he no longer thought that this compendium was the right place to criticize the work of Germain Grisez and John Finnis. But "as those two admirable gentleman know," he wrote, "this is not a recantation" (p. xi). Students interested in hearing both sides of the story may consult the essays by these authors in the 1980 and 1981 issues of *American Journal of Jurisprudence*.

of opinion ultimately reflects the dissimilarities between the perspectives of a moral realism which views ethics in continuity with a larger metaphysical description of the world and of a moral theory which considers ethics principally a matter of directing right choices in life.[121]

Moral realism centers its reflections on a contemplation of the highest wisdom.[122] The Christian moral realist approaches the moral life as part of the larger contemplative life which "consists principally in contemplation of God under the impetus of divine love."[123] Within this outlook, all Christian moral theology is fueled by the splendid intuition of Thérèse of Lisieux, who came to understand that Love alone enables the Church's members to act. What might be described as moral decisionism centers its reflections on the interior dynamics of the acting person. From this point of view, the moral life is the equivalent of an examined life, much as St. Augustine advocates when he writes: "Let each one of you consider himself: let him enter into himself, ascend the judgment seat of his own mind, set himself in order before his conscience, compel himself to confess. For it knows who he is: 'For what person knows a man's thoughts except the spirit of the man which is in him?' (1 Cor 2:11)."[124] Both posi-

121. By all accounts, Russell Hittinger seems to have begun a long-running international debate with his analysis of Germain Grisez in *A Critique of the New Natural Law Theory* (Notre Dame, Ind.: University of Notre Dame Press, 1987). Germain Grisez, "A Critique of Russell Hittinger's Book, *A Critique of the New Natural Law Theory*," *New Scholasticism* 42 (1988): 438–65, and Robert George, "Recent Criticism of Natural Law Theory," *University of Chicago Law Review* 55 (1988): 1371–429, replied to Hittinger's analysis. This exchange of views, including Hittinger's own reply to Grisez published in the same issue of *New Scholasticism*, launched a spate of journal articles, many of which appeared in *The Thomist*, and books that would require a special study to enumerate completely, let alone evaluate correctly. To my knowledge, however, Hittinger's initial appraisal and criticisms have anticipated subsequent literature on this subject even when other authors have engaged the issues more extensively. One point should be made definitively: both approaches to moral theology represent honest and satisfactory efforts to explicate what Catholic and divine faith requires us to hold about the moral life. The present author acknowledges his agreement and deep sympathy with the way that Ralph McInerny, Benedict Ashley, and their students have interpreted the Thomist tradition, and at the same time expresses appreciation for the significant contributions made by Germain Grisez, John Finnis, Joseph Boyle, and their collaborators to the defense and dissemination of Catholic moral truth.

122. For an expert presentation of the right way to approach Catholic moral theology after the issuance of *Veritatis splendor*, see Steven A. Long, *The Teleological Grammar of the Moral Act* (Naples, Fla.: Sapientia Press, 2007), especially the "Introduction," pp. xi–xx.

123. *Summa theologiae* IIa-IIae, q. 180, a. 7.

124. St. Augustine, *In evangelium Johannis tractatus* XXXIII, 5: "Consideret se unus-

tions, moral realism and moral decisionism, possess their distinguishing set of moral categories and both purport to maintain a form of moral objectivism.[125]

To cast an irenic light on the *disputatio inter doctores* over metaphysics and ethics, it is possible to recognize in the moral realists' insistence that the goods which conduce to integral human perfection themselves form part of our moral universe a continuation of Roman Catholic insistence on the sacramentality of nature. Each morally good action which includes the human person's embrace of the basic human good incarnates a moment of divine love in the world, so that to insist that such goods are premoral seems to rupture the unity of the *sacra doctrina*. On the other hand, one must admit that neither modern moral philosophy nor—and perhaps because of the then-prevailing influences in morals—the documents of the Second Vatican Council exhibit strong affinities for the relationship of moral philosophy to metaphysics.[126] On the contrary, the categories of law, the moral conscience, and human responsibility strongly characterize the ethical discourse in the second half of the twentieth century, and the Church continues to adapt these to her own purposes of moral instruction. In any event, the Christian tradition provides ample warrant for speaking about the moral life in terms of a well-formed conscience, due attention to legitimate moral norms and precepts, and the obligation to choose well in the course of one's life.[127] At the same time, both *Veri-*

---

quisque vestrum, intret in semetipsum, ascendat tribunal mentis suae, constituat se ante conscientiam suam cogat se confiteri. Scit enim qui sit: quia nemo scit hominum quae sunt hominis, nisi spiritus hominis, qui in ipso est (I Cor. 2, 11)" (PL 35, col. 1645).

125. But see the significant challenges which Henry Veatch and Joseph Rautenberg, "Does the Grisez-Finnis-Boyle Moral Philosophy Rest on a Mistake?" *Review of Metaphysics* 44 (1991): 807–30, raise against this theory, as well as the reply made by John Finnis, "Natural Law and the Is-Ought Question: An Invitation to Professor Veatch," *The Catholic Lawyer* 26 (1980–81): 266–77, to an earlier formulation of the argument that appeared in Veatch's review of Finnis's book *Natural Law and Natural Rights* in the *American Journal of Jurisprudence* 26 (1981): 247–59.

126. It should be pointed out that the Second Vatican Council did not produce a document on moral theory, and that *Veritatis splendor* completes the conciliar project as far as moral theology is concerned. For an interesting early essay on the rapprochement between modern ethical thought and the perspectives of the Aquinas, see Mark Brocklehurst, O.P., "The *Summa theologiae* and Modern Ethical Thought," *Dominican Studies* 1 (1948): 195–208.

127. John Langan, S.J., "Beatitude and Moral Law in St. Thomas," *Journal of Religious Ethics* 5 (1977): 183–95, offers a creative view of Aquinas's own moral theory when he argues that one should classify it as a kind of deontological intuitionism. Following a

tatis splendor and *Fides et ratio* have complemented the predominantly pastoral formulations found in the conciliar documents themselves by drawing our attention once again to the intimate relation that exists between moral action and the metaphysics of being.

The True Good

Both classical moral realists and the new natural lawyers agree that neither Aquinas nor Roman Catholic moral theology can interpret the end of an action as the intended effect or consequence of an action. For Aquinas, the end is that reality that constitutes the object of the act, not the pleasure, utility, benefit, or anything else which arises as its consequence.[128] So, when utilitarian moral philosophers speak about pursuing the "net social good," they can claim nothing in common with the tradition of moral realism. When students of ethics mistake teleology for a form of consequentialism, they obscure the important distinction between goods which perfect the human person and consequences which follow upon a person's action and may well harm the person. Some contemporary descriptions of teleological theories still confuse teleology with consequentialism: "The final appeal, directly or indirectly, must be to the comparative amount of good produced, or rather to the comparative balance of good over evil produced."[129] To counsel engagement with this sort of calculation about human loving seriously risks offense to the dignity of the human person. Why? This form of moral calculation offers no insurance that, in the final analysis, a specific course of action does not depreciate the life of divine charity.

The New Testament assures us that God is Love (see 1 Jn 4:8), and so the Christian believer who acts so as to embrace the end of divine charity meets God himself through the very choices that he or she makes. In the real world of salvation history, there are no neutral choices. One moves either toward God or away from Him. For this reason, it would be blasphemous to assert that acting rightly in the eyes of God could at the

---

slightly different approach to the question of Aquinas's ethical models, Steven Anthony Edwards, "Structure and Change in Aquinas's Religious Ethics," *Journal of the American Academy of Religion* 54 (1986): 281–302, argues that Aquinas employs three different approaches to the individual's relationship with God: teleology; justice; and friendship.

128. Aquinas makes it clear that the moral good is not to be identified with even accompanying pleasure, for example, see *Summa theologiae* Ia-IIae, q. 2, a. 6; q. 4, aa. 1 & 2.

129. See William F. Frankena, *Ethics* (Englewood Cliffs, New Jersey: Prentice-Hall, Inc., 1973), p. 14.

same time involve one, as a necessary part of choosing a particular course of action, in something that is opposed to the infinite goodness of God. Still, some moralists argue as if the choice of something evil, justified on the basis of some form of proportionate reasoning or the equivalent, amounts only to the shadow side of an otherwise honest effort at keeping the Commandments. The New Testament takes love seriously. "He who does not love does not know God; for God is love" (1 Jn 4:8). To pursue counterfeit loves while imagining that one loves God is like trying to move both north and south at the same time. It is an impossible feat in the natural order, and an illusion in the moral life.[130] Only the person who loves in the truth comes to know God.

The Christian believer discovers the ultimate specifying end of the Christian moral life in the promise and anticipated realization of beatific union with God. The Church instructs about the promise; the life of divine charity supplies the anticipation. Happiness is the cleaving to God as the mind's all-fulfilling object.[131] Every agent acts for an end, and an end has the meaning or nature of a good. We can thank the ascetical Dominic de Guzman for reminding the early thirteenth-century Church that her belief in the Word made flesh opposes all forms of Manichaeism. Contemporary forms of theological dualism still commit the deep-seated error of subordinating the good—for instance, of life, of human procreation, of whatever is required to sustain individual human life until natural death—to imaginary higher human goals and purposes. The Thomist axiom *gratia perficit naturam*—grace perfects nature—provides a concise statement of how moral realism conceives the relation between human flourishing and Christian beatitude. Since the transcendent God of Christian revelation

130. On the alleged "premoral" specifications of human action, see Mark Johnson, "Proportionalism and a Text of the Young Aquinas: Quodlibetum IX, Q. 7, A. 2," *Theological Studies* 53 (1992): 683–99.

131. *Summa theologiae* Ia-IIae, q. 3, a. 8. Happiness however is not a consequence of the cleaving. The Scholastics use the terms "objectual" or "intentional" to describe a subject-object activity proper to cognition and appetition. Objectual presence differs from an effect-efficient cause relationship. See *Summa theologiae* Ia, q. 8, a. 3. Oliva Blanchette, *The Perfection of the Universe According to Aquinas. A Teleological Cosmology* (University Park, Pa.: Pennsylvania State University Press, 1992), argues that the good of the rational creature extends to the good of the whole universe. He cites Aquinas's *Quaestio disputata De caritate*, a. 7, ad 5: "In the good of the universe is contained, as principle, the rational creature, who is capable of beatitude, and to whom all other creatures are ordered; and according to this it is appropriate both for God and for ourselves to love the good of the universe out of charity in the highest degree."

can never serve simply as the final consequence of my choosing him, we hold that a particular act of the divine will is required to transform human perfection into the beatitude of which no eye can see nor ear hear. This grace God alone bestows. Gregory of Nyssa compared reception of this grace to the dizziness of a man who looks down into the depths of the sea from the top of a mountain. "In the same way," he says, "my soul grows dizzy when it hears the great voice of the Lord saying: 'Blessed are the clean of heart, for they shall see God.' "[132] Because only God can fulfill the expectations of the human heart, moral realism measures human actions in accord with how completely they draw the person to union with the living God.[133]

God alone satisfies. This conviction grounds the moral theology that Aquinas develops in his *Summa theologiae*. It now remains to examine how this general axiom sustains a complete account of the moral life. Four points warrant detailed examination: in Chapter Two, we look at the ground for morals in the natural law *(lex naturalis)*, which the Church finds a worthy companion for the Gospel law *(lex evangelica)*; in Chapter Three, the process whereby the human person enters into the drama of intelligent choice; in Chapter Four, the qualifications, both of nature and grace, that enable the person to maintain a life of virtue in conformity with the Gospel; and in Chapter Five, the distinctive kind of Christian life that moral realism offers to those who live according to the truth that Christ himself announces throughout the New Testament.

Thomas Aquinas serves as our guide throughout the chapters of this introduction. But the choice of the Church's Common Doctor is not motivated by partisan theological interests. Rather it is judged that the tradition that develops within the Thomist school best illuminates what the Church holds as the perennial principles that govern the moral life. The

---

132. Gregory of Nyssa, *De beatitudinibus*, Oratio 6 (PG 44, cols. 1263–66).

133. See *Veritatis splendor*, no. 72: "The rational ordering of the human act to the good in its truth and the voluntary pursuit of that good, known by reason, constitute morality. Hence human activity cannot be judged as morally good merely because it is a means for attaining one or another of its goals, or simply because the subject's intention is good [cf. *Summa theologiae* II-II, q. 148, a. 3]. Activity is morally good when it attests to and expresses the voluntary ordering of the person to his ultimate end and the conformity of a concrete action with the human good as it is acknowledged in its truth by reason. If the object of the concrete action is not in harmony with the true good of the person, the choice of that action makes our will and ourselves morally evil, thus putting us in conflict with our ultimate end, the supreme good, God himself."

first encyclical to treat general moral principles, *Veritatis splendor*, offers ample warrant for the claim that Christian moral theology runs afoul of its basic truths whenever it departs from the foundational tenets that Thomas Aquinas set down during the course of his theological career in service to the Church of Christ. Perhaps this explains why the Pope in a later encyclical affirms of Aquinas, "In him, the Church's Magisterium has seen and recognized the passion for truth; and, precisely because it stays consistently within the horizon of universal, objective and transcendent truth, his thought scales 'heights unthinkable to human intelligence.'"[134] What better warrant to study moral theology under the tutelage of Aquinas?

134. *Fides et ratio*, no. 44.

CHAPTER TWO

Moral Realism and the Natural Law

Divine Providence and the Eternal Law

Among the theological motifs that dominate both the Old and New Testaments, the theme of God's wisdom enjoys a prominent place. St. Paul associates divine wisdom with the revelation made in Christ when he exclaims, "But we speak God's wisdom, secret and hidden, which God decreed before the ages for our glory" (1 Cor 2:7). The Christian tradition in turn accepts the canonical books of the Bible as the written expression of divine wisdom. St. Jerome accordingly counsels believers: "Love the holy Scriptures, and wisdom will love you. Love wisdom, and she will keep you safe. Honor wisdom, and she will embrace you."[1] The saints joyfully embrace wisdom as a divine gift which opens up for them everything that God has ordained for the right ordering of the world and human existence in the world. It is these holy women and men, whom the Church venerates as those who have done God's will throughout the ages, who provide moral theologians with the basic paradigms for Christian living. The lives of the saints exhibit in everyday human occurrences the eternal pattern of divine wisdom.

The holy Scriptures speak about divine wisdom under a variety of figures. The Book of Wisdom, for instance, recognizes in the water that gushed forth out of flinty rock a revelation of God's hidden counsels and of the inscrutable character of his designs. The sacred author makes a point of indicating that God used the substance of water both to punish the Egyptians, by contaminating their wells, and to benefit Israel, by providing drink in the desert. He further observes that this divine stratagem reflects both the divine justice and mercy: "For through the very things by which their enemies were punished, [the Israelites] themselves received benefit in their need" (Wis 11:5).

---

1. St. Jerome, *Epistola* 130, no. 20 (CSEL 56.3.201).

The preaching of the gospel of Jesus Christ, which marks the beginning of the new dispensation, introduces a movement from figure to reality, from the mere symbols of things, such as water, to the very reality "of the good things that have come" (Heb 9:11). The Gospel of John repeatedly teaches that Christ himself incarnates the wisdom of the Father; and it is on this basis that the Christian faith essentially distinguishes Christ from every other holy person who came before him. To cite one example, we are told that the holy persons of the old dispensation had to petition God for wisdom: "I called on God, and the spirit of wisdom came to me" (Wis 7:7). Because of his divine status, however, Christ has no need to entreat God for wisdom, for the Word became flesh, "not of blood or of the will of the flesh or of the will of man, but of God" (Jn 1:13). As the divine Word of creation and Son of the Father among us, Christ in his very person embodies the divine wisdom. Striking to the heart of the matter, John Henry Newman has observed the unique status that Christ enjoys and how it distinguishes him from Christian believers: "Recollect that our Blessed Lord was in this respect different from us, that, though He was perfect man, yet there was a power in Him greater than His soul, which ruled His soul, for He was God."[2]

Everything that Christ does for our salvation represents some aspect of his human mediation; it belongs to Christ as man to communicate divine wisdom. In his sacred humanity, Christ fully possesses and personally embodies "the plan of the mystery hidden for ages in God who created all things" (Eph 3:9). For the Christian believer, then, Christ alone remains the ultimate source of spiritual instruction and the deepest foundation of the moral life; in other terms, he forms, as St. Bonaventure reminds us, "the hidden center of the universe."[3] We can express the same truth in teleological terms. Aquinas likes to recall that "human perfection consists in cleaving to spiritual things and spurning temporal ones."[4] Because Christ alone personally incarnates the divine wisdom, he remains for all times the first spiritual "thing" to which each human person must cleave in order to discover true wisdom. In the divine plan, it is ordained

2. See his "Mental Sufferings of Our Lord in His Passion," *Discourses Addressed to Mixed Congregations*, Discourse XVI (London: Longmans, Green, and Co., 1897).

3. For a study of this Christological theme in the writings of St. Bonaventure, see Zachary Hayes, O.F.M., *The Hidden Center: Spirituality and Speculative Christology in St. Bonaventure* (New York: Paulist Press, 1981).

4. *Summa theologiae* Ia-IIae, q. 99, a. 6.

that Christ should become the object of each one's affections. Of course, the central and irreplaceable role which Christ holds in the economy of salvation leaves room for other mediators, who, though always dependent on him, each play a distinctive role in communicating the ways of divine wisdom to the world.

As the history of salvation amply illustrates, it pertains to those persons charged with presenting and interpreting Christian doctrine to point out how to use temporal things in conformity with divine wisdom. In accord with St. Paul's own explanation, Aquinas maintained that God allowed the human race to experience its own intellectual deficiencies and moral weaknesses in order to appreciate better the gratuity of revealed moral instruction.[5] It is "through the Church [that] the wisdom of God in its rich variety" is made known to the powers that govern the universe (Eph 3:10). Because of this divine dispensation, we should never make the mistake of thinking that the Christian gospel, "the power of God for salvation" (Rom 1:16), is nothing more than an ethical code attached to a specific religious tradition. To engage seriously the task of discerning what constitutes human well-being requires that one both respect and conform to the divinely revealed wisdom which orders and shapes human conduct.

Expression of Divine Wisdom

For the purposes of moral theology, we can distinguish a twofold objective in divine wisdom. First, wisdom denotes an image or exemplar, viz., the ruling notion which governs the activity of created things. It is in this sense that the Scriptures refer explicitly to the pre-existent Christ, the divine Word, as the true pattern by which "all things in heaven and on earth were created, things visible and invisible" (Col 1:16). Secondly, wisdom denotes a teleological principle, viz., one that moves every being toward its proper end or goal through the sovereign attractiveness of the end. In this meaning, Christ, "in whom are hidden all the treasures of wisdom and knowledge" (Col 2:3), accomplishes par excellence not only the task of efficiently guiding human activity to its completion, but also that of attracting and summoning this activity to himself as its sovereign and consummate end. To associate divine wisdom personally with the incarnate Son introduces another distinction about God's wise government

---

5. See *Summa theologiae* Ia-IIae, q. 98, a. 6.

of the world. Though the theologian may suitably appropriate "the power of God and the wisdom of God" (1 Cor 1:24) to the Eternal Son by reason of his origin and relation within the intra-Trinitarian life of God, it belongs to the divine nature itself to govern the universe and to ordain whatever is necessary for the well-being of humankind.[6] In other words, "the Father, the Son, and the Holy Spirit are not three principles of creation but one principle."[7]

When Aquinas discusses the eternal law in the *Summa theologiae*, he draws attention to a very important distinction for understanding Christ's relationship to the created moral order. It is simply in an appropriated sense, that is, by way of an illustrative theological convention, that we identify only the second divine Person of the Trinity with the eternal law. Why? Aquinas argues for this appropriation on the basis of the affinity between the personal name for the second person in God—namely, Word or *Verbum*—and the notion of an exemplar or image.[8] The appropriation of essential divine attributes, such as wisdom, to one of the Persons of the blessed Trinity serves only to bring out a particular aspect of the faith.[9] Forasmuch as the eternal law represents the exemplar of God's wisdom and power actually directing and moving all that exists toward

6. This doctrine is substantially represented in the encyclical letter *Veritatis splendor*, no. 43, which quotes the Second Vatican Council's Declaration on Religious Freedom, *Dignitatis humanae*, no. 3: "The supreme rule of life is the divine law itself, the eternal, objective and universal law by which God out of his wisdom and love arranges, directs and governs the whole world and the paths of the human community."

7. *Catechism of the Catholic Church*, no. 258, quoting the fifteenth-century Council of Florence (*DS* 1331) and referring back to the sixth-century Second Council of Constantinople (*DS* 421).

8. See *Summa theologiae* Ia-IIae, q. 93, a. 1, ad 2: "Whatsoever the word you can consider first, the word itself, and secondly, what it expresses. A spoken word is something uttered by the mouth of man, and expresses what it is meant to signify. The same applies to man's mental word, which is nothing other than a concept of mind expressing what he is thinking about. So it is in the life of God; the Word itself, conceived by the Father's mind, is a personal term. As appears from Augustine (*De Trinitate* XV, 14) whatsoever is in the Father's knowledge, whether it refers to the divine nature or to the divine persons or to the works of God, is expressed by this Word. Included in what is there expressed is the Eternal Law. All the same it does not follow that the Eternal Law is used as a personal term in our vocabulary about divine things, though in fact it is specially attributed to the Son on account of the close agreement exemplar has with word."

9. *Summa theologiae* Ia, q. 39, a. 7 and ad 2: "In truth the Son's name is 'wisdom of the Father,' because he is wisdom from the Father as wisdom, for each one is wisdom in himself and both together are the one wisdom."

perfection, it fulfills the conditions required for formal exemplar causality. So because of his divine status as the Logos-Son, Christ, "the image of the invisible God, the first born of all creation" (Col 1:15), embodies and displays the definitive shape or form that the order of human existence should take in the world. The Second Vatican Council's "Pastoral Constitution on the Church in the Modern World" puts it this way: "Only in the mystery of the incarnate Word does the mystery of man take on light."[10]

From the start of theological deliberation on the Incarnation of the eternal Logos, Christian apologists and theologians have sought to further the quest for the ultimate *logos* or intelligibility which undergirds and directs the created order. It is axiomatic for Christian moral theology that the regulative pattern for all right human conduct ultimately lies within the blessed Trinity. As a principle of divine life for human beings, our Trinitarian origins also display an order toward a final goal, that "most high calling" that is bestowed graciously on the human race.[11] Since this pattern especially suggests the second divine Person, who perfectly images the Father, there is something appropriate about referring to it as a Logos-pattern. It belongs especially to Christian moral theology to discern and explicate this Logos-pattern as it shapes the action of free creatures and guides human conduct.

Confusion about the manner in which the eternal Word provides the pattern for right moral conduct leads some theologians to speak about the incarnate Christ as if he were involved in the created moral order even prior to the free and gracious divine self-donation that occurs in the Incarnation. This sort of mythological Christocentrism distracts, howev-

10. *Gaudium et spes*, no. 22, as quoted in *Fides et ratio*, no. 60, where Pope John Paul II also acknowledged that this conciliar doctrine has served since his first encyclical "as one of the constant reference points" of his papal teaching.

11. *Fides et ratio*, no. 13, quoting *Gaudium et spes*, no. 22, makes the point explicitly: "Christ, the Lord 'in revealing the mystery of the Father and his love, fully reveals man to himself and makes clear his supreme calling,' which is to share in the divine mystery of the life of the Trinity." The relationship of Christ both to creation and to the eternal law which directs it depends on a common notion of manifestation or image. We find this notion verified both in Christ's personal Trinitarian name, the Word of God—a manifestation of a concept—and the eternal law's definition as a plan or *ratio*—the manifestation of God's wisdom. For a good analysis of how St. Thomas understands the doctrine of *circulatio*, e.g. *Scriptum super libros Sententiarum* I, d. 14, q. 2, a. 3, see Jan Aertson, *Nature and Creature: Thomas Aquinas's Way of Thought*, trans. H. D. Morton (Leiden: E. J. Brill, 1988).

er, from the full transcendence of the divine wisdom.[12] The New Testament asks, "Where is the one who is wise? Where is the scribe? Where is the debater of this age? Has not God made foolish the wisdom of the world?" (1 Cor 1:20). To affirm the transcendence of divine wisdom, which when applied to creation and its divine government is called the eternal law, does not depreciate the central and indispensable importance of the incarnate Word for Christian living.[13] For the ultimate regulation of the moral order finds its pre-eminent expression in the freedom which Jesus Christ, the incarnate Son, communicates to those believers who remain personally united with him. To illustrate this union, some theologians speak about the *sequela Christi,* or the following of Christ. But the appropriation of eternal law to the Word of God, the eternal Son of the Father, implies much more for the Christian believer than that the incarnate Son offers an example of good behavior for his followers to imitate.

The Swiss theologian Hans Urs von Balthasar referred to Christ as the "Concrete Norm" of the moral life.[14] By this he meant that the *exitus-reditus,* which marks out the human persons's itinerary toward God, actually centers on the person of Jesus Christ. In making this assertion, moreover, von Balthasar echoed teachings of the Second Vatican Council that we have already cited:

It is Christ, the last Adam, who fully discloses humankind to itself and unfolds its noble calling by revealing the mystery of the Father and the Father's love.... He who is 'the image of the invisible God' (Col 1:15), is the perfect human being who has restored to the offspring of Adam the divine likeness which had been deformed since the first sin. Since the human nature which was assumed in him was not thereby destroyed, it was by that fact raised to a

12. I of course distinguish this descriptive use of "mythological Christocentrism" from the far more serious charge of myth leveled against the Jesuit Pierre Teilhard de Chardin (1881–1955), who argued that the primacy of Christ, in order to be realized, must consist in an organic union of Christ with the world. See the account given by Jean-Hervé Nicolas, *Synthèse dogmatique* (Fribourg: Editions Universitaires, 1986), p. 460.

13. Aquinas explicitly affirms that the pure truth of the eternal law comprehends but transcends moral truth: "God's justice, which sets up the order of things matching the exemplar of his wisdom, namely his law, is appropriately called truth" (*Summa theologiae* Ia, q. 21, a. 3). For Aquinas and the tradition of moral realism, the eternal law is contemplative as well as practical.

14. See his "Nine Theses in Christian Ethics," in *International Theological Commission: Texts and Documents* 1969–1985, ed. Michael Sharkey (San Francisco: Ignatius Press, 1989), pp. 105–28, especially Thesis One: "Christ as the Concrete Norm."

surpassing dignity in us also. For by his incarnation the Son of God united himself in some sense with every human being.[15]

This conciliar text not only alludes to the specific, historical realization in Christ of the eternal law, but what is more important, it also exhibits the organic link in the common nature assumed that exists between the incarnate Son and the moral life of each believer.

St. Augustine accustomed the Western theological tradition to identify eternal law as a permanent expression of God's wisdom when he wrote that "that law which is named the supreme reason cannot be otherwise understood than as unchangeable and eternal."[16] And Aquinas amplified this notion when he squarely affirmed that that which establishes the origin of all that derives from the eternal law lies within God himself. In the *Summa theologiae*, Aquinas further argues that the eternal law, which he sometimes calls the *lex divina* or divine law, embodies the "ruling idea of things which exists in God as the effective sovereign of them all has the nature of law."[17] In the sense both of exemplar and of guiding principle, we can speak about divine or eternal law as an analogical expression of the divine wisdom. Because Aquinas associates this doctrine with God's providence for the world, the order of divine government directly relates to the notion of the eternal law. This divine *ordo rerum*, or order of things, undergirds the whole of the created moral order. The proposal is a large one, and cannot be compressed easily to fit the contours of a narrow-minded moralism. Eternal law represents how God knows the

15. *Gaudium et spes*, no. 22: "Christus, novissimus Adam, in ipsa revelatione mysterii Patris eiusque amoris, hominem ipsi homini plene manifestat eique altissimam eius vocationem patefacit.... Qui est 'imago Dei invisibilis' (Col 1:15). Ipse est homo perfectus, qui Adae filiis similitudinem divinam, inde a primo peccato deformatam, restituit. Cum in eo natura humana assumpta, non perempta sit, eo ipso etiam in nobis ad sublimem dignitatem evecta est. Ipse enim, Filius Dei, incarnatione sua cum omni homine quodammodo se univit."

16. See *Summa theologiae* Ia-IIae, q. 91, a. 1, *sed contra*: " 'Lex quae summa ratio nominatur, non potest cuipiam intelligenti non incommutabilis aeternaque videri.' " For the citation from St. Augustine, see his *De libero arbitrio* I.6 (PL 32, 1229).

17. *Summa theologiae* Ia-IIae, q. 91, a. 1: "Dicendum quod ... nihil est aliud lex quam dictamen practicae rationis in principe qui gubernat aliquam communitatem perfectam. Manifestum est autem, supposito quod mundus divina providentia regatur ... quod tota communitas universi gubernatur ratione divina. Et ideo ipsa ratio gubernationis rerum in Deo sicut in principe universitatis existens legis habet rationem. Et quia divina ratio nihil concipit ex tempore, sed habet aeternum conceptum ... inde est quod huiusmodi legem oportet dicere aeternam."

world to be, how he effectively conceives the ordering of everything that exists within creation.[18]

How God Knows the World to Be

Because the eternal law principally reflects the divine intelligence, it stands in relationship to divine providence as a theory of practice stands in relationship to a conclusion for practical action.[19] Consider this example. That a general has mastered the elements of military science, i.e., learned a theory of practice, does not therefore imply that the same general will win a specific military campaign, i.e., that he will successfully execute a practical action. The contingencies involved in human knowing and acting disallow positing such a necessary connection between human theory and practice. On the other hand, because God abides in utter simplicity, so that there is no real distinction between what he knows and what he does, his practical theory about things remains one with their practical realization.[20]

Because all human language falls dramatically short of representing divine truth, theology is limited in the use which it can make of univocal terms. For example, the theological deployment of the term "nature" retains a variety of analogical meanings which include the life of the blessed Trinity, the physical cosmos, and the sphere of human activity. The notion of law pertains to our human experience, and in particular to the field of jurisprudence.[21] When theologians employ the term "law," its analogical capabilities include a wide range of meanings, as one author puts it, "from the pure and eternal exemplar in the mind of God to the unsteady beat of lust in human nature."[22] In each analogical application of the term, the common note which allows for the broad deployment

18. In a very good study of the foundations and implications of a natural law order, Oscar J. Brown, *Natural Rectitude and Divine Law in Aquinas* (Toronto: Pontifical Institute of Mediaeval Studies, 1981), pp. 1–12, makes this point with reference to eternal law.

19. When Aquinas describes the nature of prudence, he takes pains to assert that the reason prudence shapes practical reason is because its *imperium* ("actus eius praecipere") moves into the order of practical reasoning, to do something. See *Summa theologiae* IIa-IIae, q. 47, a. 8, "Utrum praecipere sit principalis actus prudentiae."

20. For comment, see John Finnis, *Natural Law and Natural Rights* (Oxford: Clarendon Press, 1980), p. 391, note 35.

21. For a further discussion, see Edward Damich, "The Essence of Law according to Thomas Aquinas," *American Journal of Jurisprudence* 30 (1985): 79–96.

22. See Thomas Gilby, O.P., *Law and Political Theory*, Blackfriars *Summa*, vol. 28 (1966), p. 162.

of the term "law" centers on the notion of regulation. Thus, as objective beatitude, God remains the end-point which regulates all moral activity, and as the intelligent Origin of all that exists, God serves as the beginning of every action which, when freely ruled by grace, leads to the beatific fellowship of heaven.

There are historical reasons that persuade the moral realist to describe eternal law as how God knows the world to be. For example, a realist theologian wants to avoid interpreting eternal law by appeal to the distinction between divine "absolute" and "ordained" powers that late fourteenth-century Nominalists such as Gabriel Biel kept alive in Western theology. Biel defines the *potentia absoluta Dei*, the divine absolute power, as God's power to do whatever does not imply a contradiction, without regard to whether God has in fact committed himself to this activity— that is, without regard to *de potentia ordinata*, to the ordained power. In contrast to the infinite range of possibilities which the *potentia absoluta* foresees, the "ordained power" signifies that course of action to which God has in fact freely committed himself.[23] While voluntarism represents a basically Christian phenomenon, born of meditation upon a God who acts freely and a Christ who announces the will of the same God, its unlimited volitional emphasis does not afford an appropriate context for understanding eternal law as an expression of the divine creative wisdom that comprehends but transcends the practical order of human willling.

Since the voluntarist position seeks to ensure that God does not become subject to created morality, voluntarist theologians affirm that God does not will something because it is essentially good and right, but rather the converse. That is, in voluntarist accounts the divine willing itself determines the objects of the divine will with respect to their being good and right. Thus for such a theory it is not the divine knowledge—how God knows the world to be—which establishes the intrinsic goodness of the created moral order. But by interpreting divine wisdom as a contingent reality within God himself, voluntarist theologians must face the embarrassment which the "lawlessness" of God causes for those who argue that "the Creator of the universe and Ruler of the word can do whatever he wants to without injustice to his creatures."[24]

23. For further details, see Heiko Oberman, *The Harvest of Medieval Theology. Gabriel Biel and Late Medieval Nominalism* (Cambridge: Harvard University Press, 1963), p. 37 and note 25.

24. Oberman, *The Harvest*, p. 97, note 26.

Because moral realism understands that God is the fullness of wisdom, it outrightly rejects the voluntarist construal of how God establishes a moral order in the world. On the other hand, for realist theology to possess confidence in the Logos-pattern of the created order, in which every person can uncover an exemplar for leading a happy and fulfilled life, does not mean that Christian theology espouses a form of determinism. To put it differently, to affirm the givenness of the eternal law does not gainsay the reality of human freedom. The eternal law rather opens up the mystery of human participation in God's providence through the free disposition of our human wills "according to the purpose of him who accomplishes all things according to his counsel and will, so that we, who were the first to set our hope on Christ, might live for the praise of his glory" (Eph 1:11–12).

In every good action which merits eternal life, God and the human person fully exercise distinct but related causalities. The pattern whereby human activity and divine grace cooperate reflects a providential design for our salvation. "With all wisdom and insight he has made known to us the mystery of his will, according to his good pleasure that he set forth in Christ, as a plan for the fullness of time, to gather up all things in him, things in heaven and things on earth" (Eph 1:8–10). Although some writers esteem that the Thomist notion of predestination depreciates the place of human autonomy in the appropriation of merit, Aquinas himself warrants no such undifferentiated judgment when he analyzes the diverse exercises of human and divine freedom.[25] Rather, he advances the view that human freedom itself remains instrumentally related to the exercise of the divine omnipotence. In this construal of grace and freedom, the Thomist tradition respects the full integrity of both divine causality and human autonomy; at the same time it avoids reducing their interaction to a mutual complementarity within the same category of being, as if God does his part and we do ours.

God's wise providence active in the world covers every circumstance of human life. The eternal law applies to a world of free and, therefore, defective, fallible human beings. In the ministry of Jesus Christ, God's wisdom provides even for those moments when the human person makes a bad choice. The Gospel of John records Jesus's encounter with a Samari-

---

25. For example, see *Summa theologiae* Ia, q. 15, a. 3 and Ia-IIae, q. 91, a. 1, and q. 93, a. 1. There are obvious affinities here to what *Veritatis splendor* calls "theonomy." For further discussion, see Chapter 5.

tan woman, who, we are told, was not living according to the determinations of the eternal law. But we also learn that the "drink" that Christ
requests of the woman becomes in the believer a "spring of water gush-
ing up to eternal life" (Jn 4:14). The catechetical purpose of the passage
is clear: no personal history or present condition excludes a person from
living according to God's truth. Christ himself announces this consol-
ing message: "Let anyone who is thirsty come to me, and let the one who
believes in me drink. As the Scripture has it, 'Out of the believer's heart
shall flow rivers of living water' " (Jn 7:38). For the one who believes in
Christ, conformity to God's truth causes human freedom without con-
straining it. Conformity with Christ purifies the soul.

Eternal Law and Salvation

While it is true that Christ alone manifests the full revelation of the
Father's plan for our salvation, theologians err when they imply that
knowledge of the eternal law belongs only to those who are the benefi-
ciaries of this divine revelation. Rather, the recognition of a ruling idea
or *ratio* operative in nature derives from the notice taken of its effects in
the world. "For what can be known about God is plain to [men], because
God has shown it to them. Ever since the creation of the world his invisible power and deity, has been clearly perceived in the things that have
been made" (Rom 1:19–20).

Aquinas clearly demonstrates his sympathy for the Pauline instruction about what can be known apart from God's revelation to Israel and
in Christ. In fact, in the text of the *Summa theologiae* we can observe a special Latin term which Aquinas uses to distinguish the way that the eternal law becomes known to us from the way intelligent creatures grasp
other kinds of truths. Our knowledge of the eternal law does not emulate
the ordinary mode of gaining knowledge, which the Latin verb *scire* and
its cognates designate. Rather, such knowledge develops in a way similar
to the way the mind grasps the first principles of speculative reasoning. In
Aquinas's Latin, the eternal law is said to be "*nota*," from the Latin stem,
notare, which approximates the English verb to perceive.[26] It is interesting
to remark that Descartes also speaks about the *imago Dei* "as the *nota* of the

---

26. According to *The New Shorter Oxford English Dictionary* (1993), one definition of the
English verb "note" is "perceive"

artificer which is impressed on his work," but Aquinas's usage does not approximate a Cartesian doctrine of innate ideas.[27]

The eternal law manifests itself with greater clarity in certain creatures than in others. Participation in the eternal law, however, is not restricted to the world of nature, for to the extent that artificial things reflect human intelligence, they also manifest divine wisdom. Because they cannot choose, as it were, to place themselves outside of the order of divine providence, infra-rational creatures like created things are also bound up with eternal law. However, when some material defect impairs their full realization of the divine plan the result causes less harm than when a free creature mars the divine order by willful sin. On this account, the saint better reflects the plan of divine wisdom by living a good life than the sinner does by following bad paths.[28]

Since its purpose is to direct human conduct toward the good, human positive law should conform to divine truth. True justice should match up with the exemplar of divine wisdom, namely the eternal law. Bad laws impede human beings in society from acting in accord with God's wisdom. Natural law may be assigned the role of common minimal moral lexicon for diverse cultures and legal systems, for religious adherents and nonbelievers alike, in the hope of solving major ethical conflicts, without engaging ultimate loyalties.[29] Eternal law, however, grounds a doctrine of salvation, not social accommodation. Aquinas and the larger tradition of Catholic philosophy are correct in teaching that natural law is not merely the *product* of practical reason but the *precondition* for its right exercise. Natural law is the normative theological and metaphysical order that undergirds, makes possible, and flows into our moral logic. Through our practical moral reason we do actively participate in the divine government of our own actions. The antinomian deployment of "natural justice" and "natural right" that one finds in much of contemporary legal theory finds no support in Catholic teaching.[30] Indeed, certain axioms of liberal juris-

---

27. Descartes, *Meditations*, III, ed. C. Adam and P. Tannery, VII, 51 (Paris: Vrin, 1996): "tamquam *nota* artificis operi suo impressa."

28. See Aquinas's discussion as to "whether all human affairs are subject to the Eternal Law" in *Summa theologiae* Ia-IIae, q. 93, a. 6.

29. For a development of this consideration, see Russell Hittinger, "Theology and Natural Law Theory," *Communio* 17 (1990): 402–8.

30. For further discussion, see Ernest Fortin, "On the Presumed Medieval Origin of

prudence directly challenge God's wise plan for the world, for example, in countenancing the heinous crime of abortion.[31]

Those who consider both law and morality as properly subject to the directive function of the eternal law are to be distinguished from those who endorse the principal tenets of secular humanism and ethical idealism. Secular humanism affirms the self-sufficiency of human resources with respect to directing the course of human development; ethical idealism maintains that rational categories of understanding are sufficient for founding moral precepts. Authentic Christian moral theology, on the other hand, first recognizes the profound relationship between nature and law as part of the divine plan for drawing men to beatific union, and secondly, acknowledges that the intrinsic basis for morality reposes in the whole person, precisely in its imaging of the blessed Trinity. On this point Aquinas speaks explicitly when he affirms that in a primary way, "the order of nature does not mean the ordering of nature itself, but the existence of order in the divine Persons according to natural origin."[32] He leaves, in other words, no room for rationalist reductions about nature.

As a theological concept, the eternal law undergirds the economy of Christian salvation which is accomplished definitively by the promulgation of the new law of grace. Aquinas is equally explicit on this point when he compares St. Augustine's teaching on the eternal law with St. Paul's remark, "But if you are led by the Spirit, you are not subject to the law" (Gal 5:18). These words of the Apostle, Aquinas says, can be understood in two senses:

Individual Rights," in Ernest L. Fortin, *Collected Essays, Classical Christianity and the Political Order. Reflections on the Theologico-Political Problem*, ed. J. Brian Benestad (New York: Rowman & Littlefield, 1996), pp. 243–64.

31. Regarding abortion, the Church has strongly encouraged reform at various moments, for example, the Sacred Congregation for the Doctrine of the Faith, "Declaration on Abortion" (November 18, 1974): "It is at all times the task of the State to preserve each person's rights and to protect the weakest. In order to do so the State will have to right many wrongs. The law is not obliged to sanction everything, but it cannot act contrary to a law which is deeper and more majestic than any human law: the natural law engraved in men's hearts by the Creator as a norm which reason clarifies and strives to formulate properly ..." (no. 21). The appeal takes on stronger tones in the 1995 encyclical *Evangelium vitae*, where Pope John Paul II argues this point (see no. 90) and further stresses the urgency of promoting a just society (no. 20).

32. *Summa theologiae* Ia, q. 42, a. 3. For further information on the ontological foundations of the *imago Dei*, see D. Juvenal Merriell, *To the Image of the Trinity*, pp. 170–90.

One, that being under the law means that, while an individual is unwilling to meet its obligations, he is yet subject to its burden. So ... one is under the law who refrains from evil deeds through fear of the punishment threatened, not from love of righteousness. In this sense spiritual persons are not subject to the law for, through charity shed in their hearts by the Holy Spirit, they fulfil the law of their own will. Second, the words can be taken to mean this, that what one does by the Holy Spirit are the deeds of the Spirit rather than of the individual human being. Since the Spirit is not under the law, as neither is the Son ... it follows that such deeds, in so far as they spring from the Spirit, are not under the law.[33]

The point of view represented in this text assumes a particular conception of the old law in salvation history, and the correlative thesis that Christ's passion fulfills the old law.[34]

It is important to avoid a theological anachronism; Aquinas remains entirely innocent of the controversies concerning the alleged antinomy of law and freedom which arose several centuries after his death. The theological issue of justification as developed by sixteenth-century Reformers put this antimony in a strong and public light. Though its antecedents can be discovered in the work of late Medieval theologians, as the refutatory work of the fifteenth-century French Thomist John Capreolus demonstrates, these controversies come to occupy the center of theological debate during and after the sixteenth century.[35] But for Aquinas, and for the medieval theologians in general, the question arose in a different light. They held that the disclosure of the eternal law and its design for human happiness opens up a way that allows divine love freely to take root in the world. Their vision is symphonic. And while in the actual order of salvation, this divine love derives preeminently from the person of Jesus

---

33. *Summa theologiae* Ia-IIae, q. 93, a. 6, ad 1.

34. For more on this topic and its contemporary significance, see Matthew Levering, "Israel and the Shape of Thomas Aquinas's Soteriology," *The Thomist* 63 (1999): 65–82, as well as the author's more developed presentation in his forthcoming book *Christ's Fulfillment of Torah and Temple: A Thomistic Theology of Salvation* (Notre Dame, Ind.: University of Notre Dame Press, 2002).

35. For further information, see the relevant essays in *Jean Capreolus en son temps (1380–1444)*, *Mémoire Dominicaine*, numéro spécial, 1, ed. Guy Bedouelle, Romanus Cessario, and Kevin White (Paris: Les Éditions du Cerf, 1997). It is interesting to note that during the period of Baroque Thomism, strict Thomists argued against the position of Luis de Molina, whose distinctive antinomianism repristinated certain emphases found in the sixteenth-century Protestant Reformers.

Christ, Aquinas, as we have seen, considers the Trinitarian dimensions of the eternal law to establish the grounds for this harmony or, in the case of unrepentant sinners, the conspicuous lack of this harmony.[36]

Catholic doctrine illuminated by the work of Aquinas accepts as axiomatic the harmonious working of law and grace in the Christian life. The New Testament does not place actions which proceed from theological charity "under the law." The Gospel rather announces a reign of liberty: "Now the Lord is the Spirit, and where the Spirit of the Lord is, there is freedom" (2 Cor 3:17). Caritative actions do, however, conform to the designs of the eternal law insofar as through them Christian believers freely accomplish the work of the Holy Spirit in the world. "For the whole law is summed up in a single commandment, 'You shall love your neighbor as yourself' " (Gal 5:14). However, attempts to fulfill this commandment without due respect to the givens of the eternal law fail precisely to the extent that they disregard the order of generation in the Trinity. The Person of Love, the Holy Spirit, cannot proceed from an action that does not conform to the perfect Image of the Father's Goodness. We can thank St. Augustine for reminding us of the importance of the Trinitarian dimension of the moral life: "In the Trinity it is the Holy Spirit, who was not begotten but is the sweetness of the begetter and the begotten, pouring out upon all creatures, according to their capacity, His immense bounty and the fullness of His gifts, in order that they may keep their proper order and rest content in their proper place."[37]

In imitation of Christ who accomplished the work which the Father gave him to do (see Jn 17:4), Christian life unfolds within a pattern of obedience to the will of the Father. In his commentary on this Gospel, Aquinas even speaks about Christ as the "doctrine of the Father."[38] This means that Christ himself supplies to each of his members the concrete measure or starting point for a moral life lived under the inspiration of

36. "And this also is a natural thing, that the mind can use its reason to understand God, according to which we have said that the image of God always remains in the mind; 'whether this image of God is so overthrown,' as if overshadowed, 'that it is almost annihilated,' as in those who do not have the use of reason, 'or it is darkened and deformed,' as in sinners, 'or it is shining and beautiful' as in the just, as Augustine says in *De Trinitate*, Bk. 14" (*Summa theologiae* Ia, q. 93, a. 8, ad 3).

37. *De Trinitate*, Bk. 6, chap. 10 (PL 42, col. 931); English is from Saint Augustine, *The Trinity*, trans. Stephen McKenna, C.Ss.R., Fathers of the Church, vol. 45 (Washington, D.C.: The Catholic University of America Press, 1963), p. 214.

38. See his *Lectura super Joannem*, 7.1.3.

the Holy Spirit. The Trinitarian rhythms of the moral life reveal that the final end of human perfection coincides with the first movement of our freedom. The Book of Wisdom anticipates this slant on human destiny. We are in the hand of God, we and our words. It is he who has granted me to know both the beginning and the middle of events, the sequence of the solstices, and the succession of the seasons, the passing of the year and the place of the zodiac (see Wis 7:16–19). This movement from and toward the divine goodness arises from the depths of one's being— *interior intimo meo*. "For you did not receive a spirit of slavery to fall back into fear, but you have received a spirit of adoption. When we cry, 'Abba! Father!' it is that very Spirit bearing witness with our spirit that we are children of God, and if children, then heirs, heirs of God and joint heirs with Christ—if, in fact, we suffer with him so that we may also be glorified with him" (Rom 8:15–17). Surely these texts persuade us that one finds a properly theological appreciation of natural law only within the context of the Trinitarian ordering of human existence in conformity with the rhythms established by the eternal law.

A Christian View of Natural Law

Since the mid-1960s, controversies concerning the place of natural law in theological ethics have figured prominently in the discussions and the literature of Roman Catholic moral theology.[39] Even before the issuance of

39. In the English-speaking world, Bernard Lonergan, "The Transition from a Classicist World-View to Historical Mindedness," in *A Second Collection*, ed. William Ryan and Bernard Tyrrell (Philadelphia: The Westminster Press, 1974), pp. 1–9, presents the principal issues that continue to dominate the discussion. For further studies on Lonergan's outlook, see Andrew Beards, *Objectivity and Historical Understanding* (Brookfield, Vt.: Avebury, 1997) and, more recently, his "Christianity, 'Interculturality,' and Salvation: Some Perspectives from Lonergan," *The Thomist* 64 (2000): 161–210. Regarding Lonergan's analysis of "historical consciousness" and its relation to natural law and morality, one of the best studies is Giovanni B. Sala, *Gewissensentscheidung: Philosophisch-theologische Analyse von Gewissen und sittlichem Wissen* (Wien: Tyrolia Verlag, 1993). Also see Matthew Lamb, "The Notion of the Transcultural in Bernard Lonergan's Theology," in *Method: Journal of Lonergan Studies* 8 (1990): 48–73. Benedict M. Ashley, O.P., "Thomism and the Transition from the Classical World View to Historical Mindedness," in *The Future of Thomism*, ed. Deal W. Hudson and Dennis William Moran (South Bend, Ind.: American Maritain Association, 1992), pp. 109–21, raises some criticisms of Lonergan's position, as does John Finnis in a longer study, *"Historical Consciousness" and Theological Foundations*, Etienne Gilson Lecture Series, no. 15 (Toronto: Pontifical Institute of Mediaeval Studies, 1992).

the encyclical letter *Humanae vitae* by Pope Paul VI in 1968, moral theologians had begun to deliberate how to reinterpret natural law theory so that it might appear more congenial to those personalist considerations which had marked both the secular and religious forms of twentieth-century existentialist philosophy.[40] The reaction to the 1968 encyclical, which reaffirmed the teaching of the ordinary Magisterium on the immorality of sterilizing the mating act, signaled the beginning of a period which resolutely questioned the place of natural law in theological ethics.[41] Although the sixteenth-century Protestant Reform championed grace and faith to the practical exclusion of all other instruments of divine agency in the life of the believer, the Church still asks that moral theologians take full account of the design and ends of human nature. One author argues that the principal agents of the Reformation did not completely renounce all mention of divine law, but instead introduced the novel approach that theological ethics could enlarge upon divine law without direct appeal to the categories of human nature and natural law.[42] In any event, during the first

40. For example, Charles Curran had argued against natural law thinking as a useful factor in Church teaching in his *Christian Morality Today* (Notre Dame, Ind.: University of Notre Dame Press, 1966). At the same time, some continental theologians sought a more balanced approach to the renewal of natural law in theology—see *New Light on the Natural Law*, ed. Illtud Evans, O.P. (London: Burns & Oates, 1965)—whereas others remained skeptical, e.g., Bruno Schüller, *Wholly Human. Essays on the Theory and Language of Morality*, trans. Peter Heinegg (Washington, D.C.: Georgetown University Press, 1986), esp. pp. 1–11: "Now, as experience shows, the adjectival phrase 'natural law' is at least as ambiguous and therefore at least as open to misunderstanding as the adjective 'autonomous'. We may take as many linguistic twists and turns as we like, there is no way to avoid using homonyms." An earlier statement on natural law appears in "Zur theologischen Diskussion über die lex naturalis" in *Theologie und Philosophie* 4 (1966): 481–503.

41. Charles Curran's essay "Natural Law," in his *Directions in Fundamental Moral Theology* (Notre Dame, Ind.: University of Notre Dame Press, 1985), well represents the sort of arguments which opponents of *Humanae vitae* set forth at the time of the encyclical. For a survey of the arguments which theologians raised at the time, see Ramón Garcia de Haro, "Teologia e Scienza nella Regolazione delle Nascite," in *Teologia e Scienze nel Mondo Contemporaneo, Studia Universitatis S. Thomae in Urbe*, 31 (Milan, 1989), pp. 181–97. For further analysis of the issues, see William E. May, "The Natural Law and Moral Life," in his *An Introduction to Moral Theology*, rev. ed. (Huntington, Ind.: Our Sunday Visitor Publishing Division, 1994), pp. 43–105.

42. The author is Peter Simpson, *Goodness and Nature. A Defence of Ethical Naturalism* (Dordrecht: Martinus Nijhoff Publishers, 1987), p. 85: "The Reformation did not cause an abandonment of divine law ethics; if anything it introduced one of a more thoroughgoing kind, for it introduced a divine law divorced from the natural.... Reformation

part of the twentieth century, some Lutheran moralists, for example, were found to claim that the Catholic emphasis on natural law theory represented an example of "works righteousness."[43] Since the Second Vatican Council, however, many Catholic authors have come to adopt positions similar to those that characterized mainline Protestant views on the suitability of natural law in theological ethics.[44] This convergence of views on natural law between certain Catholics and Protestants has exacted a high price from the former. Many Catholic theologians have forgotten about the central place that human nature holds in the development of moral argument.

Misgivings about the proper place of natural law in moral argument has consolidated otherwise dissimilar groups, a re-alignment that displays its own ironies especially within Roman Catholic circles. For both revisionist moral theologians, viz., those who employ some form of proportionalism as part of their basic moral method, and the anti-proportionalists, viz., those who most vigorously uphold some form of moral absolutes, are resolved to marginalize natural law theory.[45] This phenomenon may in-

---

doctrines of total human corruption effectively prohibited attempts to provide a foundation for morality in human nature."

43. For further information, see Reinhard Hütter, "The Twofold Center of Lutheran Ethics: Christian Freedom and God's Commandments" in *The Promise of Lutheran Ethics*, ed. Karen Bloomquist and John Stumme (Minneapolis: Augsburg-Fortress, 1998), pp. 33–38. A typical expression of Luther's own attitude is found in his 1535 *Lectures on Galatians*, vol. 26 of *Luther's Works*, trans. Jaroslav Pelikan (St. Louis, Mo.: Concordia Publishing, 1963), p. 447: "Now if our sin has been forgiven through Christ Himself, the Lord of the Law—and forgiven by His having given Himself for it—the Law, that slave, no longer has the right to accuse and condemn us because of our sin; for this has been forgiven, and we have become free by the deliverance of the Son. Therefore the entire Law has been abrogated for believers in Christ." Luther's reference to the "entire Law" obviously includes natural law.

44. For further discussion of what contemporary Protestant theologians have taught about natural law, see T. Herr, *Zur Frage nach dem Naturrecht im deutschen Protestantismus der Gegenwart* (Munich: Schöningh, 1972). Also, F.-H. Schrey, "Diskussion um das Naturrecht 1950–1975," *Theologische Rundschau* 41 (1976): 59–93.

45. Hence one notes John Finnis—a stalwart defender of particular moral norms and ethical objectivity—refusing to acknowledge that natural law is truly law, maintaining instead that it is merely by *extrinsic* analogy that natural law qualifies as law. Further, he unsurprisingly acknowledges in his *Natural Law and Natural Rights* (henceforth abbreviated *NLNR*), p. 280, that he prefers to avoid the terminology of "natural law" altogether. Also see his approbation (on page 294 of *NLNR*) of Mortimer Adler's argument that natural law is law only by analogy of extrinsic attribution, found in Adler's

deed serve as testimony to the degree to which anti-metaphysical presuppositions—the legacy of Hume and Kant—persist in shaping ethical discourse.

Moral theologians generally resist being categorized as belonging to one school or another. This reluctance undoubtedly arises in part as a reaction to the custom of the casuist period (c. mid-sixteenth century to mid-twentieth century) in moral theology, when to be a moral theologian meant that one belonged to a particular school of casuistry, such as probabilism, probabiliorism, aequiprobabilism.[46] Indeed, generalizing about revisionist moral theologians approximates philosophizing about individuation: while there is general agreement that a class of revisionist moral theologians exists, it is difficult to determine what actually constitutes someone as a revisionist moral theologian.[47] In a general way, however, one can provisionally identify revisionist moral theologians as those authors who, before the 1993 encyclical *Veritatis splendor*, adopted some variety of proportional reasoning as at least one of the main features of their moral methodology.[48]

---

essay "A Question about Law," in *Essays in Thomism*, ed. R. E. Brennan (New York: Thomist Press, 1942), pp. 207–36. In extrinsic analogy of attribution, only one of the beings compared intrinsically possesses the perfection analogously predicated. Finnis (*NLNR*, p. 280) states that " 'Natural law' ... is only analogically law in relation to my present focal use of the term: that is why the term has been avoided in this chapter on Law." The mainline Thomist tradition would respond that the natural law realizes the *ratio* of law more fully than does positive law. Granted that epistemically we tend to discover moral truths before cognizing their status *as* law, this does not alter the nature of the precepts discovered, which participate in the eternal law and are divinely promulgated from creation by the governor of the commonwealth of being. For a more detailed account of the movement away from natural law, see the study by Pauline C. Westerman, *The Disintegration of Natural Law Theory* (Leiden: Brill, 1998).

46. For a brief explanation of the casuist schools, see the Appendix.

47. Philosophers easily recognize that individual instances of the same species exist, but they find it difficult to render a reasoned account for individuation; so, for example, we find so subtle a thinker as the Franciscan John Duns Scotus reduced to musing about "thisness"—*haecceitas.*

48. One demonstrable effect of *Veritatis splendor* is that the language of proportionalism has disappeared from public discourse. For example, see the exchanges in *Natural Law and Public Reason*, ed. Robert P. George and Christopher Wolfe (Washington, D.C.: Georgetown University Press, 2000). For an account of the variety of meanings that had been attached to the term "proportionalism," see Brian Johnstone, C.Ss.R., "The Meaning of Proportional Reason in Contemporary Moral Theology," *The Thomist* 49 (1985): 223–47.

Objections from Theologians

On the question of natural law, revisionist thinkers had raised two main objections. First, we find authors who rejected natural law on the basis that it exemplifies one of those global pre-scientific convictions which, for that very reason, requires critical analysis and re-appropriation before it can usefully serve the requirements of contemporary moral theology.[49] Secondly, there were revisionist moral theologians who repudiated natural law on the grounds that the theory required adherence to a metaphysical biology which, in their judgment, can contribute nothing significant to our knowledge of Christian moral truth.[50] Still, whatever their reservations about natural law, most Catholic moral theologians were willing to agree that a broadly construed natural law theory does serve as a convenient metaphor for the Catholic principle that theological ethics in prin-

49. Pre—*Veritatis splendor* proposals for accommodating classical natural law theory include that by Timothy O'Connell, *Principles for a Catholic Morality* (New York: Seabury Press, 1978), pp. 144–54, who offers a metaphorical interpretation of natural law, suggesting that the notion should be broadened to include such notes as "real," "experiential," "historical," and "proportional." In the revised edition of this textbook (San Francisco: Harper & Row, 1990), pp. 161–73, O'Connell calls these considerations "four qualities" of moral values, and he significantly changes the headings: "real," "conflict," "change," and "grounded." Richard Gula, S.S., *Reason Informed by Faith. Foundations of Catholic Morality* (New York: Paulist Press, 1989), endorses O'Connell's first approach and offers his own metamorphosis of the notion: "Natural law is reason reflecting on human experience discovering moral value" (p. 241). Again, John C. Dwyer, *Foundations of Christian Ethics* (New York: Paulist Press, 1987), strikes the same note: "Natural law is primarily *human intelligence* itself, as it strives to grasp the complexities of a situation, and as it strives to discern all of the purposes which are proper to the persons and things which are part of that situation" (p. 16). On the other hand, *Veritatis splendor*, nos. 48–50, offers its own careful analysis of the place that the human body holds in questions of natural law, and (in no. 43) quotes Aquinas's definition of natural law as a participation of the eternal law in the rational creature (see *Summa theologiae* Ia-IIae, q. 91, a. 2).

50. For example, Richard McCormick, "The Consistent Ethic of Life: Is There a Historical Soft Underbelly?" in *The Critical Calling* (Washington, D.C.: Georgetown University Press, 1989), pp. 211–32, discusses six "unwitting assumptions" that he contends easily serve to thwart the promotion of a consistent ethic of life. The first is the assumption of "biological givenness as normative," and the author cites Aquinas's treatment of the content of natural law. On the other hand, *Veritatis splendor*, no. 47, addresses charges of this kind directly: "Objections of physicalism and naturalism have been leveled against the traditional conception of the natural law, which is accused of presenting as moral laws what are in themselves mere biological laws."

ciple excludes nothing that touches the human reality—*nihil humanum, mihi alienum est.*[51]

One author summarized the view of revisionists when he wrote in the late 1970s: "The trend in natural law theorizing among Catholic theologians today is to go beyond *physicalism* and to try to achieve a larger view of human nature and human persons."[52] This summary remark reveals a common and still prevalent misunderstanding that shapes critics of natural law theory. Given the directions of modern moral philosophy, there exists the temptation to confuse the in-built structures of human nature with an inert physicalism, as if the Christian view of the body were that of a Cartesian machine. Although a sound natural law theory takes our physical being seriously, the basic grounds for natural law's claim to legitimacy rests on more than its ability to take full account of the biological and physical structures of the human person.

The emphasis that pre-1993 revisionism put on a personalist and historical-minded interpretation of natural law situated its proponents paradoxically close to another group of moral theologians. These latter, however, rejected the chief elements of the revisionists' schemes for renewal in moral theology, especially inasmuch as their proposals included types of proportionalist reasoning which distanced them from the Church's Magisterium on such issues as contraception. It is fair to identify these non-revisionist theologians as exclusively Christocentric moralists, for they hold the view that even the *praeambula* of moral theology lie within the perspectives of Christ-centered faith.[53] Such authors also remain skeptical about natural law thinking to the extent that it seems to represent a sort of autonomous discourse in moral theology. In short, those who adopt this position estimate that natural law remains external to the critical foundation of theological ethics.[54] Hans Urs von Balthasar

51. See Terence, "humani nil a me alienum puto" (*Heautontimorumenos*, act I, scene 1, line 25).

52. Philip S. Keane, S.S., *Sexual Morality: A Catholic Perspective* (New York: Paulist Press, 1977), p. 46 (emphasis mine).

53. For further discussion of the coincidences between these two groups, see my "On Bad Actions, Good Intentions, and Loving God: Three Much-Misunderstood Issues about the Happy Life that St. Thomas Clarifies for Us," *Logos* 1.2 (1997): 100–124, esp. 106–10.

54. For a clear statement of this methodology, see Marciano Vidal, *Moral de Actitudes*, vol. 1, *Moral Fundamental* (Madrid: PS Editorial, 1981), pp. 177–96: "Fundamentaciones Insuficientes de la Etica Cristiana."

champions a view like this when he consigns natural law to the realm of the pre-biblical natural order in which, on his account, the human person quite naturally fused and confused human origins from God with human origins from nature.[55]

Theologians who share von Balthasar's perspective on the theological significance of natural law frequently are content to identify natural law with that internal moral sense which is a common property of the human race. In other words, these thinkers view natural law as a philosophical expression of what the Greek tragic dramatist Sophocles portrays so well in *Antigone*, namely, the anxiety which confronts the serious individual who candidly ponders the ineluctable demands which a law of nature inflicts on mortal beings.[56] This conception of natural law reduces it to a thoroughly psychological reality, and exhibits certain affinities to the Augustinian tradition that interprets natural law as coextensive with the moral conscience.[57]

While it is possible to cite some exceptions to the rule, it remains a safe generalization that prior to 1993 natural law received little attention from the most published authors in Roman Catholic theological ethics: neither proportionalist revisionists nor exclusive Christocentrists gave sustained attention to classical natural law thinking; both, instead, developed other theological strategies for dealing with the moral life.[58] And to the extent

55. See his "Nine Theses in Christian Ethics," in *International Theological Commission*, especially Thesis 8, "Prebiblical Natural Order," pp. 119–20. For an example of a more developed foundational moral theology which takes little account of natural law, see Ramon Garcia de Haro, *Cristo, Fundamento de la Moral* (Barcelona: Ediciones Internacionales Universitarias, 1990). David L. Schindler, *Heart of the World, Center of the Church. Communio Ecclesiology, Liberalism, and Liberation* (Grand Rapids, Mich.: William B. Eerdman, 1996), adverts to natural law as part of his critique of what he calls John Courtney Murray's "dualism" (see pp. 73ff.).

56. Jacques Maritain, *La loi naturelle or loi non écrite*, ed. Georges Brazzola (Fribourg: Editions Universitaires, 1986) captures this perspective on natural law: "Antigone peut être considérée comme l'héroïne de la loi naturelle, elle qui était consciente du fait qu'en transgressant la loi humaine et en se faisant écraser par elle, elle obéissait à un commandement meilleur, à ces lois—comme elle disait—qui sont non écrites et ne sont pas nées d'aujourd'hui ni d'hier, mais qui vivent pour toujours et dont aucun homme ne sait d'où elles tiennent leur origine" (p. 20).

57. For example, see the full text from St. Augustine, *De Trinitate*, Bk. 14, chap. 4, no. 21, that is quoted partially in *Veritatis splendor*, no. 51.

58. The tags point to general directions taken by theologians, not schools formed by them. The careful work (see above, note 40) of the American theologian William E.

that these authors dealt at all with the topic, their approaches to natural law eclipsed the meaning that classical moral realism gives to *lex naturae*. This state of theological affairs generates its own sort of irony. At the same time that Christian thinkers were abandoning a theological version of natural law, secular moralists and political theorists were beginning to demonstrate considerable interest in the notion that "human nature" can play as an important explanatory conception for both moral and political theory.[59] What is more surprising, however, is that *Veritatis splendor* devoted considerable time to repudiating the post-conciliar, large-scale dismissal of natural law. This development makes it difficult for moral theologians in the Roman Catholic tradition to ignore entirely the classical formulations of natural law, although the encyclical admittedly includes references to natural law that remain susceptible to different emphases.[60]

It may be asked, to what extent would the reversals suffered by natu-

---

May of course qualifies as one of the most significant exceptions to the wide-spread neglect of natural law. Besides John Finnis (see notes 19, 44) *Natural Law and Natural Rights*, there is the philosophical work of Martin Rhonheimer, *Natural Law and Practical Reason. A Thomist View of Moral Autonomy*, trans. Gerald Malsbary (New York: Fordham University Press, 2000), which originally appeared in 1987. The philosophical climate, however, is not very congenial to moral realism in the Thomist sense, and so it can happen that students, under the speculative influence of Humean and analytic modes of thought, tend to deny the ethical significance of unified teleology, and to deny that there exists any hierarchy of goods prior to choice: which is simply to say that the *finis ultimus*—the ultimate end—is ethically disutile, a judgment very, very far from the teaching of St. Thomas Aquinas. They also can tend to forget that the matter of the human act is derived from nature and not wholly from human intention—for while the physical and moral species of an act differ, the first is one of the central causes determining the second.

59. See, for example, J. Budziszewski, *The Resurrection of Nature: Political Theory and the Human Character* (Ithaca, N.Y.: Cornell University Press, 1990); Stephen D. Hudson, *Human Character and Morality: Reflections from the history of ideas* (London: Routledge and Kegan Paul, 1990); Christopher J. Berry, *Human Nature* (New York: Macmillan, 1990). Also of interest is the collection of articles ed. John Finnis in "The International Library of Essays in Law and Legal Theory," *Natural Law* 2 vols (Sydney: Dartmouth, 1992) and the new edition of Heinrich A. Rommen, *The Natural Law. A Study in Legal and Social History and Philosophy* (Indianapolis: Liberty Fund, 1998), with an "Introduction" by Russell Hittinger.

60. Russell Hittinger analyzes the 1993 encyclical and explains how it can restore natural law to its proper place in Roman Catholic moral teaching; see his "Natural Law as 'Law': Reflections on the Occasion of 'Veritatis Splendor,'" *American Journal of Jurisprudence* 39 (1994): 1–32. For a complementary exposition, see my "Moral Absolutes in the Civilization of Love," *Crisis* 13 (May, 1995): 18–23. Both essays have been reprinted in *Veritatis Splendor and the Renewal of Moral Theology*, ed. J. A. DiNoia, O.P., and Romanus Cessario, O.P. (Chicago: Midwest Theological Forum, 1999).

ral law have surprised Thomas Aquinas? Certain authors have observed that his brief treatment of natural law arguably has generated more commentary in proportion to what Aquinas actually had to say about the notion than any other topic in the *Summa theologiae*.[61] While these suggestions should provoke further reflection, the fact remains that Aquinas does elaborate a natural law theory which lies at the heart of his theological ethics. Its main elements, moreover, provide the theoretical infrastructure for his developed theory of the moral life as a virtuous life. No serious commentator on Aquinas can overlook this feature of the *prima-secundae*.

The post-conciliar eclipse of interest in natural law is not the first time that commentators and theorists have obscured Aquinas's original conception of the natural law. In the high Renaissance, the Spanish Jesuit Francisco Suarez (1548–1617), by interpreting natural law as a teaching principally about human willing, displaced the concept of natural law from its proper place within realist theological ethics. This commentator rejected Aquinas's profound intuition that natural law represents the human person's participation or share in divine wisdom which establishes the foundation for right reason to operate. In the place of this sapiential view of natural law, Suarez responded to certain cultural coercions of the early modern period and set forth an interpretation of natural law that stressed its realization in terms of an expression of the divine will.

Suarez depreciated the ontological dimension of natural law in order to interpret it as a particular manifestation of the divine pleasure about how the rational creature should behave. Historians of natural law theory have remarked on the Suarezian turn that natural law theory took in the seventeenth and eighteenth centuries. The same historians have pointed out that the manuals of moral theology in use before the Second Vatican Council usually adopted the positions of Dominican and Jesuit theologians, who were alike strongly influenced by Suarez's interpretation of

61. Some authors even suggest that natural law holds an insignificant place in Aquinas's complete theory of morals. Noting that Aquinas devotes only a single question of six articles in the *Summa*, Vernon Bourke has observed that the notion of virtue holds a more important place in Aquinas's moral thinking than does natural law. See Vernon J. Bourke, "Is Thomas Aquinas a Natural Law Ethicist?" *The Monist* 58 (1974): 52–66. Along the same lines, also see James F. Ross, "Justice Is Reasonableness: Aquinas on Human Law and Morality," *The Monist* 58 (1974): 86–103. While these latter authors help us to grasp the substantialness of Aquinas's moral teaching, natural law, on his account, still supplies the foundation for the moral life. The virtuous life develops what is established in natural law. This means that no virtuous person can abide in contradiction to the natural law.

natural law. As such, these theologians, who produced large numbers of moral manuals, presented the Thomist doctrine of natural law along rationalist and voluntarist lines.[62]

The casuistry embedded in the Roman Catholic manual tradition greatly contributed to misinterpretations of natural law. In his *Vademecum Theologiae Moralis*, even a reliable manualist such as Dominican author Dominic Prümmer still classified sins of impurity under two headings: first, natural, viz., fornication, rape, abduction, incest, adultery, and sacrilege and second, unnatural, viz., pollution [masturbation], sodomy, and bestiality. Although Prümmer follows Aquinas's own material distinctions, this sort of presentation nonetheless reinforced the misconception that Catholic moral theology is given to consider every specific moral issue as if natural law alone supplied the ultimate determination. The manualist misconstruals of natural law also explain the tendency among some contemporary authors to think that natural law theory supplies the equivalent of a complete moral theory.[63]

Scope of Natural Law

Natural law is not the only resource needed for a complete theory of Christian morality. A realist moral theologian recognizes that natural law provides a starting point for discovering the concrete forms of moral goodness. Further, since every end exists as an end only because it is ordered to the ultimate end (*finis ultimus*), the explanation of moral normativity that is offered by natural law must in a definitive way relate this normativity to the ultimate end. Because only God truly is absolute good, God alone obligates through promulgating the whole order of subordinate ends and acts via creation. Hence the natural, and therefore obligatory, is that which is necessary in order to attain the final end. This rooting

62. In an early work, *Contraception and Natural Law* (Milwaukee: Bruce Publishing Company, 1964), Germain Grisez argued convincingly that most reaction to natural law theory actually envisions this Suarezian position. In an earlier study, *The Natural Moral Law according to St. Thomas and Suarez* (Ditchling, East Sussex: Saint Dominic's Press, 1930), the Dominican Walter Farrell also had observed the difference between what Aquinas taught and the views of Suarez on natural law. For development of the same theme, see Thomas S. Hibbs, "A Rhetoric of Motives: Thomas on Obligation as Rational Persuasion," *The Thomist* 54 (1990): 293–309.

63. See O'Connell, *Principles* (1990), pp. 251–53, "Christ and the Natural Law," who cites the lecture notes of Josef Fuchs, *Theologia Moralis Generalis* (Rome: Gregorian University, 1954), vol. 1, pp. 100–109, as one source for this reductionist view of moral theology.

of moral normativity in the absolute divine good does not locate natural law within a voluntarist framework, that is, one that makes divine will rather than intellect the whole source of moral obligation, because as established by God the order of ends flows from his will as informed by his Truth.

Natural law respects freedom. Rooting moral normativity within the divine good does not entail a denial of secondary causality. No end can be an end at all if it is not further ordered to the only end that can be sought purely for its own sake: the absolute good of the ultimate end. Similarly no created act is other than a natural but ontologically deficient imitation of God who is self-subsisting pure act. It may be argued that were there no divinely established order of ends, secondary agency would be impossible, because, without a final cause why action should be of one determinate character rather than another, action would be either unceasing or uninitiable.[64] In any case, the order of ends—like the order of acts proportioned to them—is constituted in accordance with the divine wisdom and goodness, and this order participates in the good of its transcendent source.

By maintaining the legitimacy of the natural law in theological ethics, moral realism does not therefore secretly champion a covert form of autonomous ethics. For instance, consider the argument that since natural law represents a participation in the divine law, the moral welfare of the human race requires no other divinely revealed law. To this argument, Aquinas answers that the human person participates in the eternal law in two ways. The first way presupposes a proportion with the capacity of human nature and, therefore, remains consonant with the natural end of the human creature. The second way, however, assumes the existence of a higher order, by which we are directed to our ultimate supernatural end, and to embrace this order, God's wisdom provides a divinely revealed law by which we also participate in the eternal law.[65] While it is incumbent upon realist moral theology to demonstrate that its view of the Christian moral life neither presupposes nor generates a dual conception of the moral universe, the fact remains that the eternal law represents the single divine plan for the salvation of the world. The unity of the eternal law is not compromised by the twofold manner in which human persons participate it.

In the *Summa theologiae*, Aquinas provides a straightforward, uncluttered

---

64. Aquinas argues this point in *Summa contra gentiles* III, c. 2.
65. See *Summa theologiae* Ia-IIae, q. 91, a. 4, ad 1.

explanation of natural law. He says that "natural law embodies nothing other than a participation of the eternal law in the rational creature."[66] Natural law, then, derives from the eternal law, although, since the eternal law remains identical with the divine nature itself, natural law does not exhaust the eternal law. Because he held the conviction that the ontological priority of nature provides the necessary condition for maintaining the gratuitous gift of divine grace, Aquinas argues for an intrinsic relationship between natural and eternal law on philosophical grounds.[67] This means that our understanding of human nature entails something more than a deficient abstraction, or a "remainder concept."[68] If it be the case that human nature is merely such a "remainder concept" or deficient abstraction, it is difficult to see how such a view does not compel its proponents toward holding one of two inadmissable positions concerning the nature and gratuity of God's creative action: either divine wisdom has produced an intrinsically deficient human being, that is, with something lacking in its bare essentials,[69] or God is somehow obliged to bestow something which is not due to human nature in order to complete his creation in a basic way. These two alternatives logically precede any discussion of the hypothesis of "pure nature" and the thorny question about what human nature can accomplish without divine grace or on the supposition that Adam was created outside of original justice.[70]

66. *Summa theologiae* Ia-IIae, q. 91, a. 2: "Unde patet quod lex naturalis nihil aliud est quam participatio legis aeternae in rationali creatura." However, Alasdair MacIntyre, "Natural Law as Subversive: The Case of Aquinas," *Journal of Medieval and Early Modern Studies* 26 (1996): 61–83, points out that the serenity of Aquinas's natural law doctrine was formulated in the midst of turbulent periods in thirteenth-century political and ecclesiastical life.

67. Thus, James P. Reilly, Jr., *Saint Thomas on Law*, Etienne Gilson Series, no. 12 (Toronto: Pontifical Institute of Medieval Studies, 1990), p. 14.

68. For an explanation of how moral theologians use the notion of *Restbegriff*, see Josef Fuchs, *Natural Law: A Theological Investigation* (New York: Sheed & Ward, 1965), p. 45 and Enda McDonagh, *Invitation and Response: Essays in Christian Moral Theology* (New York: Sheed & Ward, 1972), p. 34.

69. Thomas de Vio, Cardinal Cajetan (1468–1534),whose commentary on the *Summa theologiae* was printed in the Leonine edition (vols. 4–12; Rome, 1888–1906) by special mandate of Pope Leo XIII, describes five states in which human nature may be considered. See his *Commentary on the Summa theologiae, In Iam-IIae*, q. 109. a. 2.

70. For a clear presentation of the Thomist school position which developed after the Modernist crisis of the early twentieth century, see J. van der Meersch, "Grâce," in A. Vacant, E. Mangenot, and E. Amann, eds. *Dictionnaire de théologie catholique*, vol. 6.2 (Paris: Librairie Letouzey et Ané, 1925).

The key term in Aquinas's definition of natural law is "participation," or the human creature's share in the eternal law. Aquinas's use of the notion of participation in his definition of natural law possesses its own history.[71] Some authors for instance have argued that Aquinas's deployment of the notion of participation in connection with natural law exhibits Platonic influences on the Thomist doctrine.[72] For our purposes, it is also possible to translate Aquinas's *"participatio"* by the English word "share."[73] The view that human nature shares or participates in the divine pattern of all that exists forms a central thesis of a realist anthropology. Jacques Maritain, in his *The Person and the Common Good*, recognizes in the natural law the foundation not only for the dignity of the human person, but also for the establishment of the common good.

The deepest layer of the human person's dignity consists in its property of resembling God—not in a general way after the manner of all creatures, but in a *proper* way. It is the *image* of God. For God is spirit and the human person proceeds from Him as having a principle of life, a spiritual soul capable of knowing, loving and of being uplifted by grace to participation in the very life of God that, in the end, it might know and love Him as He knows and loves Himself.[74]

It is important to observe that Maritain speaks about our being capable of "being uplifted by grace." Natural law enjoys a central place in the development of moral theology, but it does not provide a substitute for the economy of salvation which comes always as a free and gracious outpouring from God and which alone makes it possible for the creature to enjoy a communication with God that exceeds the perfections of nature.

A Participation in the Eternal Law

For the purposes of moral theology, it is important to emphasize that natural law entails a twofold participation or sharing in the eternal law.

---

71. For a classical study of participation in Aquinas, see Cornelio Fabro, *Participation et causalité selon s. Thomas d'Aquin* (Louvain: Publications Universitaires, 1961).

72. See Louis-Bertrand Geiger, O.P., *La participation dans la philosophie de S. Thomas d'Aquin* (Paris: J. Vrin, 1942).

73. For example, in *Law and Political Theory*, p. 23, Thomas Gilby translates *"participatio"* as "sharing" in the key text of *Summa theologiae* Ia-IIae, q. 91, a. 2: "... et talis participatio legis aeternae in rationali creatura 'lex naturalis' dicitur." The author's translation: "Now this sharing in the eternal law by intelligent creatures is what we call 'natural law.'"

74. Jacques Maritain, *The Person and the Common Good*, trans. John J. Fitzgerald (New York: Scribner's, 1947), p. 32.

First, because the human person is capable of grasping the basic principles of practical reasoning, natural law manifests itself in human intelligence or reason. The actualization of this capacity of course supposes, as a necessary condition for its development, the everyday sense experience of material things. The initial movement of practical reason toward the good of the human person matures, if no impediment inhibits its development, into a fully developed grasp of moral science. One may distinguish between ordinary wit and the wisdom of the wise, but natural law affords every human person to participate cognitively in divine wisdom. For this reason, Aquinas says that the principles of natural law are "actually adverted to by reason."[75]

There is a second aspect to the participation that natural law achieves in each human person. Because each individual human nature embodies the divine exemplar of creative wisdom, there exists a sharing in the divine being that manifests itself in the whole person. Aquinas refers to this sharing in the eternal law as "settled convictions in [human] nature," which operate in a way similar to that of a *habitus* of a behavioral virtue.[76] This level of participation in the eternal law specifically includes the biological and psychological dimensions of the human person. According to this level of sharing, natural law expresses the structural tendencies, or natural inclinations, inherent in and proper to human nature and by which every human person is measured and ruled.

Oscar Brown offers two important considerations for interpreting Aquinas's doctrine on natural law. He first shows that when Aquinas uses the phrase "natural law precepts," as in *Summa theologiae* Ia-IIae, q. 94, a. 1, he should be understood as referring to the inclinations or structural tendencies inherent in human nature. This interpretation is required in order to respect the analogical meaning that characterizes Aquinas's general use of law as "a rule and measure" (cf. Ia-IIae, q. 90, a. 1, ad 1). Secondly, Brown insists that St. Thomas, like Aristotle, never considers practical knowledge—even as it embodies a true kind of knowledge—outside of its due context, namely the intelligent grasp of moral truth and the right appetite for human goods. And since the immediate source of our recognition and implementation of natural law remains the practical reason, it is impera-

75. *Summa theologiae* Ia-IIae, q. 94, a. 1: "... quia praecepta legis naturalis quandoque considerantur in actu a ratione."
76. Ibid., "quandoque autem sunt in ea habitualiter tantum, secundum hunc modum potest dici quod lex naturalis sit habitus."

tive, therefore, to interpret all natural law inclinations within the context of the customary dynamics of human action.[77]

For an accurate appreciation of what "natural law" means, a notional distinction is introduced between the human person and an individual human nature. In a material sense, it is true, one ordinarily identifies an individual human being with a human person, but Christian anthropology recognizes a formal difference between the two.[78] It is not easy to address this distinction. The modern penchant is to account for the uniqueness of a singular human nature by appeal to a person's spiritual activities, and so we have become accustomed to think about the human person as constituted especially by a principle that is immaterial.[79] Christian doctrine, on the other hand, obliges us to remember that the human person is composed of body and soul.

Classical Christian philosophy elaborated on the distinction between the human person and an individual human nature. The sixth-century Christian writer Boethius, for instance, aptly summarizes the difference between personal and individual human nature: nature accounts for what humankind shares in common; person, on the other hand, expresses that which makes an individual instance of humankind unique in itself and separated from all others.[80] Since one's personal identity cannot be shared with others, personhood means incommunicability, undivided in oneself and divided from all others. On the other hand, the reality of a common nature that is individuated into many members implies a kind of commu-

77. See his chapter, "Scientific Status of the Natural Law," in Oscar Brown's *Natural Rectitude*, pp. 27–60.

78. A point from theology: If this were not the case, it would be impossible to interpret adequately the Chalcedonian Christological definition.

79. For example, G. W. F. Hegel, *The Encyclopaedia of the Philosophical Sciences*, 3, trans. W. Wallace (Oxford: Clarendon Press, 1977), p. 377: "The significance of that 'absolute' commandment, *know thyself*—whether we look at it in itself or under the historical circumstances of its first utterance—is not to promote mere self-knowledge in respect of the particular capacities, character, propensities, and foibles of the single self. The knowledge it commands means that of man's genuine reality—of what is essentially and ultimately true and real—of spirit as the true and essential being."

80. For a brief introduction to the terms used in Christian anthropology, see Ambrose McNicholl, O.P., "Person, Sex, and Marriage and Actual Trends of Thought," in *Human Sexuality and Personhood: Proceedings of the Workshop for the Hierarchies of the United States and Canada, Dallas, Texas, February 2–6, 1981* (St. Louis: Pope John Center, 1981): 142–52. For an application of Boethius's distinctions, see my "Boethius, Christ, and the New Order," *Carmina Philosophiae* 1 (1992): 53–64.

nicability. As the witness of the Christian Church makes plain, Christian theology remains committed to promoting the dignity of the human person and at the same time to respecting the limits established by a common nature. While this imperative is a moral one, it nonetheless flows from the very nature of what the Church is in herself. The Church on earth forms a true communion of persons, but one cannot account for this communion in a way that justifies also calling it a Body unless each member shares the same specific nature.

In order to ensure that personal autonomy will be realized within the context of solidarity with others, moral theology must consider personal values within the context of the common good. To accomplish this goal, the moral theologian must possess some way to speak about a shared nature. Personal creativity and responsibility admittedly exemplify properties of persons, not of individual natures. But consider how the fact of a shared human nature moderates the exercise of even the most personal activities. The metier of creative design offers a helpful analogy for understanding this important element of natural law thinking. A person can demonstrate artistic genius when designing tableware, but let her try to create a fork too big for any human mouth, or a soup-spoon with holes in it, or a knife made out of soft material, and the nature of these things will thwart the success of her creativity as a designer. In other terms, even in the production of things, nature establishes limits for human resourcefulness.

However much we are involved in the creative development of human progress, the natural law challenges us to respect the fundamental design of God's wisdom. An architect may employ countless forms in the process of designing a complete house. Each element requires specific determination when it actually becomes part of the real house; for instance, a material realization of the forms of roof, of door and of doorknob, only exists in a definite place and time. Now to count as a house for human habitation the general form of house places limitations on the actual shape the composite forms must take: a roof must possess integrity; a door must be larger than a mouse hole; the doorknobs cannot have razor edges. Those moral theologians who reject the proper place of natural law thinking in the development of theological ethics because the common structures of human nature indicate universal norms for human conduct, fail to take account of the requirements which the fact of a common nature imposes on a moral theory.[81]

81. Among the many who popularize a thorough-going conceptualist view of human

The fields of medical research and public health offer a concrete example of how even the biological givens of our common human nature can supply information which a moral theologian requires in order to determine norms for promoting personal well-being. The human person is not built to sustain in a state of good health some forms of activity. A Washington physician has made this observation concerning the rapid spread of the AIDS virus.

Two fundamentals have been forgotten in all this [discussion about AIDS]. One is that the biological purpose of the sexual act is not only to transmit a body fluid. That fluid must be capable of carrying living elements from one individual into a receptive environment in the other. The full weight of evolution bears down upon sexual union to make it maximally effective in so doing. Any living agent other than sperm gets a first-class free ride in a nutrient medium. There is a long list of venereal diseases that testifies to the efficiency of this mechanism.

The second element is that there is simply no historical precedent for so many individuals sharing body fluids. Even polygamous societies typically restricted the number of wives to that which the man could support economically, and those women had no additional sexual partners.

The complex matrix of biological relationships set up by intravenous drug use and the multiplicity of sexual partners is the modern analog of a contaminated water supply. Anyone who dips into it is at risk of becoming infected. This huge reservoir of disease in so many individuals becomes a common source of infection for those who engage in the few behaviors known to transmit the disease. Biologically, humankind cannot safely sustain this kind of activity.[82]

Although this data comes from medical science, the immediate relevance for moral science is clear. The analysis points to natural law and illus-

---

nature, see O'Connell, *Principles*, pp. 222, 223: "Human nature is a philosophical concept (*Begriff* in German), a concept grounded in reality, a thoroughly justified concept, but a concept nonetheless."

82. A practicing physician in Washington, D.C., J. D. Robinson, M.D., writes in the *Chicago Tribune* (August 3, 1988). For an explanation of the philosophical warrant for taking the findings of the medical and other sciences seriously, see Benedict M. Ashley, O.P., "The River Forest School and the Philosophy of Nature Today," in *Philosophy and the God of Abraham*, ed. R. James Long (Toronto: Pontifical Institute of Mediaeval Studies, 1991), pp. 1–16. The theme has been taken up also by Anthony Santamaria, "The Parameters of Being and Acting Human: The True Case for Moral Science in the Philosophy of Saint Thomas Aquinas," Ph.D diss., University of Toronto, 1999.

trates that the providential design for human conduct which it reveals can manifest itself even at the microscopic level.

Some persons will understandably want to contend that this sort of argument simply points to the need for further technological research in order to remedy the inconveniences that presently impose themselves on those who want to engage in particular forms of sexual conduct. And because advancements in human knowledge can eventually account for even the most difficult scientific enigmas, the moral theologian will want to avoid applying to moral problems reasoning which approximates the sort of "God of the Gaps" solutions once employed, with disappointing results, in theological dialogues with the natural sciences. In other words, we should avoid considering morality as a useful but temporary explanation for those problems which science has not yet had the opportunity to resolve. Theological ethics always follows its own properly theological method. Still, an analysis of the relationship which exists between a particular kind of human behavior and its biological consequences offers an interesting example of how the design of created natures sets limits on the sorts of activity in which a human being can safely engage.[83]

In order to develop an explanation of how the natural law moves people toward the particular goods which constitute integral human perfection, realist moral theology accepts the axiom that the real and the good are coincident—or as the Latin adage expresses it, *ens et bonum convertuntur*.[84] In other terms, wherever something exists, there we find an instance of real goodness. Although authors variously explain the concrete structures in the human person which account for its movement toward the good, the classic realist position holds that desire for human perfection belongs to the category of natural desires. We distinguish natural desires from elicited desires on the grounds that the latter occur only as a response to an apprehended good, whereas the former belong to the constitution of the being's nature. Since only an elicited appetite requires knowledge, natural appetite, therefore, effectively defines and determines the subject even prior to conscious apprehension about the nature of the good thing.

83. Aquinas usually uses *"lex naturalis"* when he is speaking about natural law, but sometimes, as in *Summa theologiae* Ia-IIae, q. 94, a. 2, he chooses the phrase *"lex naturae,"* which suggests the concrete and physical aspects of human nature.

84. See *Summa theologiae* Ia, q. 6, a. 4: "... hoc absolute verum est, quod aliquid est primum, quod per suam essentiam est ens et bonum, quod dicimus Deum...."

Just as the speculative intellect develops reasoned thought from a set of indemonstrable principles basic to human knowing, so the practical intellect grasps the first principle of morality based upon the meaning, or nature, of good, namely, that which all human beings desire. The premise raises significant philosophical problems, especially with those non-naturalist views of the good such as propounded by G. E. Moore and his followers.[85] But our concern lies with how a realist moral theology accepts this naturalist view of the good as its starting point for moral action and scrutiny. Aquinas calls this endowment of practical intelligence *synderesis*. And while sometimes authors identify synderesis with conscience, which Aquinas considers an exercise of particular moral judgment, synderesis actually refers to a feature of human practical intelligence which is the source of our habitual knowledge of the first principles of moral activity.[86]

For Aquinas, the principles of natural law embody inclinations toward a course of actions to be pursued which conform to the shape of our shared human nature. By contrast, ethical idealists, emotivists, prescriptivists, and others who advance a non-naturalist account of moral action purport to validate the common principles of morality exclusively by means of mental structures that, by definition, remain independent from the biological givenness of the whole human person. This puts Aquinas decidedly within what is called the naturalist tradition in morals and politics, for he both believes that human nature is sufficiently invariant across cultures and types of social organization to be taken as a premiss in arguments seeking to justify particular courses for human behavior and, moreover, that fixed elements of human nature provide substantial enough input to function in this role. This is how shared human nature enters into a description of the moral life that can claim universal validity.

85. For a philosophical review of how this works, how it is verified in connection with evil, and, lastly, how it contrasts with non-naturalist views of the good, see Simpson, *Goodness and Nature*, pp. 148–65.

86. See *Summa theologiae* Ia, q. 79, a. 12: "Synderesis is a *habitus*, not a power, notwithstanding the fact that some have held it to be a power above reason, and others have held that it is reason itself considered as nature, not as reason." For an exposition of this approach which favors the cognitional side of natural law theory, see Vernon J. Bourke, "The Background of Aquinas' Synderesis Principle," in *Graceful Reason*, ed., Lloyd P. Gerson (Toronto: Pontifical Institute of Mediaeval Studies, 1983), pp. 345–60. The author presents a different interpretation of the meaning and role of *synderesis* in which he develops an explanation of the difference between *prudentia* and *scientia practica*.

The Inclinations of Reason and Nature

The first directive or inclination of natural law, viz., that the good must be sought and done, forms the ground for all other natural law inclinations. Accordingly, Christian moral realism gives special meaning to the principle: "Good is to be done and pursued and evil avoided." Some commentators, it is true, consider this expression of the basic principle merely a formal principle, but fail to see how it can indicate concrete directions and choices for human behavior.[87] Aquinas, on the other hand, holds that the axiom, *bonum est faciendum et prosequendum, et malum vitandum* enshrines an actual direction by way of inclination toward proper moral conduct. In other terms, the basic principle of natural law, "Good is to be done and pursued and evil avoided," remains normative for every human act; it forms the pattern of a complete and fulfilled human life.

With an appeal to Psalm 4:6, Aquinas identifies this first principle of practical reasoning as originating in the eternal law and as promoting the works of justice, that is, the whole of the virtuous life:

That is why the Psalmist after bidding us, "Offer the sacrifice of justice," and, as though anticipating those who ask what are the works of justice, and adding, "There be many who say, Who will show us any good?" makes reply, "The light of thy countenance, O Lord, is signed upon us," implying that the light of natural reason by which we discern what is good and what is evil, is nothing but the impression of divine light on us.[88]

Signed with the light of the divine countenance, the human person is able by the light of natural reason to discern what is good and evil. This capacity for moral discernment is ordered to the satisfaction of the structural tendencies inherent in human nature as well as to the avoidance of whatever impedes their fulfillment.

An adequate theory of natural law must return to the two ways in which our human nature shares in the eternal law. As the mainline Thomist tradition insists, the human person gains access to the operative principles of natural law, first, when reason actually adverts to them, and, second, when the inclinations of natural law manifest themselves in the settled convictions that abide in human nature itself. Moreover, these two

---

87. For instance, see Eric D'Arcy, *Conscience and Its Right to Freedom* (New York: Sheed & Ward, 1961), p. 52.

88. *Summa theologiae* Ia-IIae, q. 91, a. 2.

inclinations operate synergetically the one with the other. For Aquinas, this synergy of intellect and appetite involves both the rational appetite (will) and the sense appetites (the concupiscible and irascible emotions). "All inclinations of human nature, to whatever part they belong, for example our emotional responsiveness to pain-pleasure objects and emergencies, all come under natural law so far as they can be charged with intelligence."[89] If one wanted to indicate the proper place that natural law theory holds in theological ethics, it would suffice to observe that nature considered as appetite, or, as will, *natura ut voluntas*, and human intelligence jointly contribute to good moral behavior from its first origins through its final achievement in the embrace of a concrete and particular good which perfects human nature.[90]

Apart from the most common or basic principles of natural law, the structure of natural law thinking includes other common principles of natural law. At this level of natural law theory, the ontological structure of the human person determines those particular ends which each human being requires for its own flourishing. For the moral realist, anthropology illuminates human morality. But the theologian comes to know about human nature through an understanding of the basic forms of human good, that is, the various intrinsic constituents of the fulfillment or flourishing of human persons. Although some authors prefer to render a non-hierarchically ordered list of basic human goods, the Thomist position holds that three structural tendencies of human nature lie at the foundation for the moral life.[91]

89. *Summa theologiae* Ia-IIae, q. 94, a. 2, ad 2.

90. For further elaboration on the place of natural law in moral theology, see Benedict Ashley, O.P., *Theologies of the Body: Humanist and Christian* (Brighton, Mass.: Pope John XXIII Center, 1985). Anthony J. Lisska offers an interesting account of Thomist natural law theory in *Aquinas's Theory of Natural Law: An Analytic Reconstruction* (Oxford: Clarendon Press, 1996). But see also the review of his work by Alasdair MacIntyre in *International Philosophical Quarterly* 37 (1997): 95–99. William May, *Introduction*, pp. 45–49, denies that the natural inclinations constitute natural law, and argues that when Aquinas speaks about natural inclinations, he is really talking about direct and nondiscursive knowledge of the goods that perfect human persons.

91. Thus, John Finnis holds that in the inexhaustible basic human goods, such as bodily life itself, knowledge, excellence in work and play, harmony with other human persons, harmony of emotions with reason and of action with judgment, harmony with the world's ultimate cause and destiny, we can see the stable outlines of a nature which is not bounded but which has a stability such that the human race is one. For Finnis's most recent exposition of his viewpoint, see *Aquinas: Moral, Political, and Legal Theory*

A specific metaphysical paradigm undergirds the particular way in which the common principles are set forth by Aquinas in *Summa theologiae* Ia-IIae, question 94, article 2: "The order in which commands of the natural law are ranged corresponds to that of our natural tendencies." He proceeds to examine human nature under three different aspects, each one of which moves toward greater specificity: that of the general notion of substance, that of the generic notion of animal, and that of the specific property of rational or intelligent being. As a result, the moral theologian can identify three distinct areas of human well-being to which the natural law inclines each human person.

Self-preservation, the good which man has in common with all creatures: to preserve the substantial being which is possessed;

Procreation and the rearing of children, the good of the nature man has in common with sentient, but irrational, creatures: to preserve through the coupling of male and female the human species;

Knowledge of truth about God and society, the good of the nature man has in common with all intelligent beings: to act in accord with reason and to realize the potential which reason affords.

These three structural tendencies are coincident with what the Thomist commentatorial tradition, following Aquinas, calls the three primary precepts of the natural law, even though they all converge on one common primary precept, and so take on the nature of one natural law.

(Oxford: Oxford University Press, 1998), chapter 3.7, "The Way to Understanding Our Nature." In this text, Finnis amply considers natural law, but only in the section on speculative truth, which he asserts plays no foundational role in the account of moral philosophy. He offers a practical reason wholly separated from the light of speculative *adequatio* to the order of ends, and an ordering of eternal wisdom that leaves practical reason autonomously sealed off. John J. Conley, S.J., *Theological Studies* 60 (1999): 761–62, predicts that "the fidelity of this portrait to the text of Aquinas and the soft teleology of this portrait will provoke further debate," as in fact happens, for example, in reviews by Denis J. M. Bradley, "John Finnis on Aquinas 'The Philosopher'," *Heythrop Journal* 41 (2000): 1–24, and Jean Porter, "Reason, Nature, and the End of Human Life: A Consideration of John Finnis's *Aquinas*," *Journal of Religion* 80 (2000): 476–84. For an extended discussion of the way Finnis construes the political common good, see Lawrence Dewan, O.P., "St. Thomas, John Finnis, and the Political Common Good," *The Thomist* 64 (2000): 337–74.

Specific Governance of Human Conduct

To distinguish between primary and secondary precepts is a particularity of the tradition that seems to date back to the time of Aquinas. The practice does not mean that natural law spawns a materially exhaustive, formal and closed set of prescriptions and deductive entailments governing every aspect of human conduct. Because of the essential connection between natural law and virtue,[92] the realist moral theologian prefers to interpret natural law precepts as inclinations. The reason for this is supported in part by what Aquinas says about *"naturalis inclinatio."*[93] The general precepts of the natural law articulate what exist as basic inclinations in the human person to embrace the perfective ends of human flourishing. These inclinations, however, are rendered efficacious for the moral life only by the moral virtues, which articulate those things that constitute a good, human life. This articulation is not restricted to establishing logical categories, but extends to forming the actual patterns of human behavior. In other words, the general precepts of the natural law are only the cognitive foundation for the morally significant knowledge achieved connaturally in a virtuous life, a life that perfects these precepts as it perfects the inclinations they govern. It is the task of the moral theologian to identify these inclinations with the concrete human choices which perfect the image of God in each person. This means enumerating the virtues of the Christian life. Once this work is accomplished, then it is possible to affirm that "natural law precepts are absolute guides for human conduct which do not admit of exceptions."[94]

Because this vision of natural law provides broad perspectives without relying on a deductive system of moral rights and wrongs, a realist construal of natural law does not easily support a rationalist conception of natural law.[95] It is true that, since the seventeenth and eighteenth centu-

---

92. For further discussion, see Romanus Cessario, O.P., *The Moral Virtues and Theological Ethics*, 2nd ed. (Notre Dame, Ind.: University of Notre Dame Press, 2008), chap. 3.

93. *Summa theologiae* Ia-IIae, q. 94, a.3: "Since the rational soul is man's proper form, he has a natural tendency (*naturalis inclinatio*) to act according to reason, that is to say according to virtue."

94. As Ralph McInerny in fact does in *Ethica Thomistica*, p. 61.

95. Consider the optimism that must have prompted the seventeenth-century moralist Samuel Pufendorf to claim that "the knowledge which considers what is upright and what is base in human actions, the principal portion of which we have undertaken to present, rests entirely upon grounds so secure, that from it can be deduced genuine

ries, theories of natural right have adversely influenced subsequent theological interpretations of natural law—for example, by reducing it to a collection of abstract principles or formulations. But the realist doctrine of natural law that posits authentic goods as the term of human moral activity remains open to a developmental understanding of human moral potential. Provision for developing more specific details can be discovered in the common principles, although such derived principles, according to Aquinas, hold no claim to the status of full natural law inclinations.

The credit for naming the derived conclusions of natural law "secondary precepts" is generally given to the thirteenth-century Dominican lawyer Roland of Cremona (+1259); Aquinas himself, however, chose to say less rather than more about them.[96] The movement toward interpreting natural law as if it constituted a complete collection of innate jurisprudence stems from the ascendancy which canon law achieved in the late medieval Church. There is evidence that the medieval canonists were given to confuse natural law with the institutions of biblical and canon laws. There is the witness, for instance, of the twelfth-century canonist called Teutonicus. He concludes his discussion of the ninth distinction of the *Ordinary Gloss* by writing: "It is clear that whatever is found to be contrary to divine or canon law, is contrary to natural law and is to be subjected to natural law. And he [Gratian] makes here a correlation of natural law to the canonical scripture and divine laws."[97] These kinds of juridical approaches to natural law, however, risk obfuscating its nature as a participation in the eternal plan of God's wise providence for the world. Thomist moral realism, although it remains congenial to canonical precision, allows no such confusion, for it clearly recognizes that natural law represents a manifestation of God's "eternal power and divine nature, invisible though they are, [which] have been understood and seen through the things he has made" (Rom 1:20).

---

demonstrations which are capable of producing a solid science." See his *Elementorum jurisprudentiae universalis*, II, xxix; *De jure naturae et gentium*, *II*, 25 cited by L. Krieger, *The Politics of Discretion—Pufendorf and the Acceptance of Natural Law* (Chicago: University of Chicago Press, 1965), p. 39.

96. See *Summa theologiae* Ia-IIae, q. 94, a. 4. For more information, see Ross A. Armstrong, *Primary and Secondary Precepts in Thomistic Natural Law Teaching* (The Hague: Martinus Nijhoff, 1966).

97. "Patet quod quae contraria diuinae seu canonicae legi inueniuntur, iuri naturali contraria sunt, et iuri naturali postponuntur. Et facit his correlationem iuris naturalis ad canonicam scripturam et diuinas leges." Ordinary Gloss, col. 39 at (e) *Cum ergo*.

It is important that the forms of jurisprudential and of moral law not be confused: for the former rests upon most general principles, whereas the latter is always perfected in individual—and to some degree, even incommunicable—acts. Whereas the general governance of society requires abstract principles and rules and does not benefit by singular preoccupations, the particular perfection of the individual's moral character is always immersed in particular circumstances which cannot be rightly addressed through merely general rules, nor helpfully construed without virtue: without prudence, fortitude, justice, temperance, and all the other virtues which perfect human agency. Prudence enables a person to turn the singular reality of the particular case toward the ends of virtuous conduct, whereby the human creature most imitates the God whose wise and loving providence governs contingent singular effects. The Church further assures us that infused prudence with its accompanying gift of Counsel shapes the moral deliberations, judgments, and actions of each member—even, on Christ's own word, of the littlest ones among us (see Mt 11:25–26). These assurances about living the Christian moral life afford every reason to find consolation in the existence of natural law inclinations, and to trust that the light of natural reason by which we discern what is good and what is evil will faithfully illuminate them in the course of ordinary human experience.

The realist conception of natural law exemplifies a classical position in moral theology, namely, that the natural moral law endures as a concrete revelation of divine providence.[98] To the extent that it remains fully integrated into a Christian view of the moral life, natural law represents a dynamic picture of the world and at the same time fulfills the requirements of an objective moral realism.

Natural law inclinations set in motion the active use of human reasoning powers, so that it always remains incumbent on the individual to work out the moral truth in a particular situation. Moreover, such particular conclusions will not possess the same degree of connaturality with human fulfillment as the primary principles of natural law. But the basic moral issues pertaining to the right to life, to human sexual coupling, and to truth-telling in human communication all fall under the common principles of the natural law. They regulate areas of human life that are

98. For an early expression of the dynamism of natural law, see Louis Monden, *Sin, Liberty and Law* (New York: Sheed & Ward, 1965), p. 89.

indispensable to the preservation and development of the individual and of the species. And therefore it is never justifiable directly to frustrate these basic natural law inclinations.

Natural Law and the Virtues

Christian moral realism does not permit recourse to mental abstractions as a substitute for contact with the singular realities of history, society, and personal development. The natural law provides guidance for life in a real world of contingencies. Because historical and cultural determinations form the spheres in which human life unfolds individually and communally, these contingent factors fit easily into the elaboration of a natural law ethic. Examples of uneven appreciation of natural law principles at various times in the history of human conduct abound. Aquinas himself cites Caesar's *Gallic Wars* and its account of the Germanic peoples, who deemed theft allowable.[99] Still, Aquinas asserts that as principles of moral rightness in the practical reason, the common principles of natural law remain universal, ineradicable, and immutable.[100] The thrust of the natural law is always toward attainment of, and contentment in, the intelligible good consonant with human nature. This thrust and motivation flow from the intrinsically participatory relationship of the natural to the eternal law. For the natural law is nothing other than a rational participation in God's creative ordering wisdom that is the eternal law.

Of course, the application of natural law to concrete situations results in modifications, and these increase as particular circumstances become more complex. But whatever else may pertain to natural law in the changing circumstances of human history, the purpose of natural law includes each person's attainment of and contentment in the basic and unalterable human goods. Natural law thinking provides a basis for concrete moral choices, while reason shaped by prudence articulates, adjusts, and perfects

99. *De bello Gallico,* VI, 23. See Ia-IIae, q. 94, a. 5.

100. See *Summa theologiae* Ia-IIae, q. 97, a. 1, ad 1: "... natural law is a certain share in the eternal law ... and therefore it endures without change; owing to the perfection and immutability of the divine reason, which institutes nature.... Furthermore, natural law comprises commands which are everlasting...." Michael Bertram Crowe, "Human Nature—Immutable or Mutable," *Irish Theological Quarterly* 30 (1963): pp. 204–31, addresses some of the misuses which authors make of the places, e.g. IIa-IIae, q. 57, a. 2, ad 1, where Aquinas speaks about a changing human nature. For a similar expertise, see Theo G. Belmans, O.Praem., "L'immutabilité de la loi naturelle selon saint Thomas d'Aquin," *Revue Thomiste* 87 (1987): 23–44.

the natural law in fulfilled acts of specific virtues. Because "everything to which the human person is inclined by its very human nature belongs to natural law,"[101] Christian moral theology considers only a completely virtuous life as a full expression of natural law principles. Accordingly, in order fully to understand the natural law, the moral theologian must study the manner of its fruition and fulfillment through the individual moral virtues whereby natural law is rendered morally efficacious.

Are There Exceptions?

Aquinas in *Summa theologiae* Ia-IIae, q. 100, a. 8, ad 3 considers examples of suspected violations of natural law precepts recorded in the Old Testament, such as the despoiling of the Egyptians in Exodus 12:35, Hosea's taking for a wife a harlot in Hosea 1:2, but especially God's command to Abraham to sacrifice his son Isaac in Genesis 22. The Nominalist tradition, represented by the Franciscan theologian William of Ockham (d. 1349), resolved the issue by affirming the "lawlessness" of God, and fifteenth-century nominalism continued to maintain that God could dispense from all natural law precepts. Recall that in nominalist accounts of morality, the absolute divine power and freedom give God the right to designate any action as right or wrong simply by so designating it. But as we have seen, the realist tradition advances a view which does not require deciding for the good-as-willed in place of the good-as-meant. Aquinas therefore interprets these actions, to which, it is important to underscore, the authority of Scripture attaches, in a way that makes them display the divine wisdom. In the text cited above, he appeals to God's supreme authority over all creation, including human life and marriage, as grounds

---

101. See *Summa theologiae* Ia-IIae, q. 94, a. 3. Ralph McInerny devotes an interesting chapter, "Natural Law and Virtue," to this notion in *Art and Prudence. Studies in the Thought of Jacques Maritain* (Notre Dame, Ind.: University of Notre Dame Press, 1988): "If virtue is the personal appropriation of the good sketched in the precepts of Natural Law, Natural Law provides the ultimate basis for seeing our common humanity in a way that celebrates the inexhaustible legitimate differences in virtuous acts" (p. 121). For a different approach to the issue of determining the concrete moral good, see James F. Keenan, S.J., *Goodness and Rightness in Thomas Aquinas's Summa Theologiae* (Washington, D.C.: Georgetown University Press, 1992) as well as the reviews of this work by John Cuddeback in *The Thomist* 58 (1994): 342–47, and Lawrence Dewan, "St. Thomas, James Keenan, and the Will," *Science et Esprit* 47 (1995): 153–76, which call into question the legitimacy of associating with St. Thomas's account of morals an opposing distinction between goodness and rightness.

for recognizing that a new moral object now specifies the questionable acts: "Abraham, in consenting to kill his son, did not consent to homicide, since it was right that his son should be put to death by the command of God, who is the Lord of life and death. For it is God who inflicts the punishment of death on all men, just as well as unjust, on account of the sin of our first parent; and if man carries out this sentence on the authority of God, he is no murderer any more than God is." In a comment on the same episode in Genesis, von Balthasar interprets the event in a way that complements Aquinas's moral analysis: "And, lest the Isaac who was born by God's power should ever be regarded as an end in himself, God asks for him back."[102]

In this story of Abraham and Isaac, what transpires according to the Thomist account is that God's creative power changes the form of the moral object so that the apparently immoral deed can rightly be said to suit a reasonable course of activity. Abraham acts in this manner not "for himself" but exclusively as instrumental cause of an act he is otherwise forbidden to undertake simply in his own right—he is, as it were, but a "sword in the hand" of God who, as giving life, alone has rightful authority to determine life's end.[103] For Aquinas this does not mean that God dispenses from the commandment in order to accomplish a desired consequence, for Abraham acting in his own right remains bound by the commandment: it is only as instrumentally assimilated to God's direct intervention that Abraham is authorized to act materially differently than would be possible under his own recognizance. It is essential to underscore that the prerogative to intervene in the ways mentioned in the canonical Scriptures belongs only to God as First Cause and Creator of all that exists.

The variety of moral experiences which attract the attention of the contemporary student are not primarily those recorded in the books of the Old Testament. Cultural anthropologists, social psychologists, and historians of civilization contribute variously to the list of examples

---

102. Balthasar, "Nine Theses," especially Thesis 5, "The Promise (Abraham)," p. 114. For a fuller exposition of Aquinas's texts, see Patrick Lee, "Permanence of the Ten Commandments: St. Thomas and His Modern Commentators," *Theological Studies* 42 (1981): 422–43.

103. Although this authority is, on Thomas's view, rightfully delegated both to the governors of civil society and to the innocent who, though not seeking to inflict death, may accidentally do so in the course of defending themselves.

which challenge the trans-cultural and trans-historical validity of natural law. At least two factors help explain why certain people or groups of people manifest divergence from natural law principles.

First, we can consider natural law from its operational side. There the influence of unruly passions sometimes blurs even the common principles of natural law.[104] Because of the disordering consequent upon the loss of original justice, the human person cannot assume perfect self-mastery over his or her behavior. Unmanageable passions affect human behavior. While every inclination responds in some way to the notion of good, only an authentic good—ultimately discerned by right reason—provides a proper goal for liberty of choice. By way of jocund example: the American in Paris may choose to eat at a fast food counter, thereby choosing an apparent good, such as an identifiable hamburger, in place of a real good, namely, authentic *haute cuisine*; but surely some disordered passion, such as nostalgia for the American way of life, accounts for this "unnatural" decision.

By way of a more serious moral example, one notes the frequent errors which people make in identifying the proper objects for authentic sexual gratification. When a sexual partner is chosen outside of the stability that the permanent and exclusive commitment between husband and wife both generates and demands, broken relationships and hearts give testimony to the raw destructive power of intemperate passion. Such passion can lead both men and women to act, even habitually, in a way that contravenes the principles of natural law. A similar analysis can be made of persons who negate the inherent relational character of sexual relations by engaging in auto-sexual activities.

While there are many other examples of practices which allegedly demonstrate a pattern for moral behavior different than that which the natural law indicates, none of these constitute a serious challenge to the existence of the natural law. Why? Because every disordered deed yields its own punishment, each attempt to construct a pattern of moral behav-

---

104. Although I modify some of his conclusions, Michael Bertram Crowe suggests these headings in "Natural Law Theory Today," in *The Future of Ethics and Moral Theology*, ed. D. Brezine and J. McGlynn, S.J. (Chicago: Argus, 1968), pp. 78–105, and develops his discussion in *The Changing Profile of the Natural Law* (The Hague: Martinus Nijhoff, 1977). For a more recent discussion, see John Boler, "Aquinas on Exceptions in Natural Law," in *Aquinas's Moral theory. Essays in Honor of Norman Kretzmann*, ed. Scott MacDonald and Eleonore Stump (Ithaca, N.Y.: Cornell University Press, 1999), pp. 161–204.

ior outside of what conforms to God's wise providence for the human race leads to some form of moral dissolution. Rationalist closure to the divine cannot obscure the self-implosive character of vicious deeds, nor the need for the help of grace. "Quarry the granite rock with razors, or moor the vessel with a thread of silk;" writes John Henry Newman, "then may you hope with such keen and delicate instruments as human knowledge and human reason to contend against those giants, the passion and the pride of man."[105]

A second factor explaining apparent divergence from the natural law standards considers its cognitional side. If the passions can overshadow the right dictates of human reason, so likewise human intelligence in itself possesses the capacity for error. Knowledge of moral truth serves as consequential a role in the formation of right conduct as rectitude of the passions does in insuring its realization. Although the most common principle of natural law possesses a half-innate guarantee of infallibility in the habit of *synderesis,* lack of due knowledge can affect the operation of even the common inclinations of the natural law. For example, an individual or even many individuals within a culture may not yet recognize morally significant truths, for instance, that incest between brother and sister carries biologically threatening consequences to the offspring, or that persons of a despised caste and race are truly and fully human and possessed of that human dignity flowing from their status as children of God. But this does not argue for the cultural relativeness of natural law principles; on the contrary, the examples rather illustrate with imperative necessity the human mind's need to learn moral truth.

As the natural inclination toward virtue is weakened as a result of original and actual sin, it is unsurprising that the richer implications of the natural law are often obscured by disordered passion or by ignorance. This is analogous to noting that difficult mathematical problems are more resistant to solution and hence accidentally more productive of error. Where emotion, self-love, and self-knowledge enter into the contest, there should be no illusion about the manifold danger that truth may be concealed, nor about the lofty perfection and challenge of the life of virtue. Yet this is no ground for epistemic skepticism or subjectivism: the desire for genuine human fulfillment and the light of grace are persistent

105. J. H. Newman, "Liberal Knowledge Its Own End," in *Scope and Nature of University Education,* Discourse IV (London: Everyman edition, 1915), p. 112.

and active principles perfecting the natural law in virtuous action and in right judgment. The efficacious blossoming of natural law in the perfections of virtue is no more refuted by impediments and vices, than the preponderance of error in the history of science refutes truth. For deprivation of truth or virtue provides mute but authentic testimony to truth and virtue themselves. In this way, even sin obliquely points to the reality of a law for nature.

St. Augustine expresses the context in which the People of God move toward a fuller appreciation of what the Christian life entails. He writes: "Though we labor among the many distractions of this world, we should have but one goal. For we are but travelers on a journey without as yet a fixed abode; we are on our way, not yet in our native land."[106] In the native land, natural law and the inclinations that flow from it find fulfillment in the glory that Christ has asked the Father to bestow on those who have followed his way. In the light of glory will appear, to the extent that a created mind can sustain it, the true pattern of all that exists.

106. St. Augustine, *Sermo* 103, 1–2, 6 (PL 38, cols. 613, 615).

CHAPTER THREE

The Origin and Structure of Virtuous Behavior

The Voluntariness of Christian Freedom

Natural law quickens both the human cognitive and conative powers. As we have seen, it establishes in the human person the foundation for an *entente-cordiale* between the intelligent pursuit of moral truth and the human appetite for the good. In human acts, reason and will are rooted in the soul together; or again, as Aristotle observed, "they are one."[1] This unity actually represents a synergism of reason and will, as together these human powers actualize the thrust latent in the structural tendencies of human nature to reach out for a desirable end.

Since natures bear within their very composition the dynamism for seeking their own perfective good, Christian anthropology recognizes in human nature an instance of *natura ut voluntas*, that is, a nature-as-willing. Aquinas explains that *synderesis*, the operative disposition (or *habitus*) whereby the human mind holds to the first principles of practice, also transposes the human tendency to reach out for the good into the initial movement of practical reasoning.[2] Early Christian theologians such as St. John Damascene used this feature of our moral psychology as a way to express how the human desire for God, the supremely desirable

---

1. See *Nicomachean Ethics*, Bk. 2, chap. 6 (1111a23).

2. "And thus synderesis is said to incite us to good and to deter us from evil in that through first principles we both begin investigation and judge what we find" (*Summa theologiae* Ia, q. 79, a. 12). Aquinas in this same text mentions the various accounts of *synderesis* given by the early Scholastics, a notion that they had borrowed from St. Jerome. D. J. Billy, C.Ss.R. "Aquinas on the Content of *Synderesis*," *Studia Moralia* 29 (1991): 61–83 provides both an overview of the history of the notion and a good bibliography; he also underscores the important systematic point (see esp., pp. 68–73) that it is imperative to analyze synderesis with reference to its role as a primer for virtuous, and therefore, prudential, activity.

End, spontaneously wells up from within the powers of the human soul.[3]

In an account of realist moral theology, the voluntariness of human behavior signifies something about both the nature of the human person who acts and, at a most fundamental level, the moral quality of his or her actions.[4] First, as a general topic related to anthropology, voluntariness refers to the plain fact that human actions proceed from both human reason and will. Aquinas considers that human willing is related to the full panoply of natural appetites; indeed he frequently refers to the will as the rational appetite. Human beings possess the capacity to engage in a sort of reasoned appetition. Again in the lapidary phrase of Aquinas's Latin, willing embodies an inclination following upon a form as understood (*"inclinatio sequens formam intellectam"*).[5] Just as natural law inclinations arise from the specific nature that human beings possess, so also do the voluntary wellsprings of human behavior originate in both knowledge and rational appetite. Second, as a basic feature of every human action, voluntariness signifies the self-mastery which the human person can possess over his or her activity. From this capacity we are led to conclude that not only does natural law reveal the imprint of the *imago Dei*, but also that the voluntary character of human activity manifests the human person's analogical participation in that divine nature wherein knowing the good and willing the truth are necessarily coincident. A pattern of holiness is established at the very origins of human action. The more the rational creature chooses virtuously, the more he or she images God who is the cause of all voluntary movements.

Aquinas is of the view that only theology can provide a definitive analysis of human action and freedom. There is no reason to doubt that he would both agree with and appreciate the Church's present-day formulation of this thesis: "Seen in any other terms [than the mystery of the incarnate Word], the mystery of personal existence remains an insoluble

---

3. See St. John Damascene (c. 655–750), *De fide orthodoxa*, Bk. 2, chap. 24 (PG 94, col. 953).

4. Aquinas's short treatise on what constitutes the voluntary and what factors can cause the involuntary (*Summa theologiae* Ia-IIae, q. 6, aa. 1–8) precedes his discussion of the morality of human acts. The *Catechism of the Catholic Church* adopts this perspective when it teaches that "freedom makes man responsible for his acts to the extent that they are voluntary" (no. 1734).

5. See *Quaestiones de quodlibet* 6, q. 2, a.1 corpus. This text from a quodlibetal discussion illustrates Aquinas's everyday appeal to the analogical meaning of human willing, and reveals his emphasis on the embodiment of the will's spiritual activity.

riddle."[6] This fundamental Christian intuition accounts for the fact that Aquinas begins the *prima-secundae* of his *Summa theologiae* by appealing to the doctrine of the "*imago Dei.*" Specifically, Aquinas writes:

Man is made to God's image, and since this implies, so Damascene tells us, that he is intelligent and free to judge and master of himself, so then, now that we have agreed that God is the exemplar cause of things and that they issue from his power through his will, we go on to look at this *imago*, that is to say, at man as the source of actions which are his own and fall under his responsibility and control.[7]

To honor Christian teaching on the divine goodness, the moral theologian interprets human freedom as an instrument of God's wise providence for his creatures. In this respect, Christian realism radically differs from the perspectives of Greek tragedy and philosophy, which often promote a pessimistic view about the durability of goodness in human life and about the capacity of man to embrace the good.[8]

Discussion of the voluntary introduces another important consideration about the human person's movement toward perfection. While the natural desire for both human flourishing and God specify the moral life in the order of final causality, it is not the case that extrinsic causes alone move the human person. To adopt a teleological framework for morals does not require us to picture God moving human persons like marionettes. On the contrary, human actions possess a principle of motion from within their own internal structure. This distinction moves Aquinas to explain further that "the cognitive and appetitive dynamism, the internal principle of a voluntary act, may be taken as first in the class of psychological motions of desire, and still be regarded as moved by an external force according to another kind of motion."[9] In other words, by af-

6. *Fides et ratio,* no. 12.

7. See the introduction before q. 1 of *Summa theologiae* Ia-IIae.

8. For a detailed account of this view from the perspectives of both philosophy and literature, see Martha C. Nussbaum, *The Fragility of Goodness. Luck and Ethics in Greek Tragedy and Philosophy* (Cambridge: Cambridge University Press, 1986). On Nussbaum's account, a tragedy such as Euripides' *Hecuba* "shows us a case of solid character and shows us that, under certain circumstances, even this cannot escape defilement. It also [shows] us that even the good character who has not suffered any actual damage or betrayal lives always with the risk of these events: for it is the nature of political structures to change, and in the nature of personal friendship that the confident man should be indistinguishable from the trustworthy man ..." (p. 419).

9. *Summa theologiae* Ia-IIae, q. 6, a. 1, ad 1.

firming that the source of voluntary activity by definition lies within the person, moral realism denies neither that this internal principle is created by God, nor that the natural motion characterizing it—like its very nature and being—is received.

Now since the *imago Dei* is impressed on the whole of the human person—viz., the *per se unum* body-soul composite—authentic voluntary actions display human nature's inclinations to unfold harmoniously in the pursuit of an integral life of human contentment and divine charity. The Christian Gospel obliges us to seek the single goal of divine charity in every action that we perform; and even when moved by divine charity, human willing retains its truly voluntary character or nature. Realist moral theology maintains that the human person acts no less voluntarily when moved by divine grace to love God above all things, even though it denies that the human will can be effectively coerced by any outside force. This war of freedom with coercion is apparent when it is the case that some foreign agent exercises force on another human person. But it also holds true for any alleged compulsion of divine grace, for grace always respects the freedom of human choosing even as it perfects our freedom to desire only God and the things which pertain to God. To put it differently, the teaching of St. Thomas Aquinas affirms that God moves each agent with respect for its proper nature, so that when divine grace moves the human creature, the person acts freely under the impulse of the divine action.[10]

This question of freedom and of the will's derivation, both of its natural motion and of its graced perfection from God, calls for a brief excursion into the details of St. Thomas's doctrine regarding the nature of created liberty. For created freedom is not uncreated freedom, but receives both its being and its motion from God. Regarding both its outset—the motion of natural desire—and its completion—beatific union—the will is not "free" either to exist without natural desire or to possess God only to discard him. For the will naturally desires happiness, and hence is free in respect to means but not to the end, which is given by the very nature of the will as rational appetite. And in beatitude God, as infinitely perfect, so fulfills the will that there is no potency left to be dislodged from him, nor any respect owing to finitude in which he, like creatures, might be judged as in some respect not-good.

The classical Thomist understanding of human freedom is particu-

10. For a brief account of the classical thesis on grace and freedom accepted in the Thomist school, see the *excursus* at the end of this chapter.

larly important for anthropology, natural law, and our understanding of divine grace. For a natureless volition endlessly whirring in a rationalist universe separated from divine providence is the prototypical myth of "enlightened secularity." It is the myth that seeks to establish finite human reason as the highest knowable principle, and to treat human freedom as autonomously self-bestowed and self-perfective. But, to the contrary, it is apparent even from natural evidence that only the One who causes a thing's nature bestows its natural motion, and that human nature and being are created effects of God. Further, this divine bestowal of its natural motion does not violate the will but rather is the very gift of natural desire itself.[11] A thing's natural motion, like its natural being, is not self-generated. That which is positive within the volitional act—like being itself—is simultaneously most our own while yet being most a divine gift.

The Voluntary and the Free

From these introductory remarks, it should be clear that moral realism introduces a useful distinction between the voluntary and the free. Every free act is voluntary, but not every voluntary act attains the perfection of human freedom.[12] When realist moral theologians discuss the voluntary, they therefore consider the basic and indispensable conditions for human freedom. This practice affords a more comprehensive treatment of freedom than what results from a narrow focus onto the deliberate exercise of free choice itself.

Some contemporary schools of Christian ethics prefer to adopt the dominant motifs of the German *Aufklärung*, with the result that we have become accustomed to hear from some quarters about human freedom as a transcendental category which, for all intents and purposes, obscures the status and purposes of human nature as they pertain to the moral life.[13] Although the classical German idealist tradition has made freedom

---

11. For a classical locus, see *Summa theologiae* Ia-IIae, q. 9, a. 6, resp.

12. For further explanation of this distinction, see Thomas Gilby, O.P., *Psychology of Human Acts*, Blackfriars *Summa*, vol. 17 (1970), appendix 2, "Liberty within Limits," pp. 218–21.

13. "Transcendental freedom" is taken to mean one's free basic stance toward being itself, as opposed to particular individual choices which may not fully reflect this basic stance. Yet, neither the embodied nature nor the teleological ordering of human freedom is sufficiently regarded by this teaching, which construes the whole providential ordering of creature to Creator as a supererogatory detail surpassed by naked, over-

its principal value, it is quite different from Aquinas's account of free choice, as the literature of romanticism amply illustrates.[14] The Christian tradition interprets human freedom within a metaphysics of creation, and considers the profound want of the human will for happiness and the ecstatic love of God which follows upon the beatific vision as voluntary though technically non-free activities.

Since only human knowledge can grasp the exact nature of purposeful activity, it is characteristic of human beings that they can properly deliberate about an end and the relationship that a means bears to it.[15] In this ability, human persons differ from brute animals, who perceive ends, but remain largely incapable of adapting themselves to creative ways of achieving them.[16] Likewise, but for quite different reasons, angelic persons do not reflect about means, for their intuitive knowledge eliminates the need for deliberation about circumstantial means. As a result, in both angelic nature and angelic activity, the voluntary and the free coincide, although the angels remain clearly capable of choice.[17] Because the capacity to engage in intelligent behavior forms the basis for imputing responsibility, moral theologians ascribe the full weight of praise or blame only when it is a case of a person's fully voluntary activity. So when the lamb flees from the wolf, it receives neither praise nor blame; its reward consists only in its continued existence or, if it fails to flee successfully, its punishment entails death. On the other hand, we designate angels as either good or bad on the basis of their once-and-for-all choice whether to love God as the supremely desirable Good or not. With the human creature, however, willing is more complex. Before we examine the dynamics of human choosing, we need first to consider the condition *sine qua non* of freedom, the voluntary.

arching, and disembodied will. The human will does in certain respects transcend facticity, but it remains nonetheless a creaturely reality rationally specified by the whole natural hierarchy of ends, and further elevated and perfected in grace.

14. For a balanced appreciation of the contributions made by both idealism and romanticism, see Kenneth L. Schmitz, "The Idealism of the German Romantics," in *The Emergence of German Idealism*, ed. Michael Baur and Daniel O. Dahlstrom (Washington, D.C.: The Catholic University of America Press, 1999), pp. 176–97.

15. See *Summa theologiae* Ia-IIae q.6, a. 2.

16. Alasdair MacIntyre has incorporated interesting contemporary scientific research on nonhuman animals into his discussion of their reasons for action. See his *Dependent Rational Animals*, pp. 53–61.

17. See for example, the discussion in *Summa theologiae* Ia, q. 60, a. 2, "Are the angels loving as choosing to love?" where Aquinas accounts for freedom of choice in the

Indirect and Direct Voluntariness

In order to deal with questions of responsibility and imputability, the casuist tradition invested considerable energy into devising an account of voluntary and involuntary actions.[18] However, one astute observer of casuist practices has observed that many casuist authors transposed Aquinas's basic terminology, and therefore treated his distinction between the direct and indirect voluntary as one between the positive and negative voluntary. Let us define these terms. For Aquinas, the indirect voluntary simply covers two sorts of situations: first, when not acting at the proper time amounts to the willful causing of something to happen, or, alternatively, when purposefully not acting impedes something from happening. By contrast, the casuist manualists distorted this analysis. They designated willing something for itself as directly voluntary, i.e., as an instance of the positive voluntary; while they construed willing something which results from another action (as when a therapeutic operation causes an abortion) as indirectly voluntary, i.e., as an instance of the negative voluntary.[19]

The negative voluntary on the account of many manualists would constitute a kind of enacted non-action. What is important to remember, however, is that the casuist authors subtly re-directed the discussions of voluntary human behavior, so that voluntariness became identified with the highest purposes of human intention—that which is willed for itself—instead of with the fundamental movement of the human person toward the good in willing ordinate means. In other words, the casuists identified voluntariness with the ends of human striving rather than with the means thereto, and became neglectful of the idea that, as St. Thomas puts it, "the ends of human life are fixed." This development in the history of moral theology is highly significant, inasmuch as it illuminates the disposition of the casuist authors to deny that the will is by nature ordered to its final end, and identifies voluntariness with a spurious independence from the whole providential order represented by the natural law.[20]

---

angels, even though the intuitive infallibility of their knowledge always shapes their prior and natural desire for only good ends.

18. For a general discussion of the main perspectives of casuistry, see the Appendix.

19. See Thomas Gilby, O.P., *Psychology of Human Acts*, Blackfriars *Summa*, vol. 17 (1970), p. 15, note "c."

20. Servais Pinckaers, *Sources*, pp. 262–63, notes the omission of the treatise on beatitude as one of the features of the modern moral manuals: "The question was precisely

The various construals of the Principle of Double Effect represent so many ways in which moral theologians grappled with the case of effects which were caused, but not intended. And it seems significant that the history of twentieth-century proportionalism as a school of moral argumentation began with an attempt once again to puzzle out the Principle of Double Effect.[21] Consider, for example, that in the transition from pre-conciliar casuist legalism to certain post-conciliar revisions of moral theology, Peter Knauer's 1965 article, "La détermination du bien et du mal moral par le principe du double effet," holds an important place.[22] In any event, the casuists' conjectures about the negative voluntary, the *voluntarium in causa*, as it came to be known, surely accustomed moral theologians to overstate the status of individual psychological dispositions, such as personal motives and intentions, in their appraisal of morality.[23] It may also be argued that this moral version of the anthropological turn explains, at least in part, the practice of many moral theologians to ne-

---

this: whether the treatise on man's final end and beatitude had come to be considered as purely speculative and thus superfluous to moral theology."

21. For discussion of this topic from a perspective favorable to proportionalism, see Bernard Hoose, *Proportionalism. The American Debate and Its European Roots* (Washington, D.C.: Georgetown University Press, 1987).

22. See Peter Knauer's article which first appeared in *Nouvelle Revue Théologique* 87 (1965): 356–76. Two years later he published "Das rechtverstandene Prinzip von der Doppelwirkung als Grundnorm jeder Gewissensentscheidung," *Theologie und Glaube* (1967): pp. 107–33. A revised version of this article, "The Hermeneutical Function of the Principle of Double Effect," first appeared in *Natural Law Forum* 12 (1967): 132–62, and subsequently in *Readings in Moral Theology* No. 1. *Moral Norms and Catholic Traditions*, ed. Charles E. Curran and Richard A. McCormick, S.J. (New York: Paulist Press, 1979). Again, see the interesting discussion by Bernard Hoose, *Proportionalism*, esp. chap. 1, "How It Began."

23. Here is how Cardinal Cajetan, commenting on the *Summa theologiae* Ia-IIae, q. 1, a. 1, outlines the actual coordination of personal intention and the objective reality of "end" in moral action: "Therefore, in order that this matter would not remain ambiguous, I will first propose three propositions by explaining [*declarando*] them; then I will support them; and thus, thirdly, the truth will be visible. The first proposition is: to be [*esse*] in intention is not the *ratio* of 'end,' but its *condition*. The second proposition is: to be [*esse*] in execution is neither the *ratio* nor the condition of 'end,' but is *coincidical* to it [*coincidens illi*]. The third proposition is: to be [*esse*] *in the nature of things* is the *ratio* of 'end.'" ("Ut igitur res non remaneat ambigua, primo ponam tres propositiones, declarando illas; deinde probabo illas; et sic, tertio, patebit veritas. Prima propositio est: Esse in intentione non est ratio finis, sed eius conditio. Secunda est: Esse in executione nec ratio nec conditio finis est, sed coincidens illi. Tertia est: Esse in rerum natura est ratio finis" [*Commentary, In Iam-IIae*, q. 1, a. 1, no. 9].) Translation by Cajetan Cuddy, O.P. (emphasis mine).

glect the nature of the moral action itself, and to formulate principles for analyzing human moral conduct that favor heavily the personal dispositions of the agent. Aquinas includes discussion of the voluntary to show that the wellsprings of human freedom are deeper than free will, prior to free choice; when, therefore, the voluntary is impeded by factors outside an individual's control, it is a cause of regret inasmuch as the good of the human person is compromised.[24]

Enemies of the Voluntary

To sum up: a voluntary action is one which finds its principle from within the agent and which proceeds with knowledge of the end.[25] Thus, voluntariness chiefly characterizes human activity which proceeds from discursive reasoning. When it comes to making a judgment about what affects the voluntary in a given circumstance, interiority and due knowledge serve as the criteria for evaluating a human action's voluntary character. Threats to voluntary action, conventionally referred to as its "enemies," arise from anything which upsets the psychological poise or balance in either of these areas.

The pinball machine provides a helpful, albeit mechanical, metaphor for grasping the relationship of the voluntary to the free. Let the object of yesteryear's penny arcade game, namely, to score as many points as possible, represent the ultimate goal of a virtuous life. Now some intrusive factor, such as too much leaning with one's elbows, can interrupt the pinball game either immediately or at some point before the game's end. As a result of such external interference, the pinball machine tilts and the game abruptly ends. Let the intrusive factors which cause the machine to tilt stand for the enemies of the voluntary. For to one degree or another, such intrusions tilt or upset the psychological balance or poise which is required for authentically free human behavior to follow. Certain identifiable factors can affect the voluntariness of human activity, and when this happens the actions which result fall into the category of either involuntary or non-voluntary actions. Involuntary action occurs when, for instance, hijackers physically overpower a hostage and forcibly oblige the

---

24. What *Veritatis splendor* (no. 63) says about the evil done as the result of invincible ignorance or a non-culpable error of judgment applies to every instance when the voluntary is impeded, namely, a bad action, even when not imputable to the agent, still embodies a disorder in relation to the truth about the good.

25. See *Summa theologiae* Ia-IIae, q. 6, a. 1.

person against her will to shield their escape, whereas involuntary actions proceed without the deliberate will, as when a man, thinking that he is shooting wild game grouse, actually kills a neighbor's prize domestic animal. Involuntary or non-voluntary actions can be designated as authentic moral behavior only in a depreciated sense of "moral."

The classical tradition, represented by, among others, Aquinas, identifies a number of factors which affect voluntary activity. Collectively, violence, fear, ignorance, and lust constitute the *hostes voluntarii*—the enemies of the voluntary.[26] While certain elements of the theory are borrowed from classical philosophy, their application to Christian living belongs to the structure and the logic of *sacra doctrina*. When duly informed by the findings of the psychological sciences, a proper analysis of the enemies of the voluntary serves a properly theological objective. The complexities of human affairs accordingly require attention both to Aristotle's observations on how the psyche is deterred from purposeful activity, and also to the infused virtues and gifts of the Holy Spirit which direct even the most complex human activity toward evangelical perfection. The life sciences in general also may aid our understanding of how such factors as collective ignorance, societal violence, personal fear, and lust impair a person's ability to operate in a fully human way.

We know that the eternal law manifests itself in both the cognitive and the appetitive powers of human nature. The four enemies of voluntary action either restrict the requisite knowledge for deliberate human activity or intrude upon the interiority which distinguishes authentic human conduct from what happens spontaneously. Aquinas points to the substantive distinction between "human acts," which proceed from intelligence and the ensuing rational appetite, and what he calls the "acts of a human being," which arise spontaneously and therefore do not fall under a person's dominion.[27]

There are four factors to consider. Violence signifies some action imposed on a subject from the outside and against its natural bent; as such, it represents a form of coercion. Violence renders a given action involun-

---

26. For a philosopher's account of this material, see Ralph McInerny, *Ethica Thomistica*, rev. ed. (Washington, D.C.: The Catholic University of America Press, 1997), pp. 60–69, and for a fuller treatment of the Aquinas's action theory, McInerny's *Aquinas on Human Action. A Theory of Practice* (Washington, D.C.: The Catholic University of America Press, 1992).

27. See *Summa theologiae* Ia, q. 1, a.1.

tary, that is, an act which goes against willing, for the simple reason that an action so produced effectively results from the will of another person. When some form of physical violence overcomes a person, he or she becomes completely instrumentalized to the will of the aggressor.

In accord with a long tradition in Western philosophy, Aquinas contends that to the extent that the specific act of willing remains essentially a spiritual action, the will resists all forms of coercion.[28] Thus, there is a sense in which no one can force me to love anything, and as long as one seeks God in the darkness of faith which distinguishes the Christian life on earth, such radical freedom applies even to loving God. Some theological traditions emphasize the drawing power exercised by God first on the human heart and then on mind, but for the realist theologian only when God appears as he is in himself does the one who beholds this vision possess no alternative but to love him.[29] At the moment when saving faith gives way to beatific vision, our freedom of choosing disappears; in the state of heavenly glory, the supreme Object of human desire seizes the blessed in a way that completely fulfills all human voluntariness. We anticipate this as a moment of rapture, not of violence.

The second enemy, the emotion of fear, affects voluntariness in a different way than violence.[30] Fear first arises through the contending or

28. See the parallel which Aquinas makes between natural activity and voluntary activity in *Summa theologiae* Ia-IIae, q. 6, a. 5, ad 2: "To be natural means following the bent of nature and similarly to be voluntary means following the bent of will. Now an action is termed natural in two ways. First, when it is from a nature considered as an active principle; thus it is natural for fire to heat. Second, when it is from a nature considered as a passive principle, that is, because of an inborn predisposition to receive the action of an outside principle.... Correspondingly, an action is termed voluntary in two ways. First, with respect to action, or acting upon, as when one wills to do something. Second, with respect to passion, or being acted upon, as when one wills to receive another's action. This spells no violence as such, that is to say, when a subject willingly undergoes the application of an action from outside, for then he contributes to the deed by his acceptance, though not by his own effort."

29. St. Augustine argued that something can be loved which is unknown: "But then to behold and grasp God as he can be beheld and grasped is only permitted to the pure of heart—blessed are the pure in heart, because they shall see God (Mt 5:8); so before we are capable of doing this we must first love by faith, or it will be impossible for our hearts to be purified and become fit and worthy to see him" (*De Trinitate*, Bk. 8, chap. 3). There exists a tradition in Christian theology that makes our appetitive powers the site of first contact, as it were, between the human person and the divine saving initiative. When this starting point is adopted, a complementary but nonetheless different slant on the Christian life emerges.

30. See *Summa theologiae* Ia-IIae, q. 6, a. 6.

irascible emotions as a certain alarm of mind which shapes the way we react to some evil which is absent but likely to befall us. By contrast, those
evils which already have befallen an individual generate the emotion of
sorrow. The effect of fear on voluntary activity depends upon various and
complex factors. The classical example of the rich merchant at sea, however, well illustrates a typical scenario. When a threatening storm arises
without forewarning, the merchant on the high seas must immediately estimate the peril which presently endangers both his life and his merchandise. Once he determines that his life is actually jeopardized as long as
he holds on to the merchandise in the boat, fear moves him to throw the
goods overboard. While he jettisons his cargo freely, still, throwing the
goods overboard expresses voluntary action only after a fashion, for he
certainly would act otherwise if not for the sure perception that his fragile bark might sink and his life would be lost. Acting under the aspect
of simple voluntariness, the merchant would preserve both life and merchandise. Actions induced by fear exemplify the voluntary only in a qualified sense of the term, for apart from the concrete circumstances which
precipitate the fear, the individual would not have acted in such a way.

In the context of human voluntariness, concupiscence (lust) represents
the basic human desire for pleasure, but does not necessarily imply a note
of baseness, though the same term signifies both the emotion and the
vice.[31] This emotion concerns the human response to things perceived
as good but not yet possessed in joy and delight. Lust ensures that human nature remains capable of moving toward the essential goods, for example, food, drink, sexual union, required for the perfection of both the
individual and the species. Precisely because of its drawing-from-within
dynamism, lust always increases the voluntary character of an action, and
this is for the better if the action be virtuous.[32]

Theologians normally distinguish two basic kinds of lust that impinge
adversely on human action: antecedent and consequent lust. First, antecedent lust[33] signifies the case of one in whom the sudden onsurge of lust
really upsets the conditions required for realizing due knowledge of an

31. The Christian tradition uses "concupiscence" to describe an effect in the human
person of original sin, although this technical use of the term implies a more radical
dislocation within the creature than that which arises from disordered lust.

32. See *Summa theologiae* I-IIae, q. 6, a. 7. In other words, lust draws the person toward
a perceived good so that the interiority characteristic of the voluntary increases rather
than decreases.

33. See *Summa theologiae* I-IIae, q. 6, a. 7, ad 3.

end, with the result that a person acts passionately but indiscriminately. Sometimes we hear people refer to someone becoming mad with lust. No virtuous or perfective action proceeds from one who acts out of this condition, even though the cause of the antecedent lust may not be easily identified with a prior moment in the person's choosing.

Second, lust is consequent when it follows upon some form of deliberate action. Again, theologians distinguish three forms of consequent lust: first, indirect consequent lust, or the case where a person could have smoothed the passions, but did not; second, direct consequent lust, or the case where a person actively excites concupiscence of one sort or another; and third, habitual consequent lust, or the case where an individual has lost all control because of previous, repeated bad action. Since in both antecedent and consequent lust, the agent's interior movement follows its voluntary direction toward some object of desire, the lustful person is not said to act involuntarily. Instead, in cases where actions proceed from either antecedent or consequent lust, the resultant action illustrates nonvoluntary activity, that is, action proceeding from a strong interior drive while the agent lacks a keen discretionary comprehension of the object of his or her lust.

While the above-mentioned considerations obviously merit careful attention, especially when it comes to evaluating particular actions of those persons who are judged to be in some state of psychological distress, it must also be remembered that emotional upset of this kind does not constitute a desirable state for human beings. Consider the evil that disordered desires can inflict on a person. For example, the one who sins habitually against the virtues associated with cardinal temperance becomes bound to created goods in a way that conforms neither to the good of the human person nor to the evangelical virtues and Beatitudes. To pursue disordered ends with intensified passion harms a person.

Some voices, however, are heard to argue that the very fact that strong inclinations draw a person to forms of dishonorable conduct warrants reclassifying certain actions as, at least, morally neutral. The sins against sobriety and chastity supply the most commonly cited examples. Again, the arresting distinction made in *Veritatis splendor* applies also to actions whose voluntariness is impeded by violence, fear, and lust: "It is possible that the evil done as the result of invincible ignorance or a nonculpable error of judgment may not be imputable to the agent; but even in this case it does not cease to be an evil, a disorder in relation to the truth about the good."[34] This salutary warning should inform both good moral theology and sound pastoral practice.

As an enemy of the voluntary, ignorance affects the voluntary character of human behavior to the extent that human behavior means conscious and deliberate behavior. Classical moral theology distinguishes three sorts of ignorance: concomitant, consequent, and antecedent.

First, concomitant ignorance. Since, in effect, concomitant ignorance can be defined as nothing more than a coincidence, it results in a completely involuntary act. The textbook example: Two enemies intent on pursuing one another to death pause momentarily for some relaxation in the hunting fields; suddenly, while taking a few practice shots, the first one, thinking the other person to be a stag, takes aim and actually kills his enemy. Because the one who is concomitantly ignorant lacks accurate awareness of what he or she is doing, the resultant action, in this case a homicide, falls short of the fully voluntary. Still, because the result does fall within the general aim of the doer, even if it may not have been a goal at the actual moment, something like the killing of the enemy by error does not represent an entirely *involuntary* action. Voluntariness points to the inner resources of human action, and such an action—abstracting from the legitimacy of the vengeance—is not alien to the state of the killer.

Second, consequent ignorance, which means to act from voluntary ignorance. Though consequent ignorance also results in a form of involuntary action on the grounds that *de facto* the action which one performs proceeds without due knowledge, the ignorance itself nonetheless assumes the character of a voluntary act if it results from an express action or omission. The express action either yields affected ignorance—as when one avoids learning the things for which one should be held reasonably accountable—or else propagates a crass ignorance, as when one fails to take the time to master what he or she should know.[35]

Third, antecedent ignorance, which describes the state of one who acts in involuntary ignorance. Antecedent ignorance amounts to nescience, for we are not responsible for that which we envision no likely purpose to

---

34. *Veritatis splendor*, no. 63.

35. The casuists popularized a distinction between ignorance of the law (*"ignorantia juris"*) and ignorance of the fact (*"ignorantia facti"*). For further information on the significance of this distinction, consult D. Prümmer, *Handbook of Moral Theology*, trans. Gerald W. Shelton (New York: P. J. Kenedy & Sons, 1957), pp. 9–12.

be informed about. In this case, the person remains simply unaware of a particular moral truth. However, since ignorance leaves one liable to embracing evil, this state, though excusable, does not therefore portend happiness for the antecedently ignorant person. The moral realist finds no comfort in the adage "ignorance is bliss." On the contrary, only the one who learns the truth about human life and perfection knows the way to achieve this goal. The fact that some persons act in important areas of human life without due knowledge of the end prompts the moral realist to give moral instruction, not to exculpate evil.

To the extent that certain impediments tilt the poise required for human activity, the voluntariness of any action suffers impairment. The eighteenth-century English moralist Thomas Hobbes wrote that "liberty, or freedom signifieth, properly, the absence of opposition"; by opposition he means external impediments of motion.[36] Hobbes, however, only insinuates the complete dimensions of the psychological dispositions which human action requires. To render a complete determination of a particular action requires attention to more complex factors than those which concern the impeding enemies of the voluntary. At the same time, it is true that certain psychological or physical influences, such as violence, fear, lust, or ignorance, can so disturb the poise required for human freedom to unfold that no further moral evaluation is required. Still, the voluntary addresses the starting point of human behavior, not its final perfection. Those influenced by Hobbesian views on human freedom can easily forget this important lesson, and find themselves wont to interpret freedom in an overly subjective manner, without any reference to the measure that human perfection imposes on human freedom. Because of the central place that knowledge about the true good of the human person holds in moral theology, we turn now to consider the teleological dimension of human action and the guidance that revelation affords us to recognize it.

Human Action and the Guidance of Church Teaching

Since human action is the means through which the human person comes to know and love God, a complete analysis of its structure has tra-

36. See *Leviathan*, c. XXI. For a brief but accurate account of Hobbes's view on the relationship of passion to will, see Martin Rhonheimer, *La Filosofia Politica di Thomas Hobbes* (Rome: Armando, 1997), pp. 76–84.

ditionally occupied a place on the theological agenda. Aquinas follows and develops this tradition. He provides within his theological narrative of the moral life a detailed description of an integral human act, complete with an arrangement of it main psychological moments.[37] The principal interest that moral realism finds in this account resides in illustrating how virtue informs human action, not in evaluating the account's philosophical particularities. The Church in any event does not pronounce on any specific philosophical analysis. We consider the Church's moral teaching in this chapter both to emphasize that the Christian believer depends on the Magisterium for the development of personal prudence, and to suggest the manner in which what the Church teaches about the moral life informs the prudence, and indeed the conscience, of the virtuous person. In short, prudence puts reason into emotion. A brief summary of the classical outline of human action enables a comprehension of how this virtue of practical reasoning assures good human action in the concrete.

For the realist moral theologian, classes of actions possess determinable natures, and again from a realist perspective, when a person performs an action of a certain kind or nature, the action itself contributes to the shaping of his or her character. The moral equation is well known. Good or virtuous actions build good character; bad or vicious actions leave the human person in a state of moral inertia and deformity. The results or accompaniments of a particular action figure only secondarily, if at all, in a moral evaluation; the action itself already contains the form of moral goodness or badness which will affect, diversely, the doer of the deed. From a realist point of view, then, fornication is not more blameworthy and bad for its accompanying sense pleasure; and loving God is not less praiseworthy and good for its absent sensible consolation.[38]

As a general rule, the moral theologian approaches action theory with different questions and concerns than the moral philosopher. Aristotle and other ancient ethical writers provide the basic elements for the following breakdown of a human action. However, the Christian tradition, especially through St. Augustine in the West and St. John Damascene in the East, has substantially modified the original Aristotelian scheme for looking at human action.[39] Christian revelation demands this revi-

37. The discussion falls principally in *Summa theologiae* Ia-IIae, qq. 8–17.
38. Cf. Chapter Four, esp. pp. 167–70.
39. In his *Opuscula ad Marianum*, Maximus the Confessor first tried to put order into the various acts of the will. See René-Antoine Gauthier, O.P., "Saint Maxime le

sion; indeed, St. Paul himself identifies the uniqueness of Christian action when he exhorts us: "And whatever you do, in word or deed, do everything in the name of the Lord Jesus, giving thanks to God the Father through him" (Col 3:17). The account of human action that Aquinas adopts, and the commentatorial tradition develops, reflects the distinctive features of Christian revelation as this illuminates the purposes and finalities of human action. Since all that is revealed serves unto the salvation of the human race, the moral theologian is mainly concerned about distinguishing between what leads us toward godly perfection and what moves us away from it.

Aquinas's action theory forms a central component of the *sacra doctrina*, and so adopts the dynamic features of the *imago Dei* anthropology: the human creature set between God as principle and God as end. The eternal law, with its Trinitarian implications, provides the original pattern for the synergy of intellectual and appetitive powers which appears entitatively in natural law and operationally in the voluntary. God grants us an active rational share in our own government, but this activity presupposes our passive reception of being, nature, and the ordering of nature. As an exercise within moral theology, the elaboration of an action theory describes how the human person, endowed with the special prerogatives of reason and will, acts so as to reach beatitude. At the place where Aquinas introduces his action theory, he makes this theological purpose abundantly plain:

Since we cannot come to happiness save through some activity, we have now to attend to human acts, so that we may learn which of them will open the way and which of them will block it.... Some acts are of a sort proper to human beings, others are shared in common with animals. All the same, since the happiness we envisage is a blessing proper to human beings, it will be engaged more closely by activity characteristically human than by their animal activity.[40]

Confesseur et la psychologie de l'acte humaine," *Recherches de Théologie Ancienne et Médiévale* 21 (1954): 51–100. In his *De fide orthodoxa*, Bk. 2, chap. 22, St. John Damascene follows Maximus's lead.

40. See the introduction at *Summa theologiae* Ia-IIae, q. 6. For a fresh account of this material and its place within Aquinas's overall conception of the virtuous life, see John Dominic Corbett, O.P., *Sacra Doctrina and the Discernment of Human Action* (Washington, D.C., 1999), a thesis submitted to the Faculty of Theology at the University of Fribourg (Switzerland).

The authors within the Thomist commentatorial tradition have contributed to the following analysis of the distinguishable moments that compose each human action. Their purpose has been to illustrate how human reason and appetite combine to direct what moral agents accomplish.[41] In pursuing this goal, these authors expound on the principle that in human acts, reason and will are rooted together; or to return to Aristotle's intuition, "they are one."[42]

Psychological Structure of the Human Act

In a most general sense, moral realism distinguishes between interior and exterior acts of the will.[43] The interior acts are called elicited acts of the will; elicited means exercised by a power immediately. Such acts include intention, choice, consent, and the other acts that make up a complete human action. A fuller discussion of the elicited acts of will and intellect follows in this section. Exterior acts of the will are those acts which involve the exercise of capacities that mediate the willing, as when sinews and nerves and flesh transmit a volition into an exterior act like bicycling or mountain climbing. In these examples, the will commands or imperates another human capacity in order to achieve its goal. To take account of these two forms of action, the Scholastics distinguished between "elicited" and "imperated" acts of the will.

Authors within the commentatorial tradition have outlined the twelve moments that compose a complete human action (depicted in the chart on the following page), and though the description may mislead, these moments also have been called the "twelve acts of the mind." As noted above, the present interest in identifying these elicited acts is to trace the interaction of knowing and loving as it unfolds in the composition of a human action. Although intellect and will interact causally on one another, their elicited acts do not individually represent full causes of human action. *Actiones sunt suppositorum*, as the scholastics put it: actions rightfully belong to the whole person. Persons act, whereas intellect and will

41. For more information on how the commentators systematized Aquinas's unsystematic discussion of this material, see Joseph Romiti, S.J., *De Processo Evolutivo Doctrinae de Actu Humano Completo* (Mediolani: Gregorianum, 1949).

42. Cf. note 1 above and *Nicomachean Ethics*, Bk. 2, chap. 6 (1111a23).

43. For a detailed philosophical discussion of the issues considered in this section and the next (pp. 118–24), see Stephen L. Brock, *Action and Conduct: Thomas Aquinas and the Theory of Action* (Edinburgh: T&T Clark, 1998).

The Structure of the Human Act

About the end (*circa finem*)

VOLITIO	INTENTIO		FRUITIO
1. Perception	3. Judgment (synderesis)		11. Performance
2. Wish	4. Intention		12. Completion

About the means (*circa ea quae sunt ad finem*)

PRUDENCE:	COUNSEL	JUDGMENT	COMMAND (*imperium*)
	5. Deliberation	7. Decision	9. Command
	6. Consent	8. Choice	10. Application
	Subjective appropriation of the means		*Effective realization of the means*

always remain individual capacities or powers of the acting person. If we consider this principle within the larger field of theological inquiry, more than one cause exists for any human action. In fact, the theologian is able to identify at least three full causes active in the production of a human action: God, the human persons at work, and the real objects in the universe about them.[44] While the moral theologian must also attend to the interaction of grace and freedom, the following discussion principally concerns the last two of these causes, the acting person and his or her engagement with moral objects.

Within a teleological view of human purpose and agency, it is customary to divide the twelve moments which compose a human action between those which bear upon the end and those which bear upon the means.[45] The schema above includes the principal headings within the

44. See Gilby, *Psychology of Human Acts*, p. 214.

45. Some authors refer to this division as founded on the order of intention and of execution respectively; others, however, question the usefulness of the schematization.

traditional schema; these are arranged under two architectonic considerations, viz., the order of intention and the order of execution.

As a first consideration, we can summarize the unfolding of the order
of intention by using three verbs in the tense-independent infinitive form
as key words: to wish (velle), to enjoy (frui), and to intend (intendere). In the
list that follows, these divisions are listed under the heading of the appropriate derivative noun.

Wish (volitio): At the root of all voluntary activity we find the basic attraction of human appetite for the good as perceived (1, 2). Accordingly, the
first determination of the will involves a good which is presented and
judged as an end to be attained (3).

Enjoyment (fruitio). The end also forms the beginning of human action.
Voluntary activity follows after the "intended" fruition of the good-
to-be-sought. The end moves us toward the simple enjoyment of the
end as possessed. Between volitio and fruitio (11, 12) lies the dialectic of
the discursive voluntary.

Intention (intentio): In order for the end to exercise its drawing power, it
must be somehow present to us. In a realist context, intention carries
the very strong meaning of making present the "intended" end (4).
Simply to wish for a good end does not suffice; we intentionally pursue
the end even as the end draws us toward itself. Note that just as the natura ut voluntas signifies human nature-as-willing, so intention expresses
human nature's basic tending toward its perfective form or end.[46]

For example, John Finnis, "Object and Intention in Aquinas," The Thomist 55 (1991): 3–10,
thinks that the traditional schema betrays more than illustrates Aquinas's analysis of
human action, whereas Jean Porter, "Desire for God," pp. 48–68, wonders whether human cognition can really serve as an ordering principle of a moral life driven toward
beatitude. It would be difficult, however, to find much support for these demurrals in
more than 500 years of commentatorial tradition on Aquinas.

46. See Summa theologiae Ia-IIae, q. 10, a. 1: "For the will wants, not only its own immediate object, but also all that corresponds to each of the other powers, and to the whole
of a concrete human nature ["ad totum hominem"]. By nature man wills all that matches
his entire ability, not just the will, for instance to know the truth, to be, to live, and so
forth, indeed all that relates to the integrity man was born to have ["consistentia naturalis"]:
the universal object of the will embraces all these as so many particular goods." The exact nature of intention is treated in q. 12 where, as a further precision, Aquinas clearly
distinguishes it from the circumstantial motive why a person does something.

The scholastic commentator Cajetan contends that each of the above-mentioned moments in a human action bears upon the end. He argues that a perfect knowledge of the end requires these three elements: first, that the end be a good loveable for itself (*volitio*); second, that there exists no further good or order to be sought (*fruitio*); third, that everything else bears upon pursuing the end (*intentio*).[47]

Under the full weight of human desire for the good, the human person is left to ponder the various concrete ways that can lead to the attainment of a particular good. We can conveniently consider two further phases or sub-divisions, at this point: the first phase deals with a subjective appropriation of means,[48] and the second phase includes the effective realization of means.

As a second consideration, we can summarize the order of execution with the following key words: (5, 6) to select (*eligere*), (7, 8) to choose (*consentire*), and (9, 10) to implement or use (*uti*).

The subjective appropriation of means: Free choice or judgment (*librum arbitrium*) (8) concerning means constitutes the final moment in this movement. But free choice depends on the causality of right reason, and this chiefly happens through prudence, which strengthens deliberation (5) and practical judgment or decision (7). The tradition also points out a distinctive disposition in the will known as consent (*consensus*) (6), viz., the poised reflection concerning the selection of means which mediates between deliberation and decision.[49]

The effective realization of means: Before the actual command (9) achieves its goal of embracing the end, there occurs a bringing to bear of the will's resources. Aquinas calls this the *usus activus* or application (10). This moment immediately and effectively results in the achievement of the

---

47. Cardinal Cajetan was the first scholastic commentator to attempt to put order into the account Aquinas gives of human action. See especially his *Commentary, In Iam-IIe*, q. 12, a. 1. and q. 16, a. 4.

48. In some renditions of the scheme, commentators calls these an "immanent activity about means." It seems better, however, to keep these steps (5, 6, 7, 8) clearly within the order of execution, in order to indicate better that these moments concern means which remain *outside of the will intending the good.*

49. For a philosophical clarification concerning the role of deliberation, see Daniel McInerny, "Deliberation about Final Ends: Thomistic Considerations," in *Recovering Nature: Essays in Natural Philosophy, Ethics, and Metaphysics in Honor of Ralph McInerny*, ed. Thomas Hibbs and John O'Callaghan (Notre Dame, Ind.: University of Notre Dame Press, 1999), pp. 105–25.

end under the direction of the *imperium*, which effectively brings to bear the will's power to set human powers in motion.

The groupings provide a convenient way of picturing a human act from within a teleological perspective, that is, one where human action embraces real being, and does not stop short at a choice of it. No pretense is made to construct the equivalent of a behaviorist's model of human action. On the contrary, the schema serves to illustrate the dynamic inter-penetration of mind and will and the mutual action and reaction ("refluence") of their partial acts on one another. For this reason, one may imagine the twelve-step diagram rather like a baroque swirl than like the organs of a dissected frog. Think about Gianlorenzo Bernini's altar columns under the dome of St. Peter's Basilica, instead of an anatomical display where every nerve and muscle is held by pins in a fixed place.

The interplay of the two basic capacities of the rational soul, intellect and will, remains a constant feature of the outward movement of this dialectic. From within the psychological structure of the human act, authentic human freedom arises. This freedom is rooted in perception, wish, judgment, intention (1–4), begins to appear in deliberation and consent (5, 6), but is constituted by decision (traditionally identified with the act of conscience), and choice (7, 8). Afterwards, freedom disappears in the *usus activus* (application, 10) as this develops consequent to command (9). In other words, once the person says "Do this," he or she leaves behind the order of a free choice of means, and returns, as it were, to the order of the end. We apply ourselves to its performance (11) and experience its enjoyment (12). Significantly, Aquinas the theologian likes to describe this moment as one of enjoyment (*fruitio*), delectation (*delectatio*), joy (*gaudium*), and rest (*quies*). Each one of these terms suggests a contentment and excellence that the reasoning creature ultimately finds only in God.

Human Choosing and Christian Freedom

To the extent that the Greek concept of freedom undergoes a radical transformation as a result of contact with Christian revelation, the theology of human freedom serves as a good example of what the 1998 encyclical letter *Fides et ratio* has called Christian Philosophy.[50] Free choice, it is true, accounts for an action's ultimate praiseworthiness or blamewor-

---

50. "The term seeks rather to indicate a Christian way of philosophizing, a philosophical speculation conceived in dynamic union with faith" (no. 76).

thiness. But the movement toward exercising full human freedom begins with our spontaneous, and therefore non-free, wants or desires; it terminates, for weal or woe, in a non-deliberative condition of attainment. In the realist schema of things, human freedom represents one value in the overall account of acting within a Christian moral teleology. St. Paul helps us adopt this perspective when he admonishes the Galatians: "For you were called to freedom, brethren; only do not use your freedom as an opportunity for the flesh, but through love be servants of one another. For the whole law is fulfilled in one word, 'You shall love your neighbor as yourself'" (Gal 5:13–14).

Aquinas echoes this teaching when he places a higher premium on the moral perfection of the human person than on an individual chooser's right to exercise freedom. However uncongenial it may be to some contemporary political ideals, the Christian believer knows that making the right choice always counts for inestimably more than being free to make choices.[51] Servais Pinckaers explains what he labels the "freedom for excellence" by showing that its origins repose in the qualities that perfect the human being. "The natural root of freedom," he writes, "develops in us principally through a sense of the true and the good, of uprightness and love, and through a desire for knowledge and happiness."[52]

Central to a realist conception of freedom remains the conviction that human choosing in itself does not constitute an ultimate value for human existence. When the ultimate Good—for *natura ut voluntas* (nature-as-willing) inclines toward God as Supreme Good—appears in beatific vision, our human freedom will discover no alternative but to embrace God, the supreme cause of beatitude. For the journey of Christian faith and the wayfarer who follows it, this eschatological destiny measures at each turn the deployment of authentic Christian freedom. The Christian tradition insists that true freedom remains ordered toward God; and the saints illustrate that only godly choices can authentically perfect our liberty and make us truly free. Because the specific goods which perfect the reasoning creature created in the *imago Dei* count first for human happiness, Christian theology mainly regards freedom as a special quality of an action, in-

51. Ignatius Smith, O.P., "Aquinas and Some American Freedoms," *The New Scholasticism* 21 (1947): 105–53, pointed out more than fifty years ago that it is difficult immediately to translate this theological principle into political theory.

52. Pinckaers, *Sources*, p. 357, and his general discussion of the freedom for excellence, pp. 354ff.

stead of an absolute ideal that crowns every action. This principle applies to even those choices that people are wont to consider most personal, for example, the use of marriage. The Christian religion holds that for a person to find union with God constitutes an infinitely greater blessedness than for a person to secure the right to choose among a range of options.

Romanticism of whatever stripe exalts a freedom that is measured only by its own possibilities, and those theologians who mistake this ideology for the teaching of the New Testament are inclined to elaborate a moral theory based chiefly on the categories of freedom and responsibility. The axiom "our ends are in the beginnings" undergirds moral realism and its approach to human conduct. Within the full perspective of the Christian mysteries, the Triune God remains the first, efficient, and final Cause of all human being and becoming. Revelation, not rational psychology or secular anthropology, provides the warrant for this claim. The universe of human activity—from the first rational act of the child to the most advanced achievements of technology or politics—constitutes a world of secondary causes. Since it forms part of the Christian belief about creation and divine providence, St. Paul frequently reminds his hearers of this fundamental truth, for example, when he tells the Corinthians, "It is God who gives the growth" (1 Cor 3:7). A teleological structure provides the best framework to interpret the Christian moral life. Teleology not only manifests itself in the true End of human existence, it also influences the way that the human person acts to achieve this goal.

The Guidance of the Church's Magisterium

Because of the importance which the Christian life places on achieving the proper goals in life, the Church values the charism of infallibility which marks her teaching office. We can best appreciate the purpose and necessity of a Magisterium in morals if we consider the fragility of human reasoning left to its own resources. A revealed doctrine about *mores* belongs to the patrimony of the Christian Church and establishes for her the right to speak, even in the public domain, both on matters which pertain to human happiness and on those which pertain to Christian perfection.[53]

---

53. In other terms, Christian perfection is not a category which belongs to an elite group within the Church, though at some periods authors consciously sifted out spirituality from the main body of moral teaching. For example in 1930, a Belgian publishing

It is human need, not institutional hubris, that explains, at least in part, the Church's legitimate request of all Christian faithful for their religious assent and submission of heart and mind in matters about the moral life.[54] Magisterial authority, which belongs principally to the Roman Pontiff and the bishops in union with him, serves true freedom. "The service to the Church which the Magisterium renders is thus for the benefit of the whole People of God called to enter the liberty of the truth revealed by God in Christ."[55] The claim of course runs against the cultural assumptions that undergird liberal, procedural democracies. But the Church is not a democracy, and the relationship of the members to her visible Head does not compare with the relationship of citizens in democratic republics to their elected officials.

Although one can point to certain moments in the Church's history when conciliarist movements reached particularly high peaks, the true spirit of Catholicism has always resisted attempts to democratize the Church. The reason for this instinctive retreat from democratization lies in the fact that Catholicism preaches truths which unaided reason is unable to uncover. By definition, Christian belief transcends the ordinary expectations of human reason and sense. And the only humanly compelling reason for belonging to a Church which proposes for belief truths which touch upon not only sacred realities, visible and invisible, but also one's personal moral life lies in the conviction that God himself guarantees the reliability of these truth claims. Although certain fundamentalist

---

house edited selections from the *Summa theologiae* under the title *Selecta ad Theologiam Ascetico-Mysticam e Summa Theologica Divi Thomae Aquinatis* (Malines: H. Dessain, 1930). The following order of presentation is observed: First, On perfection (IIa-IIae, q. 184); On the gifts of the Holy Spirit (Ia-IIae, q. 68); On the Beatitudes (Ia-IIae, q. 69); On the fruits of the Holy Spirit (Ia-IIae, q. 70). Second, selections from the *secunda-secundae* on the theological virtues of faith, hope, and charity and the gifts associated with them.

54. Certain misunderstandings about freedom of choice seriously affect how some contemporary theologians regard the religious *"obsequium,"* (cf. The Dogmatic Constitution on the Church, *Lumen gentium*, no. 25) or assent required of Christian believers in matters of magisterial teaching on moral issues. See the informative study of John R. Connery, S.J., "The Non-Infallible Moral Teaching of the Church," *The Thomist* 51 (1987): 1–16. More recently, the papal declaration *Ad Tuendam Fidem* has sought to clarify what is required of the Christian believer; see Pope John Paul II, Apostolic Letter Motu Proprio, *Ad Tuendam Fidem* (1998), by which certain norms are inserted into the Code of Canon Law and into the Code of Canons of the Eastern Churches.

55. Congregation for the Doctrine of the Faith, *Instruction on the Ecclesial Vocation of the Theologian*, no. 14 (1990).

Christian bodies share this conviction, they do not also share the clearly formulated doctrines which the Church proposes as precise objects of faith. Since these doctrines serve as external guarantees (the interior guarantee being God himself) of the unity of faith, Catholics welcome them, including those doctrines that pertain to morality. Doctrines about faith and morals enable the Church to exist as a catholic Church, even when Catholic teaching is difficult to explain and uphold in certain cultural contexts.

Among its legitimate aspirations, moral theology seeks to understand the true and full meaning of the texts of Scripture and other authoritative expressions of the Church's faith, so that the Christian people will receive and accept God's revelation in all its richness. As the Second Vatican Council reminds us, the "primary and perpetual foundation" of theology, and, therefore, of moral theology too, remains the written Word of God, understood together with sacred Tradition and as authentically interpreted by the Church's living teaching office exercised in the name of Jesus Christ.[56] The teaching authority of the Church provides a service of truth for all men and women, for it presents to the world a divinely authenticated instruction about what constitutes proper human conduct. Because the need for right instruction about human affairs increases, not decreases, with the complexity of scientific and technological advances, the mission of the Church in the world daily gains importance for the well-being of the human family.

The Church's mission to provide catholic or universal instruction also explains, for example, why in Roman Catholic moral theology, sexual preferences are considered less important than what makes for good sex, and why "compromise" moral theology in general does not find a congenial hearing. Who would want to enact a compromise with beatitude? To claim that the Church holds the true course to human happiness and can point it out infallibly rests on an article of faith. "I believe in the Holy Spirit, the holy catholic Church, the communion of saints ..." Only when it is realized that God guarantees the truthfulness of what the Church teaches can one dispel the suspicion abetted by some that the Church's moral instruction is restrictive instead of beatifying.

56. *Dei verbum* 24 and 10. For further explanations of the role of Catholic theology within the Church, see Avery Dulles, S.J., "Criteria of Catholic Theology," *Communio* 22.2 (1995): 303–15, and J. A. DiNoia, O.P., "Communion and Magisterium: Teaching Theology and the Culture of Grace," *Modern Theology* 9 (1993): 403–18.

To possess a filial confidence in the Church's moral teaching comes as a grace from God, but the right philosophical considerations can dispose a person to receive the grace. In his championing of reason against unreason, Pope John Paul II points up the relationship between a philosophy that accepts a universal knowledge of the good and the preservation of the human good: "It should never be forgotten that the neglect of being inevitably leads to losing touch with objective truth and therefore with the very ground of human dignity."[57] At the same time, the Pope can encourage a fruitful exchange among persons who hold different views: "To believe it possible to know a universally valid truth is in no way to encourage intolerance; on the contrary, it is the essential condition for sincere and authentic dialogue between persons."[58] The contemporary climate of intellectual egalitarianism sometimes makes it difficult to persuade people that firm adherence to moral truth does not threaten to encourage divisive, even bellicose, attitudes. Christians nonetheless must be prepared to confront the problems of the contemporary world with a confidence born of the strong convictions about truth and dialogue that Pope John Paul II has encouraged us to adopt.

We can still learn from the Socratic fallacy. To know the truth does not mean that every Christian does the truth; to account theologically for the reality of personal sin and failure introduces dogmatic considerations about voluntary fault and its consequences. Human thought boggles before the mystery of evil, and confrontation with sin leaves one depressed without appeal to the supernatural mystery of the Cross of Christ. Moral theology points to the primal revolution in which man separated himself from God as well as the remedy for it that bursts forth from the crucified side of Christ. For the moment, however, it suffices to note that the Church can communicate to the world candidly and convincingly God's own truth about human conduct. Today particularly, men and women need this kind of truthful teaching, not only because the well-being of their lives depends on it, but also because the secular culture offers so many distractions from moral truth. Because of the cultural deformities, the moral theologian especially must take up again St. Paul's challenge to the Corinthians: "We destroy arguments and every proud obstacle raised up against the knowledge of God, and we take every thought captive to

57. *Fides et ratio*, no. 90.
58. *Fides et ratio*, no. 92.

obey Christ" (2 Cor 10:4–5). Only an organic vision of the truth will enable Christians to address in an effective way the long elenchus of moral dilemmas which, if not resolved, truthfully, will continue to threaten the well-being of the human race.

The Primacy of Prudence for a Virtuous Choice

According to realist moral theory, the entire subject matter of morals revolves around instruction on the virtues and growth in a virtuous life. In order to deal with the requirements of catechetical instruction, the Christian tradition customarily reduces the large number of virtues that distinguish the practice of the Christian life into two categories: the theological virtues and the cardinal moral virtues, sometimes called the human virtues. The theological virtues include faith, hope, and charity; the cardinal moral virtues, prudence, justice, fortitude, and temperance. Aquinas, a principal exponent of virtue-centered ethics, asserts that the virtues do more than provide convenient categories into which moralists or catechists can organize their instruction about the moral life. Virtue, in other words, supplies more than a description of moral goodness. As developed within the Thomist tradition, the virtues constitute real sources of human action, working in both efficient and final causality. They are true dispositions for action, operative habits (*habitus*) that energize both the quest and the attainment of a happy life.[59] To return to the subject of Christian freedom, only the exercise of free choice shaped by virtue guarantees that a person reaches the goal of complete happiness.

Since the virtues serve as real sources of human action, their operation observes the basic dynamic that governs all human action. The practice of the theological and moral virtues enables a person to both pursue with intelligence and embrace with discrimination the real goods of supernature and nature that are intended by God to perfect human existence. The effect of virtue on human behavior is best displayed in those moral virtues that regulate the movements of both the rational and sense appetites:

59. See the introduction at *Summa theologiae* Ia–IIae, q. 49: "Having discussed action and feeling we now turn to the sources of human action within and without the agent. The sources of action within the agent are capacities and *habitus*; capacities were considered in the *prima pars*, but *habitus* remain to be discussed [in the *prima-secundae*]. We shall deal first with *habitus* in general; and then turn to those particular *habitus* such as virtues and vices, which are sources of human action."

justice in the will, fortitude in the contending emotions, and temperance in the impulse emotions.

Moral behavior means intelligent behavior; no virtuous behavior exists apart from conformity with a measure of moral truth. To put moral truth into human behavior is the work of the first cardinal virtue, prudence. This virtue in fact embodies a kind of knowing, as a long-standing intuition of the Christian tradition testifies. For example, the seventh-century Iberian theologian Isidore of Seville (d. 636) fittingly associates in his *Etymologies* the origin of the word *prudentia* with knowledge about provident conduct. Prudent persons look ahead in order to ensure that what they do achieves the good; put otherwise, prudence is knowing what to want and what not to want. The cardinal virtue of prudence shapes human deliberation with respect to the proper means for reaching an end, and what is equally important ensures that the person in fact embraces the end. From the perspectives of moral realism, the adjective "prudential" applies to every good moral action performed.

Prudence and Practical Reasoning

The virtue of prudence, a distinct *habitus* of the intellect, informs the exercise of the Christian life. Without possessing prudence, a person can neither behave well nor develop a good character. A retrospect on the tradition reveals that casuistry's emphasis on the role of conscience relegated prudence to a subordinate place in accounts of the moral life. But once the perspectives of casuistry no longer governed the practice of moral theology, and the intellectual environment became more congenial to virtue theory, authors again considered the role of prudence in guiding the virtuous life. Servais Pinckaers insists that moral theology renewed according to the wishes of the Second Vatican Council requires a correct understanding of this virtue and its function in the formation of human actions.[60] Prudence forms the theoretical nerve of a teleological conception on the moral life. It shapes human actions in accord with the dictates of right reason, so that human intelligence can easily discover the truth about human and divine perfection.

Since prudence ensures that an action both embodies the complete

60. Servais Pinckaers explains the history of the transformation of prudence and its significance for moral theology in *Sources*, pp. 249–53; for a systematic treatment of prudence, see my *The Moral Virtues and Theological Ethics* (Notre Dame/London: University of Notre Dame Press, 1991), chap. 4.

form of moral goodness and represents the truth-claims of moral science, this cardinal virtue plays a large and ambitious role in sustaining the Christian moral life. In itself, prudence remains a virtue, a perfection, of the intellect. Prudence puts truth into human conduct. But when it enters the constellation of the moral virtues, prudence takes on the character of a moral virtue. Prudence shapes human action. Together prudence and the moral virtues enable a person to choose what conforms to the dictates of right reason (moral truth) as well as what embodies authentic human good. The Thomist claim about the function of prudence differs from that, for instance, of John Duns Scotus (c. 1264–1308), who taught that prudence remains a kind of pure knowing.[61] By defining it as a simple intellectual virtue that provides direction for the moral life, but not formation of the powers of the soul, Scotists effectively suspended what moral realists refer to as prudence's unitive function. Again, this means that prudence informs the behavioral virtues, while these virtues in turn strengthen prudence.

In its conspicuous Nominalist version, the opinion that conscience denotes a merely cognitive moral faculty historically owes much to examples of reductionist intellectualism, or the penchant to explain morality exclusively in terms of the person's reasoning skills.[62] In the traditional teaching, however, it is held that a Christian character develops harmoniously in accord with both moral truth and rectified appetites. Recall that accounts of the moral life from the patristic and high medieval periods located conscience under prudence and thereby in conjunction with the other moral virtues. But reductionist views of prudence, such as one that identifies *tout court* moral judgment with rational conscience disembodied from virtue, overlook the important role that the development of moral virtue plays in directing human affairs. Theorists who argue that conscience plays an autonomous role in the moral life depreciate the im-

---

61. For further discussion, see Mary Elizabeth Ingham, "Practical Wisdom: Scotus's Presentation of Prudence," in *John Duns Scotus: Metaphysics and Ethics*, ed. L. Honnefelder et al. (Leiden: E. J. Brill, 1996), pp. 551–71. And for a discussion of the psychological theory that this view of prudence supposes, see Tobias Hoffmann, "The Distinction between Nature and Will in Duns Scotus," *Archives d'Histoire Doctrinale et Littéraire du Moyen Age* 66 (1999): 189–224.

62. See the expert discussion of this point by H.-D. Gardeil and Servais Pinckaers in their "Éditions de la Revue des jeunes" commentary on *Summa theologiae* Ia-IIae, qq. 6–21 in *Les actes humaines*, vols. I & II (Paris: Les Éditions du Cerf, 1997).

portance of a rational measure to direct and shape the movement of *appetite* toward good ends. Even when this emphasis is accompanied by insistence on the obligation to have an informed conscience, the presentation of the Christian moral life is truncated. Consider how the Nominalist preference for will-acts emerges in the moral perspectives dominant in the spiritual writers of the late medieval period. The piety of this age, sometimes referred to as the *via moderna* (modern way) to distinguish it from what had developed during earlier Christian centuries, encouraged persons to choose proper Christian conduct, but reflected minimally on the flowering of acquired and infused *habitus* under the direction of right reason. Rather than enabling the perfection of the whole person, morality thence retreats from its roots in right appetite into a deracinated pure rational paradigm inadequate both to the composite body-soul character of the person and to a theology informed by the Incarnation. Consider, for example, how the spirituality of Thomas à Kempis (c. 1380–1471) reduces sanctity to renunciation of self as a condition for union with God.[63]

To the extent that they exhibit a mistrust of nature as a source of moral wisdom, moral theories which rely exclusively on individual conscience restrict the parameters within which moral decision-making transpires. Such theories in effect deny reason's capacity to grasp a universal truth about the good and to apply it to particular circumstances. The Church has recognized the dangers inherent in this tendency and their relationship to larger metaphysical issues dealing with metaphysics and morals:

Once the idea of a universal truth about the good, knowable by human reason, is lost, inevitably the notion of conscience also changes. Conscience is no longer considered in its prime reality as an act of a person's intelligence, the function of which is to apply the universal knowledge of the good in a specific situation and thus to express a judgment about the right conduct to be chosen here and now. Instead there is a tendency to grant to the individual conscience the prerogative of independently determining the criteria of good and evil and then acting accordingly. Such an outlook is quite congenial to an individualist ethic, wherein each individual is faced with his own truth different from the truth of others.[64]

---

63. See P. Pourrat, *Christian Spirituality in the Middle Ages*, trans. S. P. Jacques (London: Burns, Oates, and Washbourne, 1924), pp. 252–64.

64. See *Veritatis splendor*, no. 32, a text which appears again in *Fides et ratio*, no. 98.

Conscience-centered accounts of the moral life favor recourse to theoretical reason in order to ground moral behavior, or they combine elements of deontology with a sense of obligation in order to spell out the requirements of the moral order. While encouraging the free exercise of choice, theories of this kind also promote an individualism that is irreconcilable with authentic Christian personalism and the community structure in which alone it can flourish.

A proper understanding of conscience does not introduce a covert system for bracketing general moral truths when it is judged that particular circumstances or personal convictions justify a conscientious exception to a general norm. The exercise of Christian conscience always falls under the sway of prudence, the virtue that unites truth and love. A Christian theological view of prudence combines the intellectual emphasis of classical philosophy—for example, as expressed in the Aristotelian doctrine of *phronesis* or practical reasonableness—and the conative leanings represented in the Christian tradition especially by St. Augustine, and so keeps truth and love together. In his discussion on musical measures, St. Augustine observes how love as *delectatio* became as it were a weight for his soul; authentic love orders the soul, so that where the heart dwells, there also one finds delectation.[65] St. Augustine's experience applies to the moral life: Who would turn to a spendthrift for advice about budgets or to a profligate for the truth about pleasures? The dependence of conscience upon prudence is indicated by the very nature of conscience as a rational act of moral judgment concerning what is to be done here and now. For to be probative, such judgment must be existentially conformed to the truth of the proposed act, agent, and circumstances: all of which is impossible without the integrating work of prudence.

The cardinal virtue of prudence provides, as it were, the *locus* for concrete moral decision-making; its proper exercise ensures that our decisions lead to what alone can satisfy a human nature created in the *imago Dei*. By placing prudence at the center of moral practice, realist moral theology avoids the anxieties that certain moral theologians cause both themselves and others by accepting a fundamental tension between subjective conscience and objective law. Aquinas, however, recognizes the irreducibility of all forms of sheer moral knowledge which, even when elab-

65. See St. Augustine, *De musica.* Bk. 6 (PL 32, 1081–194 at 1179): "delectatio quippe quasi pondus est animae."

orated in highly refined moral theories, remain incapable of moving into the order of execution or real action. The view that conscience by itself provides the faculty for translating moral knowledge into actual practice also runs counter to the evidentiary fact that, sometimes even over a long period of time, people act against their deepest instincts of conscience.

As a virtue of the intellect, prudence shapes the discursive development of practical reason. Prudence is not love essentially, but *causaliter*, that is, love motivates prudence; charity prompts the mind to be discerning about God's law.[66] "The unspiritual man does not receive the gifts of the Spirit of God, for they are folly to him, and he is not able to understand them because they are spiritually discerned" (1 Cor 2:14). In the field of human endeavors, the ultimate cause remains the common end of the whole of human life, so that the person who discerns well about the whole of the good life deserves to be called prudent in an unqualified sense. On this account, infused prudence shares some of the characteristics of that wisdom which supplies the supreme measure for human life. St. Paul considers that he imparts this truth "in words not taught by human wisdom, but taught by the Spirit, interpreting spiritual truths to those who possess the Spirit" (1 Cor 2:13). And Maximus the Confessor likens Christ to a lamp which dispels "the gloom of ignorance and the darkness of evil," and the Church to the lampstand from which the word of God fills the minds of all those who live in the world with divine knowledge.[67]

Prudence concerns itself with translating moral wisdom into practical action, into actually doing something concrete about engagement with the good. Aristotle impressed this notion onto the Western moral mind. In the *Nicomachean Ethics*, he observes:

For we say that deliberating well is the function of the intelligent person more than anyone else; but no one deliberates about what cannot be otherwise, or about what lacks a goal that is a good achievable in action. The unconditionally good deliberator is the one whose aim expresses rational calculation in pursuit of the best good for a human being that is achievable in action.[68]

66. Aquinas modifies the practical intuition of St. Augustine which he expresses in *De moribus ecclesiae catholicae*, Bk. 1, chap. 15 (PL 32, col. 1322).

67. St. Maximus the Confessor, *From an Inquiry Addressed to Thalassius*, quaest. 63 (PG 90, cols. 667–70).

68. Aristotle, *Nicomachean Ethics*, trans. Terence Irwin (Indianapolis: Hackett, 1985),

The Christian tradition recognizes that the philosopher's "best good" is revealed to us as the *summum bonum*, the highest Good in an unqualified sense. Only God matches that description.

Since prudence always remains interested in the *agibile*, the doable, its concern must extend to individual cases.[69] Aristotle's realism remains coolly confident about the ability of prudence to form sound practical judgments, but the Christian thinker must also recall the Book of Wisdom when it warns that "our counsels are uncertain" (Wis 9:14).[70] Christian practice then does not reproach the prudent man for failing in unforeseen and exceptional cases, but only when he fails in matters that fall under common experience. Still, prudence aims at regularity in sound moral judgment and practice.

It is on this basis, in fact, that prudence qualifies as a *bona fide* moral virtue, namely, that it charges a person's conduct with moral truth, so that the person actually embraces a concrete moral good.[71] Having accepted Aristotle's definition, the Christian scholastics continued to speak about prudence as the right order of doing something—*recta ratio agibilium*.[72] The rectitude or rightness of prudence rests on the authentic end of human existence.[73] As a *ratio*, prudence constitutes a perfection of human intelligence; it consists in reasoning. Prudence possesses its own logical structure, which is ordered to consider proper relations among things involved in human conduct. At the same time, prudence develops a right order

---

Bk. VI, chap. 7 (1141b10–14). For further discussion of Aristotle's view, see M. Mauri, "Aristotle on Moral Knowledge," *Studia Moralia* 30 (1992): 227–46.

69. For a technical study of Aquinas's psychology as it relates to the operation of prudence in the internal senses, especially the *vis cogitativa*, see Thomas V. Flynn, O.P., "The Cogitative Power," *The Thomist* 16 (1953): 542–63.

70. In St. Thomas's Latin Vulgate, "incertae sunt providentiae nostrae;" in a modern rendition from *The New Oxford Annotated Bible with the Apocrypha* (New York: Oxford University Press, 1991): "For the reasoning of mortals is worthless, and our designs are likely to fail...."

71. Moral virtue renders good the doer and his or her acts. However, the intellectual virtues enable us only to think or to make something properly; so, the intellectual virtues—wisdom, science, and understanding—are virtues only in this qualified sense of the term. See my *The Moral Virtues and Theological Ethics*, chap. 3.

72. See *Nicomachean Ethics*, Bk. 6, chap. 5 (1140b20).

73. Aristotle's *orthos* for straight or erect takes on the meaning of that which is exact, correct, true, or authentic. In a similar way, the Pauline notion of rectitude reflects a more profound meaning than a morally straight path for Christian life, since it refers to the fullness of Christian love and life.

for doing; it is about practical intelligence in the order of action. Aquinas distinguishes prudence from art, but the metaphor of virtue as a craft helpfully expresses his notion of what prudence achieves.[74] If we think of virtue as a craft, then prudence sees to it that the prudent person assembles a good life, in the same way that artistic talent ensures that an artisan crafts a worthy artifact.

Prudence and the Good Ends of Human Perfection

How does prudence effectively direct the virtuous life? In his general treatment about prudence, Aquinas remarks that "prudence directs the moral virtues not only in the choice of the means, but also in appointing the end."[75] The actual working out of prudence in a concrete circumstance results in instantiating the good end of human virtue. The Latin verb *praestituere*, which ordinarily means "to appoint beforehand," can also bear the meaning of "to enact," as when one enacts legislation. In this sense prudence effectively establishes a virtuous act. But prudence does not appoint the ends of the moral virtues, but only arranges those activities of ours that serve to reach them. Natural law establishes the end of the virtues; their realization embodied in the good choices and character of virtuous people reflects how God knows the world to be. Aquinas summarizes this feature of his general virtue theory and at the same time suggests its coalescence with the view that natural reason reflects divine wisdom:

The end of the moral virtues is theirs, not as though they themselves appoint it, but because they stretch out to it as set for them by natural reason. In this they are helped by prudence, which opens the way and arranges the steps to be taken. We are left with the thought that prudence ranks above and charges the moral virtues, yet it is put forth from synderesis, rather as insight into principles advances into scientific knowledge.[76]

The text prompts the Christian moral theologian to maintain confidence in the natural order of the virtues, which represents an outgrowth and expression of natural law. Although their holiness depends on a free

---

74. For a penetrating discussion of this metaphor, see Alasdair MacIntyre, *Three Rival Versions of Moral Enquiry*, chap. 3, "Too Many Thomisms?"

75. *Summa theologiae* Ia-IIae, q. 66, a. 3, ad 3.

76. *Summa theologiae* IIa-IIae, q. 47, a. 6, ad 3. By "natural reason," Aquinas of course means natural law and its expression in the virtuous ordering of human life.

bestowal of supernatural grace, the saints still exhibit a variety in their lives that gives particular expression to how God knows the world to be.

The moral virtues themselves contain the principles required for a person to embrace specific good ends of human perfection as these are variously related to one or another of the virtues. When they fulfill this function in the virtuous person, the moral virtues carry out the inclinations of the natural law, but with a particular discernment of the good-as-meant. In other words, prudence enacts a form of discursive moral reasoning that remains bent on the discovery of the intelligent good, the good-as-meant. When prudence enables one to discover the right way to implement a particular moral virtue, then the prudent person has discovered the mean of that virtue, tailored to his or her specific condition and circumstances.

Cajetan smartly distinguishes a twofold notion of "mean" for a moral virtue, the simple mean—or the rational measure defining the virtues—and the mean materially considered, that is, the particular human good achieved through the virtue. As Cajetan writes, "in the formal sense, mean designates the simple definition of a mean, but in the material sense, it designates the *res* which embodies the mean of virtue." He then concludes that "the first sense of mean remains a good of reason, but the second sense denotes the good *res*, the good thing itself, as existing in the intelligent good, the good-as-meant. The first kind of mean constitutes the end of the moral virtues, but the second kind of mean supplies what is ordered to the end."[77] Thus the practical reasoning of prudence does not stop at choice, but leads naturally to the embrace of the good thing. Christian prudence observes Aristotle's intuition that prudence is a truth-attaining rational quality, concerned with action in relation to the things that are good for human beings.[78]

The virtue of prudence builds upon synderesis, the *habitus* of the practical intelligence which supplies a fundamental moral sense concerning the pursual of good. It is possible to distinguish three major moments in the development of moral knowledge: first, a pre-scientific grasp of mor-

---

77. *Commentary, In IIam-IIae*, q. 47, a. 7, no. 1: "formaliter, pro ipsa medii ratione; materialiter, pro re denominata media.... Primo modo est bonitas rationis ; secundo modo est res bona bonitate rationis. Primo modo est finis moralis virtutis, secundo autem est id quod est ad finem."

78. See *Nicomachean Ethics*, Bk. 6, chap. 5 (1140b20), trans. H. Rackham (Cambridge: Harvard University Press, 1947).

al principles which constitutes the level of universal moral reflection; second, the scientific elaboration of reasoned opinion about moral matters which defines the legitimate concerns of ethics; and third, the judgment we make when we apply moral principles to concrete situations. This judgment, which is sometimes called the judgment of conscience, produces a special kind of moral knowledge, namely, knowledge about what is to be done here and now. As a form of moral knowing, as *Veritatis splendor* points out, conscience always serves the wider aims of prudence and is regulated by universal moral truth. The judgment of conscience, even though it deals with particular and immediate conditions in the moral life, still remains *in pura cognitione*—in a state of simple cognition. Virtuous choice depends on more than knowledge.

The moral realist recognizes what harm a poorly informed conscience can cause the person who acts from it. Because questions of subjective culpability are not the first ones addressed in a realist assessment of moral action, the fact that some people remain invincibly ignorant about certain moral truths provides no consolation. An error about what makes for proper human conduct, whether the person holds the erroneous view as the result of vincible or invincible ignorance, thwarts the exercise of the virtue of prudence. An erroneous conscience can find no validation or verification in a properly developed moral science, nor in a moral precept, nor, for that matter, in practical reasoning itself. Accordingly, the person who acts on the basis of an erroneous conscience acts badly, and every bad or disordered action brings its own punishment. So the young adolescent who judges that she receives too small a weekly allowance in comparison with that given to her peers, and, therefore, clandestinely removes money from the household's common funds, may convince herself that she is acting in good conscience. But in acting this way, the young girl particularly fails to develop the good of filial piety, which ensures, among other important goods for human life, the development of honest and trusting communication between parent and child. *Fides et ratio* dissuades moral theologians from implementing moral philosophies that are either subjectivist or utilitarian; it is never right to promote individual conscience as sufficient for final decision-making in the moral life.[79] A wrong decision about what course of action to take not only enacts a mis-

79. See *Fides et ratio*, no. 98.

take about what to do, it also, as the example of the young girl illustrates, removes from a person a good end that human well-being requires.

Prudence commands our behavior, and for the moral realist the act of command proceeds from the intellect, not from the will. As the final and main act of prudence, command instantiates the goal of reasoned direction of conduct. When moral truth and properly rectified appetites support the command of prudence, the prudent person enjoys a certain infallibility that his or her conduct achieves the maximum of goodness. But command forms the final moment in the working of prudence.

In the order of discovering the means, to the practical reason belongs first, the deliberation about suitable means (counsel [5]), second, the making of a practical judgment (decision [7]), and third, the regulation of a moral action to the extent that command (*imperium* [9]) actually ordains the instantiation of a moral choice. Prudence shapes this movement at each of the three critical moments in which the intellect exercises its own causality on human choosing.

Counsel, judgment, and command compose the three acts of cardinal prudence. As integral acts of the one cardinal virtue, each one of these prudential acts is shaped by a distinct virtuous *habitus* so as to ensure that the unitive function of prudence prospers in the real world of human endeavor. Good counsel, or *eubulia*, shapes the mind to undertake a proper deliberation about what options are available for pursuing a given good. Judiciousness, or *synesis*, and farsightedness, or *gnome*, aid the act of judgment; the former helps in matters of ordinary routine and the latter provides the wit to judge in the exceptional circumstance. *Prima facie*, these virtues which are allied to prudence may seem to replace it, but the fact remains that sometimes it happens that a well-judged deed is put off or done carelessly or improperly. That explains why the crowning of sound judgment requires a principal virtue which is well and truly imperative; that virtue is cardinal prudence itself.[80]

There is a reciprocal relation between the moment of deliberation and the emotions; good counsel belongs especially to the rectified person. If we consider how bad emotion adversely affects the development of good counsel, we catch a glimpse of how the unitive function of prudence works in the moral life. If one is emotionally unwilling to realize a

---

80. See *Summa theologiae* IIa-IIae, q. 51, a. 3, ad 3.

particular goal—for example, when a student is loath to spend the time required for study in his discipline—this indisposition adversely affects the student's capability for proper deliberation as to how to arrange for studying. Because one is not conformed to the end of the virtue of studiousness, the practical reason experiences difficulty in deliberating when and how to achieve the good of studiousness.

The scholastics recognized that the emotions could gain such an upper hand in a person's life that one's whole vision of the moral life would reflect the ubiquity of disordered passions. In this circumstance, prudence, as a virtue which promotes the right notion about doing things, faces a serious deterrent. Soothing of frazzled emotions of course occurs in different ways; and the believer always maintains free access to the grace and sacraments of the Church. But if one continues in a state of serious emotional tussle with a good which forms an integral part of human perfection, then the person risks falling victim to the vicious circle of imprudence. This means that instead of good counsel guiding an individual's deliberation to the desired consensus about means to pursue, the practical reasoning process deadlocks and the development of sound practical judgment is largely, if not entirely, impeded.

The Christian Art for Living

In his textbook of Christian virtues and vices, Gregory the Great sketches in broad strokes how disordered passion affects the operations of the practical reason. We find this extremely forthright analysis in his *Moralia*, the reforming Pope's allegorical commentary on the Book of Job:

From avarice there springs treachery, fraud, deceit, perjury, restlessness, violence and hardness of heart against compassion.... From lust are generated blindness of mind, inconsiderateness, inconstancy, precipitation, self-love, hatred of God, affection for this present world, but dread or despair of that which is to come.[81]

This instruction persuades us to exercise caution about introducing a sharp distinction between the moral state of the person and the moral

---

81. See St. Gregory the Great, *Morals on the Book of Job*, Bk. 31, chap. 45 (Oxford: John Henry Parker, 1844), where the author comments on the text of Job 39:25, "When the trumpet sounds, the horse says 'Aha!' He smells the battle from afar, the thunder of the captains, and the shouting." Chapter 45 of the same work contains the classic source for the seven deadly vices.

quality of the person's actions. Personal dispositions affect immediately the capacity of a person to pursue a proper course of moral conduct. The tradition accepts as axiomatic that a person's moral character deeply shapes perceptions about proper directions for the moral life.

Imprudence marks the person whose emotional state promotes either undue haste in seeking good counsel or the making of precipitate judgments about a course to be taken. Imprudence also marks an inconstant spirit, one which easily gives up on the decided-upon course. Aquinas signals negligence as the general cause of imprudent behavior; in this case the person exhibits "a certain slackness of will which results in the reason not being solicitous about coming to effective decisions on things which ought to be done and how they ought to be done."[82]

In addition, sham or mock prudence thwarts spiritual development, because it employs human shrewdness and craftiness for the purposes of obtaining ends which fall short of the good ends of human perfection. Spiritual writers accordingly identify these vices against prudence as carnal prudence, when one seeks finite goods with a passion rightly reserved for God alone, or cunning, guile, and deception, when one employs means which are not true, but feigned and specious, in order to achieve some objective. The authentic Christian outlook develops from another perspective. For it embodies Christ's warning that "no one can serve two masters ... both God and mammon (Mt 6:24) and, at the same time, his encouragement: "Look at the birds of the air" and "Consider the lilies of the field" (Mt 6:25–34).

When these counsels are observed, prudence flourishes. In the prudent person, we observe one whose emotional life remains well-ordered, and whose deliberation about means provides the basis for an accurate decision as to the making of a good choice. When this happens, the prudent person benefits from the full virtuousness of prudence. For the one who exhibits a developed ability in each of the crucial areas of moral reasoning, the virtue of prudence exemplifies the attainment of a highly refined moral culture. The integral parts of prudence suggest some of the qualities one expects to discover in the prudent person: good memory,

---

82. *Summa theologiae* IIa-IIae, q. 54, a. 3. The whole question recapitulates the patristic moral teaching concerning the dangers of *accidie*—apathy about spiritual well-being—which for the early Church Fathers constituted a fundamental nemesis, thus, sometimes identified with the devil that prowls at noon, for spiritual development.

the capacity for insight, readiness to learn, inventiveness, and a certain soundness in applying general principles to the variety and uncertainty of particular cases. And because prudence rounds off a good action, prudent persons also observe foresight, circumspection, and caution in carrying through the command of prudence.[83] In short, for the virtuously prudent person, intelligence and human appetite perform harmoniously toward the accomplishing of good human activity.[84]

Toward the end of his career, St. Thomas reflected on the place which prudence and good counsel holds in the life of the Christian believer. The verse of the Psalm, "May he grant you your heart's desire, and fulfill all your plans!" suggested this reflection on the way prudence effectively directs the moral life.

First, "May he grant your heart's desire," we interpret to mean what you will, as this bears upon the end, as if the Psalmist were to say, may God lead you to the end which you yourself intend. The End is God, as it is written in Proverbs 10:24, the desire of the righteous ends only in good.

Secondly, "Fulfil all your plans," which we interpret to mean those things which are ordained toward the end [his quae sunt ad finem]. Because we are unable to foresee everything our counsels are feeble, as the Book of Wisdom 9:14 puts it, the reasoning of mortals is worthless, and our designs are likely to fail. God, however, is there to confirm us toward the Good. He does this in a twofold way: first, by directing our counsels which should be concerned with actively seeking eternal life, as in John 16:24, "hitherto you have asked nothing in my name; ask, and you will receive, that your joy may be full" and, secondly, by his giving us what we need in order to pursue our good counsels toward the joyful possession of himself.[85]

---

83. For information on the parts of virtues, see *Summa theologiae* IIa-IIae, q. 48, where Aquinas describes integral parts or components of a virtue as "the qualities combining to shape a virtue's finished performance."

84. Imprudence, on the other hand, means bad activity. This vice can result from either disordered passions, vicious habits, or deficiency in moral learning. Just as one can explain the manifest absence of natural law inclinations in certain cultures and peoples at certain times by appealing to defects in moral knowledge or to corrupt customs and habits, so one can discover the root of individual imprudence either in the lack of due moral knowledge or in a state of habitual vice.

85. The text is found in the *Postilla super Psalmos*, 19, no. 2 (Vivès edition, vol. 18, p. 336). Following the Gallican Psalter as contained in the Vulgate edition of the Bible, Aquinas comments on Psalm 19:5: "tribuat tibi secundum cor tuum et omne *consilium* tuum confirmet."

This commentary on the Old Testament illustrates Aquinas's keen appreciation for the association that exists between the human virtues and the Christian way of life. He encourages us to build effectively upon both nature and grace. At the same time, the commentary conveys the general sense of how the prudent person enjoys a life of human flourishing and how, even as a wayfarer, the Christian experiences in faith the joy that awaits total fulfillment in heavenly beatitude.

The foregoing account of prudence informs the teaching of the Church. *Veritatis splendor* teaches that "in every sphere of personal, family, social and political life, morality—founded upon truth and open in truth to authentic freedom—renders a primordial, indispensable and immensely valuable service not only for the individual person and his growth in the good, but also for society and its genuine development."[86] Aquinas comments on the various forms of prudence which correspond not only to the good of the individual, but also to that of the family and of the state; these are monastic or individual, domestic, and political respectively. In the Church, we see the ultimate realization of prudence when the members heed St. Paul's exhortation: "In your minds you must be the same as Christ Jesus" (Phil 2:5).

With few exceptions, modern moral philosophy follows one of two directions: first, schools of emotivism propose sincere feelings as the ultimate moral criterion, and second, schools of moral cognitivism propose a variety of ways for the intellect to dictate a course of action. Various factors in the history of moral philosophy account for the fact that few theories recognize two crucial truths: first, that rational principles no matter how well defined cannot adequately ensure that a particular human action really instantiates moral goodness; secondly, that the appetites in themselves lack the ability to develop a full moral measure, even though one may allow that they contain the germ of virtue. Authentic prudence cultivates an intelligence measured by moral knowledge and capable of shaping human behavior toward virtuous ends as these are grasped by a rectified appetite.[87]

Prudence belongs to the development of the moral life. As an infused and an acquired virtue, it depends on both the revealed and ratio-

---

86. *Veritatis splendor*, no. 101, but see as well the preceding paragraphs in nos. 96–101.

87. For a discussion of how prudence influences even in exceptional circumstances, see my "Epieikeia and the Accomplishment of the Just," in *Aquinas and Empowerment: Classical Ethics for Ordinary Lives*, ed. G. Simon Harak (Washington, D.C.: Georgetown University Press, 1996): 170–205.

nal sources of moral wisdom. Through prudence and the moral virtues, our activity corresponds to the authentic ends or goods of human nature—this is called conformity with the "thing" or *res*. Such conformity with the complete number of good human ends shapes the character of a virtuous person who, because of the psychological power contained in the *habitus*, easily and surely achieves the goals of human life. Unlike the good musician who may "learn" how to play a false note, the prudent person cannot voluntarily act imprudently. In other words, he can never act against his own good. Because prudence integrates moral knowledge and rectified appetites in order to provide concrete and particular norms for human behavior, prudence remains a key virtue for the formation of a person's moral character. All of the moral virtues require prudence because this moral virtue guarantees the production of a virtuous action in the practical order. Insofar as correct moral reasoning combines with rectified appetite for good ends, a virtuous action infallibly results. But this state of affairs defines the saint, whose prudence always remains genuine (not sham or motivated by carnal ends), general (not restricted to a limited field of human endeavor), and complete (not favoring one or another act of prudence). In other words overall, the saints best illustrate prudence. They are the people who have taken good counsel, made good judgments, and, above all, remained resolutely effective in commanding a virtuous life. No wonder the Church reveres them as those who have done the will of God throughout the ages.[88]

A Brief Speculative Excursion into Freedom and Providence

What is more personal to us than our existence and our freedom? Yet we do not bestow either upon ourselves, but receive them. This discloses the foundation for an understanding of *graced* motion and desire, which is analogous with God's bestowal of natural volitional motion and desire. Just as God creates the will and gives to it its natural motion as a free rational appetite without in any way violating it, so grace uplifts and perfects without violating the rational appetite, freeing it from defection.

---

88. See *The Roman Missal*, Eucharistic Prayer II: "... et omnibus Sanctis, qui tibi a saeculo placuerunt, ..." English translation: "... and with all the saints, who have done your will throughout the ages."

Insofar as the will receives its natural motion from its Creator, and hence is naturally moved freely to act, it cannot simultaneously *not* be acting. And insofar as it is naturally moved freely to act thus-and-so it cannot *simultaneously* not-act thus-and-so. But unless freedom is defined as repugnance to the law of identity and noncontradiction, there is no detraction of freedom in noting that creaturely freedom receives its being, nature, and natural motion from God. No matter how one explains the causality operative in particular volition, to choose "A" is not not-to-choose "A". Human freedom consists in the incapacity of any finite good to compel the will, not in a spurious exemption from divine providence or independence from the gift of its own being, nature, and desire.

By way of clarification, two senses of "power" traditionally are considered important for understanding how volitional freedom is consonant with the divine gift of the will's natural motion and graced perfection. These two pertinent senses of "power" classically are designated as the "divided" sense and the "composite" sense *(sensu diviso* and *sensu composito)*.

The first such sense of "power"—the divided sense—indicates how it is that we retain a power to do something which is incompatible with our present condition. For instance, even while sitting, in the "divided" sense one retains the power to stand—because one really is capable of standing, although not at the same time that one sits (for this would contradict the nature of sitting and the nature of standing). It is in the divided sense that the will has the power to act differently than it does when freely acting under the perfecting suasion of grace and subject to God's imparting of its natural motion.

For example, God moves me to an act of worship here and now; but I retain the power to do something else—to think risible thoughts, animadvert on politics, and so on. One is not slavishly incapable of rational desire, but rather the very perfection of rational desire enables the will to be fixed on an object, and while it is freely moved to be so fixed, it cannot not-be fixed. Similarly, in the divided sense one retains the power of conscious sight while sleeping—but one does not consciously see and sleep at the same time. It is in this sense of "power" that the will retains the power to act diversely vis à vis God's imparting of the natural motion of the will. Insofar as the will is naturally and freely moved to do "x", it nonetheless retains the power to do "y", but in the divided sense and not simultaneously.

The composite sense of "power" by contrast indicates the compossibility, or simultaneous possibility, of two acts. And in this sense, freedom does not require that one retain power to act differently *in sensu composito*. For instance, human freedom does not require that one be free to stand precisely while sitting, because this is a contradiction in terms. Human freedom does not require that when one is desiring one not-be desiring, for this is a contradiction in terms. It is no part of human freedom that when I freely move—through the divine gift of the natural motion of the will and through its graced perfection—toward some salutary act, that I can simultaneously and equally not move toward the salutary act. It is no imperfection of freedom that it may be fixed on an object, for—in the divided sense—it retains the power not to be fixed on any finite object.

So, insofar as here and now I am freely and naturally moved by God as with the imparted natural motion of the will, I cannot not-be moved here and now. This implies that here and now, when we freely desire something through the interior motion bestowed by God upon the will, either naturally or by grace, we cannot simultaneously not-desire it, because this would constitute a contradiction (desiring while not-desiring, being freely moved while not being freely moved). In this composite sense then, manifestly the will is not free to do other than it is moved to do, because the will is not free not to be a will.

Insofar as God efficaciously and freely moves the will, the will is freely moved, just as insofar as I freely and efficaciously move I am moving. The created will simply lacks the power not to be a created will, which would be not freedom but nihilation. Hence the efficacy of God's grace in no way compromises human freedom, although it does indicate that human freedom is created and natural rather than deific and self-sufficient. Evil enters in with the defectibility of the creature, and God is not the author of defect. But any being or good in creaturely action is first from God, and secondarily from the creature, and this pertains first and foremost to the good of our own free assent.[89]

---

89. Several texts from Aquinas help to articulate this teaching. Hence we find St. Thomas writing: "God, therefore, is the first cause, Who moves causes both natural and voluntary. And just as by moving natural causes He does not prevent their acts being natural, so by moving voluntary causes He does not deprive their actions of being voluntary: but rather is He the cause of this very thing in them; for He operates in each thing according to its own nature" (*Summa theologiae* Ia, q. 83, a. 1, ad 3). This teaching clearly explicates the truth that God's bestowal of the will's natural motion does not contradict voluntariness, but is rather the very cause of voluntariness, which neither

This theme of the dependence of creaturely activity upon God in both the orders of nature and of grace is a defining theme of the theological teaching of St. Thomas, and in diverse philosophic formulations— emphasizing the infallible attraction of the good rather than motion— of the Augustinian tradition as well. It is quite arguably the essential and most delicate issue of Christian anthropology, and the central point of its variance with all rationalisms or what Maritain called "anthropocentric humanisms." It may even be argued that the historical challenge to this Thomist-Augustinian tradition[90] constitutes an historically intra-Catholic source for radical ideological secularism, as contrasted with extra-Catholic sources (continental idealism, phenomenalism, materialism).

Since the will is specified by the intellect, and the intellect can judge any finite good in some way not to be good, the will cannot be constrained by any finite object. Hence it retains freedom, in the divided sense, with respect to any finite good. By contrast, were the will once to cleave to the Perfect Good, it would be so utterly fulfilled as to render it incapable of aversion to God because utterly perfected and actuated: there would be no respect in which God could be seen by the intellect as not-

---

exists, nor has natural motion, apart from the Creator and First Mover. Aquinas also writes: "No created thing can put forth any act, unless by virtue of the divine motion" (Summa theologiae Ia-IIae, q. 109, a. 9, resp.). And, again: "To be moved voluntarily, is to be moved from within, that is, by an interior principle: yet this interior principle may be caused by an exterior principle; and so to be moved from within is not repugnant to being moved by another" (Summa theologiae Ia, q. 105, a. 4, ad 2). Further, he writes: "... we must come at length to this, that man's free-will is moved by an extrinsic principle, which is above the human mind, to wit by God, as the Philosopher proves in the chapter on Good Fortune (Ethic. Eudem . vii)" (Summa theologiae Ia-IIae, q. 109, a. 2, ad 1). And, again: "But not only is every motion from God as from the First Mover, but all formal perfection is from Him as from the First Act. Hence the action of the intellect, or of any created being whatsoever, depends upon God in two ways: first, inasmuch as it is from Him that it has the form whereby it acts; secondly, inasmuch as it is moved by Him to act" (Summa theologiae Ia-IIae, q. 109, a. 1, resp.). The translations in this note are taken by exception from the older (1911–25) English translation of the Summa by Father Laurence Shapcote, though attributed to the Fathers of the English Dominican Province (New York: Benziger Brothers, Inc., 1947).

90. Posed originatively in good faith by the Spanish Jesuit Luis de Molina (1535–1600), but later developed so as to bracket the providentialist sense of human freedom, which arguably constitutes the most important anthropological point of departure between Christian and rationalist teaching. Within the setting of modern philosophy, the writings of Pope John Paul II have aimed to restore a sense of God's providential guidance to theological discussions about human freedom.

good insofar as God truly were seen. Further, the natural desire for perfect happiness ensues simply upon our volitional nature as flowing from reason. There is no liberty with respect to it because the will is defined by its status as rational appetite of the Good: this is what it means to be a will. Yet how could the will constitute a rational appetite if, intuitively possessing the Supreme Good, at that very instant it could remain unperfected, fugitive in its taste of the good?

Any finite good is in some respect—*qua* finite—not the supreme fullness of the good, and hence may be deemed not-good even when it is here and now good for us. Our defects may warp our freedom, leading to disordered appetite and rejection of those finite goods that objectively would aid in our perfection.[91] Hence it is only through defective freedom and the rejection of finite created "emissaries" of God—created grace, the sacraments, good works, the holy Scripture, sacred Tradition, holy persons, places, and things—that we are capable of rejecting God, and not "face to face." Yet the necessary condition for the sight of God is that we conform our acts and lives to the right order of creation he ordains in nature and grace.

91. It is true that God always retains the sovereign power to save us from defect, but his healing gifts are bestowed not only in mercy but in justice: God's mercy and justice are not rightly formal motives either for presumption or despair, but for humility and self-abandonment to God.

CHAPTER FOUR

The Form of a Good Moral Action

Christian Realism and the Form of the Moral Good

Christian teleological ethics illustrate the sort of intrinsic morality that alone is worthy of the kerygmatic proclamation of God's kingdom that Christ enacts through the mysteries of his life, death, resurrection, and glorification. The relationship between salvation and the moral life is not an accidental one. The New Testament scholar Rudolph Schnackenburg indeed refers the entire moral teaching of the New Testament to the eschatological fulfillment that Christ both announces in his preaching and realizes in his person and life. "Because [Christ] proclaims God's kingdom as imminent, indeed as present, palpable, and effective in his own person and works," writes Schnackenburg, "he therefore demands also a new morality which is in keeping with the time of salvation and thus must also completely 'fulfill' the old law (Mt 5:17)."[1] For the Christian believer, then, the moral life implies more than that a person measures up to a standard of ethical ideals. To live the moral life means to abide with the crucified and risen Christ. Christian ethics evaluate human actions and a person's capacity to perform good ones with an eye on Christ's satisfactory death that once and for all has achieved God's promise of salvation for the human race.

Theological Warrants

The Belgian theologian Servais Pinckaers stresses that the Christian moral life springs from the radical foundation of God's grace and flourishes only through sustained personal union with Jesus Christ; he further insists that the Sermon on the Mount establishes a principal locus for the moral

---

1. See his *Christian Existence in the New Testament*, vol. 1 (Notre Dame, Ind.: University of Notre Dame Press, 1968), p. 172.

teaching of the New Testament.[2] At the conclusion of his Sermon on the Mount, Christ exhorts his disciples: "Be perfect, therefore, as your heavenly Father is perfect" (Mt 5:48). But Christ requires of his disciples only that which, in the measure of the divine goodness, he himself bestows on them. Moreover because of this freely bestowed gift, those who follow Christ can contribute to the actual establishment of a world of divine "goodness and loving kindness" (Ti 3:4). Confidence in the divine generosity underlies the development and dominates the insistencies of Roman Catholic moral theology, and at the same time justifies the expectation for achieving that moral excellence Christ asks of his disciples. To fulfill this expectation, Christians should approach each of their specific actions as if it were a distinct sacramental expression of God's love.

The Christian faith proclaims that the first fully personal expression of divine love and kindness dawns in the world at the moment of the Incarnation. At the very instant when "the Word became flesh" (Jn 1:14a) in the womb of the blessed Virgin Mary, God raised up a fallen world through the power of the Holy Spirit "through whom God's love has been poured into our hearts" (Rom 5:5). In his discussion of the historical beginnings of the new covenant, Aquinas recognizes this same bestowal of the Holy Spirit as the principal characteristic that differentiates the old law of covenantal promise and obligation from the new law of Gospel grace and freedom.[3] "So before all else," he insists, "the new law is the very grace of the Holy Spirit, given to those who believe in Christ."[4] The deepest reasonableness of an intrinsic morality resides in the uniquely Christian confession that, since each justified soul becomes a temple of the Holy Spirit, the demands of love are never too great to fulfill.

St. Augustine explains that Jesus personally embodies a divine love which possesses no cause other than the divine goodness itself, and that this very same grace overflows to the members of his Body: "The predestination of the saints is the same predestination that reached its greatest glory in the Saint above all other saints."[5] Since Christ personally en-

---

2. In addition to the pertinent sections of *Sources*, see his more popular presentation of these themes in *The Pursuit of Happiness—God's Way*, trans. Sr. Mary Thomas Noble, O.P. (New York: Alba House, 1998).

3. *Summa theologiae* Ia-IIae, q. 107, a. 1, ad 2.

4. *Summa theologiae* Ia-IIae, q. 106, a. 1.

5. St. Augustine, *De Praedestinatione Sanctorum ad Prosperum et Hilarium*, chap. 15, 30–31 (PL 44, cols. 981–83).

acts the divine goodness in our human history, that is, because he "lived among us," everything that the member of Christ does, insofar as it flows from Christ, prolongs the original Incarnation of God's love throughout the course of the ages. In a certain sense, Christian moral theology establishes the authentic forms in which Christ himself appears again and again in the graced lives that believers originally receive in Baptism, and in which they continue throughout a lifetime punctuated by reception of the other sacraments of initiation, forgiveness, and service to the communion. The Letter to the Romans announces this pattern: "Therefore we have been buried with him by baptism into death, so that, just as Christ was raised from the dead by the glory of the Father, so we too might walk in newness of life" (Rom 6:4). In other words, because Christ "lived among us," Christians believers likewise are able to live as God's children, "heirs of God and fellow heirs with Christ, provided we suffer with him in order that we might also be glorified with him" (Rom 8:17).

Because only authentically good actions reflect this uninterrupted outpouring of divine goodness in the world, the Church insists upon a morality that takes seriously the intrinsic quality and nature of each human action. In his *Confessions*, St. Augustine grappled with this intuition when he wrote that, "at a certain moment, we were pushed to do good after your Spirit conceived the good in our hearts, but before that time, it was to doing evil that we were inclined, when we had abandoned you; but you, only God, good God, never stopped doing good for us."[6] Bear in mind that extrinsic accounts of the moral life emphasize the responsible self and a set of ethical norms or values to which one either adheres or is compelled to follow, whereas intrinsic morality, in the sense used here, takes account of the self, the regulation of law, and the interior energies or resources necessary for a person to conform his or her actions to the good that the law dictates. The personal appropriation of moral truth means that the moral norm is not only observed but that the truth itself further shapes the various powers or faculties of the soul, making the one who embraces the truth a virtuous person. Catholic theology appropriates this work of sanctification to the third divine Person of the Trinity, the Holy Spirit. Specifically, the Church confesses that the Holy Spirit, who is also known as the Gift of truth, really conceives goodness in the hearts of believers. For this reason, Christian moral theology repudiates every variety of moral extrin-

---

6. St. Augustine, *Confessiones*, Bk. 13, chap. 36, no. 38.

sicism on the grounds that such outlooks ultimately constitute a reductionism with respect to the working of divine grace in the creature.

Since the New Testament commends without reservation the service of love (cf. Jn 15:12), theological ethics must adopt an uncompromising attitude toward anything that contravenes authentic human love. The First Letter of John even employs the metaphor of murder to summarize whatever runs counter to the good of the neighbor. "The children of God and the children of the devil are revealed in this way: all who do not do what is right are not from God, nor are those who do not love their brothers and sisters.... All who hate a brother or sister are murderers, and you know that murderers do not have eternal life abiding in them" (1 Jn 3:10, 15). This strong comparison between harm to one's physical life and harm to one's spiritual life, by hating the neighbor, poignantly illustrates to what extent our moral conduct, when not in conformity to the truth, adversely affects the well-being of other persons.

Though the Christian tradition promotes the realization of divine love in the world, it will not allow us to speak undifferentiatedly about love. In fact, artless attempts to fashion a complete moral doctrine out of the whole cloth of New Testament *agapē* frequently result in caricaturing the Christian life. Recall that in his "Canterbury Tales," the fourteenth-century English poet Geoffrey Chaucer ironically places the insignia *"Amor vincit omnia"* on the golden broach of a worldly Prioress.[7] But the authentic Christian tradition, especially represented in St. Augustine, brooks no such flippancy about sinful activity; sin embodies "self-love even unto despising God."[8] St. Augustine accordingly advises that "we should be displeased with ourselves when we commit sin, for sin is dis-

---

7. See Geoffrey Chaucer, *The Canterbury Tales*, ed. Walter W. Skeat (London: Oxford University Press, 1951), Prologue, 158–60: "Of smal coral aboute hir arm she bar / A peire of bedes, gauded al with grene; / And ther-on heng a broache of gold ful shene, / On which ther was first write a crowned A, / And after, *Amor vincit omnia.*" Perhaps the most celebrated effort to move Christian ethics in this direction is that of Joseph Fletcher's *Situation Ethics: The New Morality* (Philadelphia: Westminster Press, 1966), which aimed to ground ethics on the basis of the axiom: "Love fulfills the mandate of the Christian life." Albert R. Jonsen, "Casuistry, Situationism, and Laxism," in *Joseph Fletcher: Memoir of an Ex-Radical* (Louisville, Ky.: John Knox Press, 1993), 10–24, acknowledges the affinities between the situationism of Joseph Fletcher and the neo-casuistry advanced by some Catholic thinkers. For a Catholic effort to establish "mutual-love ethics" as normative for Christian life, see Edward Collins Vacek, "Divine-Command, Natural-Law, and Mutual-Love Ethics," *Theological Studies* 57 (1996): 633–53.

8. St. Augustine, *De civitate Dei*, Bk. 14.

pleasing to God; then we will in some measure be in harmony with God's will, because we find displeasing in our self what is abhorrent to our Creator."[9] St. Augustine stands in an unbroken history of holy doctors and teachers who demonstrate the seriousness with which the Church warns against sinful behavior. Because mistakes about how to distinguish moral good from sinful behavior jeopardizes the well-being and holiness of her members, both actual and potential, the Church can never retreat from preaching and teaching the full truth about the good of the human person.

The Placement of the Moral Good

In order then to fulfil its mandate as a scientific, that is, a full and complete account of the Christian moral life, moral theology confronts straight on the task of delineating the substantive contours in which love and hate can abide in human actions. This requires first of all placing moral action in its proper context within the divine scheme of things. One author sketches out the large picture in the following way:

This rightness [of a given action] is measured by the eternal reasons in the mind of God, partially translated for us in the precepts of natural law. Conclusions are drawn by moral science from these precepts, which conclusions set out the general requirements for the art of politics and legislation in Church and State. The rightness is finally brought to the point of particular action through the judgment of individual conscience.[10]

It is impossible for the theologian to evaluate any moral action without reference to the divine saving instruction, which is one with "the eternal reasons in the mind of God." This means that every moral agent is also a practitioner of the *sacra doctrina*, and so must situate, ultimately through the particular determinations of prudence, each one of his or her moral actions within the comprehensive setting of the eternal law, natural law inclinations, and the determinations of common moral wisdom, as these latter may bear upon a specific course of action.

The Second Vatican Council continues the Church's conviction about the value of an intrinsic morality when it affirms that the doctrine of

---

9. St. Augustine, *Sermo* 19, chaps. 2, 3 (CCL 41, cols. 252–54).

10. Thomas Gilby, O.P., *Principles of Morality*, p. 167. Gilby employed the phrase "natural law precepts," whereas the interpretation of Aquinas followed in this book prefers to speak about natural law inclinations or principles.

creation requires us to recognize the intrinsic goodness of all things that make up the temporal order. Created realities "are not only helps to the final end of human beings, but have their own value given them by God, both in themselves and taken as parts of the integral temporal order: 'God saw all that he had made and it was very good' (Gn 1:31)." The Council goes on to affirm that "this natural goodness receives an added dignity from the relation of these things to the human person for whose use they were created."[11] This outlook on the goodness of creation, rooted in the truth of the sacred Scriptures, establishes the grounds for the way that a Christian provides even a philosophical analysis of human actions. One author perceptively remarks on the distinctive place that human actions hold in the created world: "The creator's regard for creatures' being-in-the world is not restricted to ordinary categorical relations, but is directed fundamentally to a distinctive kind of transcendental interrelationship. For the mode of the world is that it have its being in the acts of its creatures."[12] Human actions, then, are unlike any other events in the world. Through them the divine purposes of the Creator are made manifest in those creatures who alone on earth are capable of personal communion with the Persons of the Blessed Trinity.[13]

Catholic teaching requires that an adequate moral theology describe the "proper mode of the world ... in the acts of its creatures," and demonstrate as well the morality inherent in these human acts. Just as Genesis recounts that God knowingly causes the substantial goodness and beauty of created things, so the human person participates in this creative power through his or her virtuous actions. The prescriptions of theological ethics seek to ensure the actual production of true and beautiful things in the sphere of human activity. Or to paraphrase Aquinas on this central

---

11. The Second Vatican Council's "Decree on the Apostolate of the Laity, *Apostolicam actuositatem*, no. 7: "Omnia quae efficiunt ordinem temporalem ... non solum subsidia sunt ad finem ultimum hominis, sed et proprium habent valorem, a Deo eis insitum, sive in seipsis considerata, sive uti partes universi ordinis temporalis: 'viditque Deus cuncta quae fecerat, et erant valde bona' (Gn 1:31). Haec eorum naturalis bonitas specialem quandam dignitatem accipit ex eorum relatione cum persona humana in cuius servitium sunt creata."

12. Kenneth Schmitz, *The Gift*, p. 112.

13. For further discussion, see Romanus Cessario, "The Trinitarian Imprint on the Moral Life," in *The Oxford Handbook to the Trinity*, ed. Gilles Emery, O.P., and Matthew Levering (Oxford: Oxford University Press, 2011), pp. 487–92.

point of Christian doctrine: a good action displays beauty which manifests the ordination of reason.[14]

The creative ordination of reason does not impose a sort of arbitrary *a priorism* on human initiative. Because good moral conduct always conforms to how God knows the world to be, each virtuous action which is committed at the proper time, in the right circumstance, and which embodies the full measure of prudence achieves the whole subsistence of a moral value. According to the conception of realist moral theology, however, moral value is not imputed to an action on the basis of an extrinsic principle, such as positive law, human convention, or public opinion. Neither does it originate in our personal assumptions about the moral life, or in our strong feelings about a moral issue, or in our untutored intuitions about what makes for right conduct. The Christian realist recognizes authentic moral value in an action only when the action fully participates in the eternal law.[15] Thus, *Veritatis splendor* repeats the age-old wisdom of the Judaeo-Christian tradition: "Patterned on God's freedom, man's freedom is not neglected by his obedience to the divine law; indeed, only through this obedience does it abide in the truth and conform to human dignity."[16]

Because the original order of the created world shares in the truth and goodness which belongs first and preeminently to God, human reason is able to distinguish virtuous conduct in the intelligent good (the good-as-meant) from vicious conduct, which always implies the lack-of-good-as-meant. We fathom the importance of attaining moral truth when we consider the warning that the Gospels give about falling into the darkness, and we are impelled to seek moral truth from the assurances that Christ himself speaks in the Johannine Gospel: "I am the light of the world; anyone who follows me will not be walking in the dark, he will have the light of life" (Jn 8:12). Intrinsic morality forms part of the Gospel teaching in an inalienable way. Because Christ himself communicates the light

14. See *Summa theologiae* IIa-IIae, q. 145, aa. 2, 3: "inquantum quemdem habet decorem ex ordinatione rationis."

15. See *Summa theologiae* Ia-IIae, q. 71, a. 6: "When it is said that all sins are evil but not because they are prohibited, that prohibition is to be understood as an act of positive law. If the prohibition is understood in terms of the natural law, then all sins are evil because they are prohibited, since the natural law comes from the eternal law, and acts of positive legislation come from the natural law."

16. *Veritatis splendor*, no. 42.

of life to his members, the Church never compromises with moral evil.[17] Recall that the actual practice of Christian love transports the reality of the Incarnation into the world of everyday human conduct. This explains why St. Augustine held the view that in the Sermon on the Mount Christ already handed over every precept suitable for guiding the Christian life: "The one who wishes to meditate with both piety and perspicacity on the Sermon which our Lord delivered on the mountain, such as we find it in the Gospel of St. Matthew, will undeniably discover there the perfect charity of the Christian life."[18] The five main themes which St. Augustine discovers in the text from the Gospel of Matthew provide a basic charter for a specifically Christian moral realism.[19]

Aquinas considered the moral philosophy of Aristotle useful for Christian moral theology only to the extent that sound philosophy provides a means to express and safeguard the great teaching on the Beatitudes. For within the schema of Aquinas's moral realism, all created moral goodness exists by reason of an intrinsic participation in the highest good which is God.[20] The Christian moral realist knows that the realization of perfect charity initially depends on our ability to observe and specify the intrinsic difference between good and bad human acts. When moral realism speaks about an intrinsic morality, it does not promote a species of moral essentialism, as if moral evil existed in the things-out-there. Some moral theologians interpret the phrase "intrinsically evil" (intrinsece malum) as if the Church were suggesting that morality is tied up with a world of pre-determined bad things. But as Aquinas points out, the term "morality" derives from mores, from what people really do, and so properly belongs only to the world of human activities.[21] The use of the term "object" in moral

17. See the Dogmatic Constitution of the Church, Lumen gentium, no. 9: "While it transcends all limits of time and confines of race, the Church is destined to extend to all regions of the earth and so enters into the history of mankind. Moving forward through trial and tribulation, the Church is strengthened by the power of God's grace, which was promised to her by the Lord, so that in the weakness of the flesh she may not waver from perfect fidelity, but remain a bride worthy of her Lord, and moved by the Holy Spirit may never cease to renew herself, until through the Cross she arrives at the light which knows no setting."

18. St. Augustine, De sermone Domini in monte, Bk. 1, chap. 1 (PL 34, cols. 1229–31).

19. St. Augustine, De sermone Domini in monte (PL 34, cols. 1229–1308). For a discussion of these themes, see Pinckaers, Sources, pp. 141–67.

20. See M.-D. Roland-Gosselin, "Le Sermon sur la montagne et la théologie thomiste," Revue des Sciences Philosophiques et Théologique 17 (1928): 201–34.

21. See Summa theologiae Ia-IIae, q. 58, a. 1. Aquinas actually makes the point to explain

theology should not lead one to imagine that moral theologians divide the world between good and bad objects, as if the metier of moral theology could be compared with the sorting out of black and white chess pieces.

As developed in the Christian tradition, actions are specified by their "objects." The Church, moreover, recognizes that the analysis of objects elaborated by St. Thomas Aquinas still retains its value.[22] Aquinas relies conceptually a great deal on moral objects, but he of course stipulates that an object does not acquire its moral character except when it becomes engaged with purposeful human behavior. If we consider the term etymologically, "ob-jectum" signifies something which is thrown up against something else. Aquinas recognizes that one can identify these objects according to species and kind, but this sort of classification happens according to an entirely different set of rules than those which govern the classification of physical beings. Still, as Aquinas points out, there abides a reciprocal relationship between moral purposes and natural things: "Moral ends befall natural things; and conversely the meaning of a natural end influences a moral end."[23] Specification of a moral action, however, always follows upon the human person's acting in the world and, thereby, engaging a variety of real goods which belong to the world of nature and which are able potentially to contribute toward human contentment.

The Scholastic authors captured this teaching in once-familiar axioms. Real objects-in-the-world interacting with the moral agent serve as drawing final causes of human action: Every agent acts for the sake of an end.[24] They also function in the line of exemplar causality, viz., as the specifying formal cause of a human action: Every agent acts so as to produce what is like itself.[25] The relationship of human acts to objects remains *ad aliquid*, that is, an opening out of a subject to an object, of the

---

why the moral virtues are tied to inclination: "Now 'moral' virtue is named from 'mos' in the sense of a natural or quasi-natural inclination to do some particular action."

22. See *Veritatis splendor*, no. 78: "The morality of the human act depends primarily and fundamentally on the 'object' rationally chosen by the deliberate will, as is borne out by the insightful analysis, still valid today, made by St. Thomas (see *Summa theologiae* Ia-IIae, q. 18, a.6)."

23. See *Summa theologiae* Ia-IIae, q. 1, a. 3, ad 3: "Fines autem morales accidunt rei naturali; et e converso ratio naturalis finis accidit morali." This text is significant for discussions of "physicalism."

24. See Aquinas, *Summa contra gentiles* III, c. 2: *omne agens agit propter finem.*

25. See Aquinas, *Summa contra gentiles* II, c. 11 (3); c. 53 (5): *omne agens agit sibi simile.*

self to the other person, and ultimately of the human person to God.[26] In general, modern moral philosophy reacts in an allergic fashion to the view that some final and ultimate goodness can actually cause goodness in human actions.[27] The foundational figures of the period have spoken out against teleology. For instance in the seventeenth century, Thomas Hobbes thought that he could announce the demise of the notion with impunity: "There is no such *Finis ultimus* (utmost ayme) nor *Summum Bonum* (greatest good) as is spoken of in the Books of the old Morall Philosophers."[28] The Christian tradition, however, maintains the view that not only should every human action aim to embrace the good, but in order to do so, every human action must acquire the pattern of the good. The end both draws and specifies.

The Concrete Form of the Moral Good

In order to identify the concrete form of the moral good, the Christian moralist considers at least three principal causes that shape and explain human activity. According to the terminology which has become customary since the twelfth century, we refer to these sources of morality as the object, the end, and the circumstances of an action.[29] In any human action, the complete form of moral goodness derives from the interplay of these three constitutive elements which determine the action's moral character. In pursuing this matter, Aquinas applies the Neoplatonic adage *bonum ex integra causa, malum ex quocumque defectu:* The good is from the ordered and complete set of perfected causes, whereas from any defect

26. For a succinct statement of the general theory, see Thomas Gilby, O.P., *Principles of Morality*, p. 166: "The form of morality consists in a relationship to the perfect and intelligible good which is the ultimate end of human activity, and to the subordinate goods, *ea quae sunt ad finem*. It is a relationship, *ad aliquid*, πρός τι, an opening out [of] subject to object, of the self to an 'other' which above all is God. A relationship of conformity means that the activity is morally good, a relationship of nonconformity, or rather of disconformity, means that the activity is morally bad."

27. For instance, G. E. Moore and moral philosophers like R. M. Hare who took their cue from Moore's observation that Good can never be equated with any of the things sought as good.

28. The text is cited in Alasdair MacIntyre, *A Short History of Ethics* (New York: Macmillan Publishing Co., 1966), chap. 10 at p. 138, which also treats Luther, Machiavelli, and Spinoza.

29. The *Catechism of the Catholic Church* retains this language (see nos. 1749–56), and the Encyclical *Veritatis splendor* offers further explanations (see nos. 71–83) when it discusses the "moral act."

Metaphysical Levels of Being	Levels of Goodness in Moral Act
Specific Definition, i.e. genus with specifying difference, e.g., rational animal, elephant, ball game.	Specific Determination, i.e., object (*finis operis*), [moral objectives], e.g., judicial execution of the innocent, adultery, perjury.[30]
Individuation, i.e. specific nature with individuating matter, e.g., this man, this grey elephant, last night's baseball game.	Individual determination, i.e., circumstances, e.g., the judicial execution of a Christian missionary, adultery with your brother's wife, perjury against the poor. [31]
Personhood, i.e., the ultimately subsisting personal reality, undivided within itself, incommunicable, and divided from all others, e.g., my uncle Russell.	Personal determination, end [intention], e.g., to execute judicially an innocent man in order to save his family from destruction, to commit adultery in order to escape a death penalty, to give alms in order to be well thought of by others.[32]

whatsoever evil ensues. In other words, he argues that in order to possess the full form of moral goodness, each of the three elements must be complete and good, but in order for the action's form to be deficient, it suffices that only one element fall short of the mark. Thus each human action possesses a definite and identifiable moral nature.

Christian theology implies a specific metaphysics of action. In order to illustrate how an action instantiates a definite moral nature, we can draw a comparison between the nature of a human act and the metaphysics of created personality. Philosophers discern a relationship between the triplex goodness that informs a human action and the levels of being that distinguish the human person.[33] A concrete human action falls under the

30. See *Summa theologiae* Ia-IIae, q. 18, aa. 2 & 4.
31. See *Summa theologiae* Ia-IIae, q. 18, aa. 3, 10, 11.
32. See *Summa theologiae* Ia-IIae, q. 18, a. 4.
33. In *Summa theologiae* Ia-IIae, q. 18, a. 4, Aquinas it is true refers to a fourfold goodness in each human action. There, however, he counts the "level" of genus, for example, in man, the category of "animal," as a distinctive level in classifying human action.

category of actions in general; but just as there is no such thing as a generic person, likewise generic actions do not actually exist. Still, we are able to recognize this deed as a brave action and this woman as, for example, Aunt Alice, only on the basis of an appeal to a more general category of things which includes all actions and all living beings.

The chart on page 153 sets up the relationship between metaphysical distinctions of being and the levels of goodness that can exist in human actions. This comparison of the metaphysics of human personhood with the levels of goodness that human actions can attain provides a general view of how moral realism approaches evaluation of human action. This general view remains indispensable both for the metaphysics of morals as well as for moral epistemology, that is, for how an action receives its concrete moral nature and how one can identify those moral natures as ones that are satisfying or unsatisfying with respect to human fulfillment.[34]

There exists a real world which contains a variety of good things, or what Aquinas calls the *res naturales,* and the human person remains free to engage them properly or improperly.[35] Practical judgments draw on theoretical insights and theoretical insights motivate practical operations. A Swiss friend invites me to lunch on the shore of Lac Leman. He inquires of the maître d'hôtel, and learns what is best in the day's catch. Without an existing fish and the expectation that it would be delicious he would not have chosen to order it. It is true that without having wanted to have a fine meal, my host would not even have considered the goodness of fishes or other kinds of food. But we were hungry, wanted to eat, he wanted to show me a fine day, to express gratitude, etc. This wanting which suffuses practical reason makes the ontological goodness of the fish immediately relevant for his acting, and so we settle down to enjoy a delicious *loup de nier.* At the same time, the satiety or *quies* that other luncheon customers share with us confirms that the waters of Lac Leman conceal a storehouse of piscatory *rei naturali* that will never lose their relevance for moral theology. Were my clerical friend, however, to opine, "There are so many good, wonderful things on earth which do not motivate my practical operations, even though I theoretically know of their goodness: the

34. For further and related discussion of Aquinas's "virtue epistemology," see Thomas S. Hibbs, "Aquinas, Virtue, and Recent Epistemology," *Review of Metaphysics* 52 (1999): 573–94.

35. See for example, *Summa theologiae* Ia, q. 2, a. 3: "Ergo est aliquis intelligens a quo omnes res naturales ordinantur ad finem, et hoc dicimus Deum."

contents of safes, beautiful girls, jewelry in Zurich's Bahnhofstrasse, fine cars like a Rolls Royce, etc.," I would have to reply that the knowledge of their goodness becomes practical as sparking my appetite and motivating practical deliberation. And so any of these objects may be considered as speculative "precisively" or "nonprecisively." They are "precisively speculative" inasmuch as the speculative object is indifferent to whether my desire is sparked thereby or not, and when we simply consider the object as such. They are "nonprecisively speculative" precisely inasmuch as the knower does not lose his voluntary, appetitive nature while knowing, so that this speculative object may indeed spark desire, and so cause the object to be engaged in a new and practical way as object of desire and terminus of operation, a judgment embedded in wanting.

Aquinas develops his view on moral objects along lines inspired by his reading of Aristotle, whose construction of the moral order as objectively discernible is drawn from the plain evidence of men and women acting and interacting in the world. Aristotle understood that morality concerns the basic realities that contribute to human existence, such as food for consumption, weapons for defense, property for security, and so forth. Aquinas develops this philosophical vision, drawing inspiration from the anti-Manichaean temper of the Dominican Order to which he belonged. Among the Order's foundational objectives, it aimed to overcome the profound theoretical skepticism, though not always practical reluctance, that the medieval Albigensians had adopted concerning the basic goodness of created things, such as sexual intercourse, ample food and drink, entertainment and amusement, and so forth. In defining the moral world, Aquinas describes an order of things—an *ordo rerum*—which remains fundamentally good and which free human beings can use to discover both a full measure of human happiness and the God of happiness. In addition, when we attain this contentment, more is involved than the cessation of a natural desire, more, that is, than what we encounter in the contented cow chewing its cud or in the bright metaphysician intuiting being. The pursuit of happiness sets up a moral objective to grasp and hold, not merely a *bonum*, but a true good-as-meant, something which possesses a *ratio bonitatis*. Recall that the proper burden of love is always the good-as-thing, not simply the mental reason for being good.

In its native constitution, this order of things reflects divine providence, viz., how God knows the world to be. Aquinas spells out the significance of this moral order in a text where he explains that some human acts are right according to nature and not merely because they are prescribed by law. In an important chapter from the *Summa contra gentiles*, Aquinas first affirms that those things which are prescribed by divine law are right, not only because the law stipulates them, but also because they are in accord with nature.[36] At the end of a series of arguments, Aquinas explores the main contention that guides Christian realism and distinguishes it from the various forms of secular morality: no person can successfully reject God as the point of final rest, so that whatever leads toward God is naturally good and whatever leads away from God is naturally bad.

Because the charity of God abides forever, Christian *agapē* is distinguished by stability and duration. Charity leads to God, for "no one can be known, except in function of the friendship which one bears him."[37] Yet one cannot fail to note that changes of philosophical outlook have altered the way that theologians engage in moral argumentation within the Christian Church. It is easy, for instance, to distinguish the voluntarist model, broadly construed, and its account of divine charity from the way that a moral realist describes the enactment of divine charity.[38] First, conformity to any positive law, whether civil or ecclesiastical, does not in itself guarantee the fullness of moral good. Granted that good positive law should always respect the form of the moral good, it is clear that jurists and legislators are not always guided by objective truth. Second, the mutual agreement of the governed, for example, the sort of convention that Rousseau's *Social Contract* promotes, does not alone suffice for establishing the moral good.[39] Government according to the will of the governed obviously presumes conformity to moral truth in those governed.[40] Third,

36. See *Summa contra gentiles* III, c. 129.

37. The text comes from St. Augustine, *De diversis quaestionibus LXXXIII*, q. XI, 5 (PL 40, col. 82) as quoted in Ceslaus Spicq, O.P., *Charity and Liberty in the New Testament*, trans. Francis V. Manning (New York: Alba House, 1965), p. 59.

38. See Bonnie Kent, *Virtues of the Will: The Transformation of Ethics in the Late Thirteenth Century* (Washington, D.C.: The Catholic University of America Press, 1995), but also my review in *The Thomist* 61 (1997): 473–77.

39. For a perceptive analysis of Rousseau, see Mary Ann Glendon, "Rousseau and the Revolt against Reason," *First Things* 96 (1999): 42–47.

40. For further information on "The Social Contract," see Maurice Cranston, *The Noble Savage: Jean-Jacques Rousseau 1754–1762* (Chicago: University of Chicago Press, 1991). This London School of Economics professor provides a thorough outline of Rousseau's social, political, and religious programs.

the evolution of social or historical consciousness cannot substantially alter the form of the moral good, for human nature cannot lose its specific characteristics while still remaining human nature. Fourth, God does not impute rightness or wrongness to basically neutral actions according to the arbitrary assertions of his will.[41] God's objective charity toward us lies at the heart of the Christian religion, and so moral realism regards charity not merely as inspiring the good deeds of God's children, nor simply as mothering the practice of religion, but as constituting the very being and the life of the Christian believer.[42]

The good-as-meant, that is, the good as right reason practically achieves it, constitutes the first and prior moral determinant of human activity. Virtuous action does not proceed without a discovery of the good-as-meant. On the other hand, if we try to impose personal values on the lack-of-good-as-meant—to repackage practical denial of moral order as justified by serving some personal aspiration—we engage in the moral equivalent of imagining a barking man or an autosexual person. Why? Because the fixed measure of human action derives from the fixity of the natural order of human ends.

Consider an example from everyday experience. Human communication does not occur without an intelligent exchange of words, viz., by using a *vox significativa*, as the Scholastics designated the verbal (or non-verbal) signs that we use to communicate. Similarly, human sexual acts are meaningful according to their ordering to fixed ends. The exercise of human sexuality outside the norms established for Christian marriage falls short of realizing its nature as a legitimate form of human sharing and procreation. In these examples, performing the marital act with someone other than one's proper spouse is tantamount to attempting communication with another person through the use of unintelligible sounds—for the end rendering the acts meaningful is not present. There exists a definite measure according to which the use of created things is proper to human life, and if one chooses to set aside this measure, the actions themselves harm the human person, as is evident in the various forms of frustration which oftentimes accompany bad and dishonest con-

---

41. Nor, as explained above (cf. Chapter Two, pp. 95–97) do the biblical cases where this may seem to occur (e.g., Abraham's sacrifice of Isaac, Hosea's concubinage, Israel's despoiling of the Egyptians) compel one to hold for divine imputation.

42. For more on this, see Ceslaus Spicq, O.P., *Charity and Liberty in the New Testament*, pp. 83ff.

duct. Authentic Christian moral discernment must always follow this realist norm.

The New Testament describes a Church which communicates a unity
of faith and morals to her members, so that "if one member suffers, all
suffer together with it, if one member is honored, all rejoice together with
it" (1 Cor 12:26). By its nature as a universal discourse, Christian morality
discloses an essentially ecclesial way of life. Indeed, St. Paul always incorporates his moral catechesis within the framework of an instruction concerning the mystical Body of Christ.[43] While the New Testament does
consider the case where personal intention depreciates the moral worth
of even a good action (cf. Mt 6:2–4), Christian theology fundamentally
envisions a community where each one's personal intentions remain ordered to the common good: "There is one body and one Spirit just as you
were called to the one hope of your calling" (Eph 4:4). The communion
of charity that marks the true presence of the Church accordingly supposes that its individual members do not postulate private worlds of moral meaning or act upon arbitrary norms for personal conduct. Authentic
charity implies communion. "Do not be conformed to this world," St.
Paul entreats the Romans, "but be transformed by the renewing of your
minds, so that you may discern what is the will of God—what is good
and acceptable and perfect" (Rom 12:2).

Because the fullness of ecclesial communion requires an equally full
communion in love, Christian moral theology invariably finds itself at
odds with those political philosophies that promote the broadest views
concerning individual freedom and autonomy. For the Christian, personal liberties, even if guaranteed by civil constitutions, never serve as an excuse for falling short of "what is good and acceptable and perfect." Liberty does not in itself guarantee the fulness of moral goodness; nor does
it, in and of itself, sufficiently embrace the moral constituents of the common good so necessary for political right order.[44] Rather is it the case

---

43. See the observations which follow Rom 12:4–8, 1 Cor 12:12–30, or Eph 4:4–16.

44. John Paul II makes the point strongly in *Evangelium vitae*, esp. nos. 68–74. For example, "Democracy cannot be idolized to the point of making it a substitute for morality or a panacea for immorality. Fundamentally, democracy is a 'system' and as such is a
means and not an end. Its 'moral' value is not automatic, but depends on conformity to
the moral law to which it, like every other form of human behavior, must be subject: in
other words, its morality depends on the morality of the ends which it pursues and of
the means which it employs" (70).

that rightful liberty itself is defined in terms of the fixed order of human ends. The existence of ordered liberty within society is itself a function of that natural hierarchy of ends that defines the common good (and without which, the common good would be either nearly contentless, merely instrumental, or wholly subjective—none of which provides an adequate understanding of a distinctively political order).

In order to foster the moral harmony which both characterizes the Christian life and ensures the authenticity of communion among its members, as well as for reasons of evangelical pedagogy, the Church makes its own the certitude that one can make general statements in morals whose truth-claim is not bound up with personal examples. The Second Vatican Council clearly endorsed developing objective criteria for evaluating moral actions,[45] and the teaching office of the Church assumes that in morals, much as with other dogmas of faith, one can make meaningful general statements. An examination of the historical record of course reveals that the Church has engaged more frequently in solemn definition about dogmatic matters than about moral ones.[46] This does not mean that the Church has not taught authoritatively about morals, but rather that the vast majority of the Church's official moral instruction falls under the umbrella of the ordinary Magisterium.[47] In any event, the historical

45. See *Gaudium et spes*, no. 51, where the Council explains why an evaluation of motives and even good intentions are not sufficient for determining what constitutes a good course of action in the Christian life.

46. Some authors claim that the Church has never solemnly defined a specific moral norm, but the teaching of Trent on polygamy provides a counterexample: "If anyone says that it is permissible for Christians to have several wives at once, and that this is not forbidden by divine law (Mt 19:19ff.), *anathema sit*" (Session 14, canon 2 [*DS* 1802]). More recently, the condemnations of direct and voluntary killing of an innocent human being, especially in procured abortion, of suicide, and of euthanasia in *Evangelium vitae* (see esp. nos. 57–67) offer examples of moral teachings as secondary objects of infallible teaching.

47. As *Lumen gentium*, no. 25, makes clear, this does not mean that what the Church has not solemnly defined has not been infallibly taught. For a discussion of this controverted issue in contemporary moral theology, see John Ford, S.J., and Germain Grisez, "Contraception and the Infallibility of the Ordinary Magisterium," *Theological Studies* 39 (1978): 258–312, and the reply by Francis Sullivan, S.J., *Magisterium: Teaching Authority in the Catholic Church* (New York: Paulist Press, 1983), pp. 119–52. Germain Grisez returned to the question in his "Infallibility and Specific Moral Norms," *The Thomist* 49 (1985): 248–87. See my brief account in *Catholic Dossier* 6.3 (May–June 2000), 5–8 of the levels of infallible teaching as stipulated in the "Profession of Faith" and "*Ad Tuendam Fidem.*"

tradition of common instruction in morals implies that one can legitimately employ general statements in morals without at the same time remaining at the level of the indeterminate and nebulous.[48]

Finding Goodness in Objects, Ends, and Circumstances

Moral realism couches its general moral discourse in language which supposes that, just as particular natures possess their own identifying forms, so also specific moral actions possess their identifying forms.[49] We speak of the moral nature of a given human action. General statements in morals designate moral forms. The moral theologian, moreover, can verify these statements without their being bound up with an example of a particular action or with a specific person's motive. To affirm that we can know the form of moral goodness apart from particular instances is not to assert that such forms exist in the world only as pure logical types.[50] On the contrary, the form of the moral good is found in a world of general moral meanings, of historical happenings, and of express personal motives. The technical vocabulary of moral theology upholds this conviction when it speaks about identifying a specific moral action with reference to moral objects, circumstances, and "ends" or intentions. The usage is found in the *Catechism of the Catholic Church:* "The object, the intention, and the circumstances make up the 'sources,' or constitutive elements, of the morality of human acts."[51]

The Moral Object

Because the terminology of objects, ends, and circumstances, enjoys a long-standing usage in moral theology, it is imperative to understand its proper meaning. First, then, we consider the nature of the moral object. As I have said, the standard methodology for delineating a human action includes specification by object. In order to understand fully this way of

48. For an adaptation of this teaching to the Decalogue, see Patrick Lee, "Permanence of the Ten Commandments," pp. 422–43.

49. For historical and systematic considerations of this theme, see Servais Pinckaers, O.P., *Ce qu'on ne peut jamais faire* (Fribourg: Press Universitaires Fribourg, 1986).

50. Critics of the English moralist R. M. Hare point out that his attempts to develop a science of morals remain precisely at the level of the abstract.

51. *Catechism of the Catholic Church*, no. 1750.

identifying an action, we must learn what constitutes a specifying object. Recall that etymologically the word "ob-ject", from the Latin *ob* (against) and *jacens* (throwing), suggests an activity, namely, to throw something up against another thing. In order to specify an action as a particular type of action, we first consider the interplay of a given motion with some thing. For example, we could not imagine the action of fishing without reference to a fish (even if none is caught!), or slicing without an apple (or some such cutable thing), or doing metaphysics without *ens ut ens*. Objects specify actions; the formal object specifies an operation as its end, term, or principle.

In order to show how different objects specify different specific kinds of activity, consider the generic action of hitting any object, such as baseballs, nails, and your best friend's back. Each one of these objects diversely specify the generic action of hitting; thus, we can distinguish three different formal actions: playing baseball, doing carpentry, and encouraging a friend. The natural material object of any capacity, such as self-motion, is the whole range of objects in which the form of the object may be found. In simpler terms, I can choose to hit anything that is hitable. Furthermore, the nature of the object itself enters into the psychological shaping of the formal action, and, therefore, shapes the correct performance as well. For example, swinging a baseball bat, hammering a nail, and slapping someone's back each entail determined kinds of hitting. If a zealous friend were to strike somebody in the same way that a major league player swings at his pitch, the recipient would most likely say that he was a victim of battery rather than the beneficiary of a friendly gesture. This kind of a moral evaluation, moreover, would not require appeal to the zealous friend's motive or purpose, for the "end of the action" itself contains sufficient moral meaning in order to make a judgment. For instance, forcefully hitting a friend in the back with a baseball bat is naturally not an act of friendly encouragement, irrespective of anyone's motive.

Certain moral theologians, it is true, today argue that the principal moral analysis of a given action rests in a detailed examination of the consequences which it produces. But in the example given above, the "friendly" battery does not ensue as the mere consequence of a bad motive or purpose; rather, the specific action first of all emerges in the formal object itself. The "end of the object" describes, then, the whole intentional order which unites an action with its proper object, so that we can determine how the action conforms to the good ends of human existence. And for this reason, one author chooses to speak about moral objectives, instead of moral objects, so that the expression will better signify the dynamic aspect of the theory.[52]

A realist approach to theological ethics requires an adequate account of moral objects. Moral actions concern real things: doing justice deals with concrete property in the same way that playing baseball involves real balls and bats. Chastity pertains to real flesh in the same way that carpentry involves real nails and wood. In short, "object" designates a specific reality which shapes the moral life and provides an identifiable description of a moral situation. For example, consider such actual descriptions of moral objects as "an innocent life," "another person's spouse," "partner-less sexual activity," "non-truth in a courtroom." Each of these objects identifies a potential ingredient for moral action. When we associate these objects together with a specific kind of activity, we arrive at an adequate conception of what someone is doing. So, for example, *to take directly* "an innocent life" constitutes murder; *to have sexual relations with* "another person's spouse" constitutes an adultery; *to obtain* "sexual gratification without the mediation of a proper partner" constitutes masturbation and other unchaste acts; *to speak* a "non-truth in a courtroom," i.e., under oath, constitutes perjury. In other terms, one can adequately define certain kinds of actions by reference to moral objectives so as to establish a recognizable class of actions, e.g. murder, adultery, auto-erotic behavior, perjury, about which one can make a judgment as to whether or not such a kind of action contributes or not to the perfection of the human person.[53]

The world as it exists offers real objects which take on a moral significance by the way in which we reasonably act toward them.[54] This sort of determination occurs before such personal motives or purposes as the

---

52. E.g., T. C. O'Brien, *Faith*, Blackfriars *Summa*, vol. 31 (1974), pp. 178–85, translates the Latin *"objectum"* as "moral objective."

53. *Veritatis splendor* adopts this view: "Reason attests that there are objects of the human act which are by their nature 'incapable of being ordered' to God, because they radically contradict the good of the person made in his image" (no. 80).

54. For a certain clarification of this important issue, see Martin Rhonheimer, " 'Intrinsically Evil Acts' and the Moral Viewpoint: Clarifying a Central Teaching of *Veritatis Splendor*," *The Thomist* 58 (1994): 1–39 and "Intentional Actions and the Meaning of Object: A Reply to Richard McCormick," *The Thomist* 59 (1995): 279–311. The articles have been reprinted in *Veritatis Splendor and the Renewal of Moral Theology*, ed. DiNoia and Cessario.

love of God or hatred of the neighbor supplies the final, personal determination. Though secular existentialism opposes this claim, Christian moral theology rejects the idea that arbitrary assertions flowing from one's subjective view of the world can supply moral rectitude to an act that is disordered vis à vis its object. The creature does not create his or her world; the creature interacts with a world created by God. So only in the abstract is a category of morally neutral actions even thinkable, for in the real world wherein actions exist, every deliberate act either is ordered duly or is not. Efforts by certain post-conciliar moral theologians to rationalize a world of pre-moral/non-moral/ontic evil are built upon the un-real hypothesis that there are not actions which in themselves and by nature are specifically good or bad. Such an hypothesis, however, contravenes sound moral teaching. The teacher of Catholic truth can never countenance the commission of a *malum culpae* (an evil of fault); on the contrary, he or she is bound always to expose what is disharmonious with the true good of the person.[55]

The Deformity of Sin

The Christian tradition actually recognizes only two categories for evil. The first, the evil of punishment *(malum poenae)*, denotes the punishment which one suffers as a result of sin, and the second, the evil of fault *(malum culpae)* denotes the actual transgression or sin. A sinful action is one that neither conforms to truth nor embodies goodness; sin is a privation of the due order that should inform a human action. As both the Scriptures and Tradition testify, the deformity of evil present in the world derives from the original sin. In Adam the original sin instantiates fault and brings punishment, but for the race of Adam, original sin brings only punishment. The *Catechism of the Catholic Church* usefully explains that "original sin is called 'sin' only in an analogical sense: it is a sin 'contracted' and not 'committed'—a state and not an act."[56] The pun-

---

55. Recall that the Church explicitly teaches, e.g., *Gaudium et spes*, no. 51, that the moral quality of a human action "ought to be determined by objective criteria, derived from the nature of the person and of human acts" (... sed obiectivis criteriis, ex personae eiusdemque actuum natura desumptis, determinari debet ...). *Veritatis splendor* expands on this theme, and appeals to moral theologians and to the Church's pastors (see nos. 109–17) to conform their teaching and instruction to sound moral doctrine.

56. *Catechism of the Catholic Church*, no. 404. See also no. 405: "Although it is proper to each individual, original sin does not have the character of a personal fault in any of Adam's descendants."

ishment for the human person consists in a deprivation of original holiness and justice, and the consequent disordering of the human capacities, intellect and appetites, both sense and rational.

One is not able to relate immediately certain punishments of original sin to personal moral agency, for example, earthquakes, famines, natural disasters. But even these signs that visible creation has become hostile to man are associated with the sinful and broken condition of the human race. In the actual economy of salvation, all punishments due to original sin, including disease and physical catastrophes, can be interpreted only in the light of the Christian doctrine of redemptive suffering.[57] Christian moral theology must attend to whatever is required to restore fully the *imago Dei* present in each human being; this working out of salvation entails the progressive restoration of the Godly image. Because Christ has promised to remain with his Church until the end of time, the Church is able to sacramentalize not only the good things that we do but also the evil that we endure. Ethical schemes that do not take proper account of the nature of the human person and of human actions are less suited to appreciate this sacramental dimension of the Christian moral life.[58]

Some Everyday Illustrations

Because Christian theology accepts the goodness of the created order as such, realist moral theology remains confident about establishing moral truth in the conformity of an action with its object, in the same way that realist epistemology looks for truth in the conformity of the mind's concept with what really exists in the world. The person who has begun to delight in the flesh of another person's spouse can recognize that he or she has begun to walk down a path that leads to frustration, not perfection. Why? Because neither the eternal law, nor the natural law, nor the form of the moral good-as-meant allow one to incorporate such activity into a reasonable pattern of human living. Such an act no more represents a perfective procreative relation, than the deceitful acts of a hit man, who

57. For further information on Christian soteriology and the doctrine of original sin, consult *Catechism of the Catholic Church*, nos. 396–412, and my *The Godly Image* (Petersham, Mass.: St. Bede's Publications, 1990).

58. *Incarnationis Mysterium*, Bull of Indiction of the Great Jubilee of the Year 2000, esp. nos. 9, 10, exemplifies the sacramental aspect of the moral life when it explains the practice of the Jubilee indulgence. For a critical analysis of a non-realist proposal for human action, see William E. May, "Aquinas and Janssens on the Moral Meaning of Human Acts," *The Thomist* 48 (1984): 566–606.

shakes hands and smiles like a friend while leading a marked man to his doom, represent genuinely friendly acts. In each case the perfective object necessary to render these deeds good is lacking.

To ensure that one recognizes the perfective object of an action, weighing consequences is excluded as a principal criterion for making a moral judgment about a specific action.[59] Neither reward nor punishment in itself stipulates the form of the moral good. What happens consequent to an action is not the correct place to focus an evaluation of the goodness of the action. Moral drunkenness occurs before physical inebriation. For one sins against sobriety at the moment that one chooses to exceed the right measure which *recta ratio* determines as a limit for drinking intoxicating beverages. Fornication happens when unmarried persons choose to engage in sexual relations. This choice normally follows the arousal of passion, but may precede the actual illicit embrace and consequent experience of sexual gratification. To allow the concupiscence of the eye destroys purity of heart whether or not the fixed gaze settles on a satisfying object. In sum, the consequences of an action do not figure directly in the reckoning of moral goodness or badness.[60]

To explain sin by appeal to objects does not mistake physical states for the moral order. The removal of a cancerous organ specifies a different moral object from the removal of a healthy one. And although the physical symptoms are identical, when a doctor anesthetizes a patient for surgery we identify a different moral object than when a college student on a Saturday night drinks to excess. To lose completely one's self-control and consciousness through an intemperate use of alcohol falls below the standard of human dignity; such drunkenness is morally bad, bad by reason of its object *(ex objecto)*. But to accept the same physical conditions before serious surgery, even by the same means if no other anesthesia is available, would be entirely correct. The end of the work, the *finis operis,* is one thing in plain drunkenness and another in anesthetic intoxication, and this difference depends on something more than a mere physical description of a state or action. To comprehend the truth of this claim requires only that one be able to distinguish between dissipation and surgery. St. Cyril of Alexandria reminds the Christian to respect the nature of things: "If anyone here present is thinking of putting God's grace to the

59. See *Veritatis splendor,* no. 77: "But the consideration of ... consequences, and also of intentions, is not sufficient for judging the moral quality of a concrete choice."

60. See *Veritatis splendor,* nos. 71–79.

test, he is deceiving himself, and he does not understand the nature of things."[61] In making an examination of conscience, this warning finds suitable applications under the headings of each of the Commandments.

A realist moral theology does not imply an unbending, rigid, or antipersonal stance toward the delicacies of the moral life. Moral objects remain the foundation-stones for human freedom, in the same way that the natural law provides the foundation for the grace of the new law. We have the witness of Tertullian: "Freedom in Christ has done no injury to virtue. There remains in its entirety the law of piety, sanctity, humanity, truth, chastity, justice, mercy, charity and purity; and blessed is the man who will meditate day and night upon this law."[62] Freedom in the moral life functions instrumentally, that is, it accompanies the performance of actions which remain in conformity to, and therefore respect, the contours of a common nature. Freedom, however, cannot transform a bad action into one which perfects human existence. Free and mutual self-giving, for instance, can never transform the cohabitation of unmarried couples into an acceptable form of courtship. The latter affords a period of virtuous preparation for the "one flesh" of marriage, whereas the former anticipates the conjugal union without the protection of publically (and for the baptized, sacramentally) pronounced vows.

Appeal to the supreme place of conscience in the moral life can direct people away from paying due attention to moral objects, even though Aquinas acknowledges the possibility that an erroneous conscience can influence, and even excuse, someone in a particular case. Exculpation however does not preserve the person from missing out on some feature of the human good. For example, the extreme case of an infallibly erroneous conscience does not render an imperfective act perfective, but merely points toward the preservation of a certain stultified innocence born of ignorance and lacking the achievement of moral goodness. That is, it regards imputation of fault, and in no way the integral goodness of the act. Just as the goodness of excellent driving is incompatible with running over one's mother-in-law owing to an accidental slipping of one's foot upon the pedals—although this accidental slipping would refute imputation of malice or fault—so morally decisive ignorance is incompatible

---

61. *Catechetical Instruction*, 1, 2–3. 5–6 (PG 371, cols. 375–78).

62. *De pudicitia*, VI, 4: "Libertas in Christo non fecit innocentiae iniuriam. Manet lex tota pietatis sanctitatis humanitatis veritatis castitatis iustitiae misericordiae benevolentiae pudicitiae. In qua lege beatus vir qui meditabitur die ac nocte (Ps 1.2)."

with the moral goodness to which we are called. And just as driving instructors seek to overcome habits which may lead to such accidents, so
moral instructors strive to eradicate ignorance that can deprive actions
and agents of their due moral goodness.

By way of conclusion on moral objects in measuring sinful comportment: some actions, properly defined by their appropriate objects, always
possess a deformed moral character no matter what circumstances or intentions lie wrapped up with them. Though typological generalization
by means of moral objects plays an important role in moral analysis, it
accounts for only one of the three required determinations. Complete
evaluation of a moral action requires due consideration of the *circumstances*
and *intentions* which accomplish it. Properly defined, murder constitutes a
bad kind of action. The doctor in a deserted place who snips the fatally-
wounded accident victim's spinal cord may appeal to a personal end—in
the sense of individual purpose or motive—which rational enquiry cannot uncover. He may even argue that this particular action belongs to
another category than murder because the end of the deed (*finis operis*)
should not be compared with wilful murder of a healthy person. But if
his case requires a judgment before a civil court, the reasons known only
to God ordinarily will not warrant acquittal. Feeding the hungry always
embodies a good action even if pride or vain-glory diminishes its meri-
toriousness in the one who gives alms. In some cases, however, too much
attention to purification of motive can obstruct the performance of good
actions, and so the tradition practiced in the Society of Jesus wisely counsels *age quod agis*—go on doing what you are doing.

The Church insists that happiness remains the goal of all human activity, and this conception dominates the moral life. The unity of the
Church's members requires agreement among them about the goodness
and the badness of moral objects. We are all journeying toward a single
destination which is the new Jerusalem, and while on journey we must
keep the true end before us, for as C. S. Lewis warns, "those who are go-
ing nowhere, can have no fellow travelers."[63]

Personal Intentions

A second consideration about the evaluation of human action involves
the matter of personal intention. The terms used in the discussion first

---

63. See *The Four Loves* (London: Fontana Books, 1963), p. 63.

require a word of explanation. The catechetical tradition uses the word "end" to designate not only the goals toward which all things move, but also the personal purposes or motives of those agents pursuing these goals. While some confusion is possible, it is an enriching function of the truth of moral teleology that it recognizes a relationship between the end of the agent (*finis operantis*) and the end of the deed (*finis operis*), to the extent that both of these ends are meant to harmonize in the production of a good action.

Debate about the question of the extent to which personal intention contributes to objective criteria in the evaluation of an action enjoys a long history in Christian ethics. The twelfth-century logician Peter Abelard pointedly raised the issue in his *Ethics: or Know Thyself*, where he argued that morality consists in intention alone and that the things we do, the actions we perform, remain—apart from our intention in performing them—morally neutral.[64] It is generally agreed that Abelard let his philosophical thinking run ahead of his Christian convictions; indeed the New Testament itself offers a warning against calculation on the basis of intention when the Gospel of John disapprovingly records the reasoning of the high priest Caiaphis who was willing to sacrifice the Innocent One in order to save the Jewish people from the menace of the Roman authorities (cf. Jn 11:49–50). So we are not surprised to discover Aquinas flatly asserting that "one can never justify a bad action on the basis that it was performed with a good intention."[65]

But how does Christian realism figure the end of the agent (*finis operantis*) in the moral analysis of human actions? First of all, moral realism distinguishes the deep meaning of "end" as personal motive or purpose from the accidental meaning of "end" as suggested by the circumstance of "why." The circumstance of "why" refers only to the accidental reason why something happens instead of why it did not happen. In the sense of a circumstance, the why of an action lies outside of the agent's personal choosing, i.e., a certain flow of historical happenings settles why this event took place or that event did not occur. To account for eating fresh shellfish by appeal to the fact that one was passing time on Cape Cod does not reveal one's personal intention.

64. For a fuller treatment of this topic, see Ralph McInerny, *Ethica Thomistica* (1997 ed.), chap. 5, esp. pp. 83ff.

65. See his *Collationes de decem praeceptis*, chap. 6. *Veritatis splendor* incorporates this teaching into its account of intrinsically evil acts, see esp. nos. 81, 82.

When we speak about personal intention as an "end," for example as we actually find it used in the phrase, "object, end, and circumstance," the term "end" designates something different from either the circumstantial why of an action or the teleological bent of nature as such.[66] We have already observed that there is an element of conscious willing which forms part of the constitution of the moral object itself. In this sense, how I choose to hit a baseball necessarily, viz., by reason of the object, differs from how I choose to hit my friend on the back; or, to put it another way, the moral object itself materially shapes a person's choosing. While this choosing already expresses something of my personal willing or intention, it does not account for the full measure of my personal intentions, i.e., of what I am intending to accomplish by my action. This is to introduce that in each unimpeded voluntary action, we can discern a *double movement of the will.*

In his discussion of the moral character of a human action, Aquinas actually speaks about a double activity of the will. He takes pains carefully to explain the relationship between the "end [which] is properly the object of the interior voluntary act" and the "exterior act [that] takes its species from the object with which it is concerned." Because a certain amount of confusion on this point still exists among theorists, it will be useful to study fully the text.

In the voluntary action there are two acts, namely, the interior act of the will and the exterior act, and both of these acts have their objects. The end is properly the object of the interior voluntary act, and that with which the exterior act is concerned is its object. Therefore, just as the exterior act takes its species from the object with which it is concerned, so the interior act of the will takes its species from the end as its proper object. However, that which is taken from the side of the will relates formally to that taken from the exterior act, because will uses the members in action as instruments, nor do the interior actions have the note of morality except insofar as they are voluntary. Therefore, the species of the human act is formally considered taken from the end and materially considered taken from the object of the exterior action.[67]

---

66. As we have seen, Aquinas himself reserves the term "intention" to signify the deep-seated inclination of a nature toward a specific end, triggered by perception, wish, and the judgment of *synderesis.* In this sense, *"intendere"* belongs to the order of the end, rather than to that of the means.

67. *Summa theologiae* Ia-IIae, q. 18, a. 6.

We need to consider the implications of this text in order to work out some of the issues that divide moral theologians.

The mention of a material-formal distinction prompts some moral theologians to interpret Aquinas as if he considered external actions—the material consideration—to hang like outer appendages on inner states, i.e., on the formal consideration of the will's activity. But this reading fails to grasp the thorough-going coherence of Aquinas's realist conception of human action. Moreover, such an interpretation depends upon a dichotomization of the formal and material which, since it is introduced mainly in the seventeenth century, remains foreign to his *Weltanschauung*.[68] In order to express the difference between a moral object and personal motive or purpose, moral theologians, it is true, traditionally distinguish between the *finis operis*, the end of the action, and the *finis operantis*, the end of the agent. While this distinction remains legitimate, it is still possible to employ the distinction in an overtly Platonic way, and to argue that an action receives the significant portion of its moral meaning from the "end" of the agent.[69] But for the moral realist, as has been underscored, the end of the work itself gives substantial definition to the form of the moral good, and this must be integrated into the fully personal meaning of intention. An act is integrally good only by the rightness of all its constituents, while it is flawed by any defect (*bonum ex integra causa, malum ex quocumque defectu*). Hence the matter of an act may be such that it is not congenial to the form of an agent's purpose, just as clubbing with a baseball bat is not congenial to the form of the purpose of expressing friendly comradery. The *finis operantis* receives its matter from the *finis operis*, and is limited thereby. For matter must be proximate to the reception of form—the matter of a wooden desk is not fit suddenly to become the matter of gold. Likewise, moral theology is not moral alchemy, and human intention cannot make inherently distelic acts to be naturally perfective.

Recall that for the moral realist, the object of intention remains a telic good that reason judges to be perfective or fulfilling of the kind of agents that we are. Since human reason itself must conform to the requirements of objective moral truth, all forms of personal capriciousness

---

68. For a lucid resumé of Aquinas's teaching, see McInerny, *Ethica Thomistica*, pp. 85ff.

69. Thus, those who advance a view about pre-moral evil, appeal to the standard teaching on the relationship of *finis operis* and *finis operantis*.

are ruled out. Still, as T. S. Eliot recalls in *Murder in a Cathedral*, the purification of a person's "end" or motivational purpose remains a desidera-
tum even for something as objectively good and circumstantially correct
as martyrdom.[70] Given that an action is specified by its proper object, we
can consider three species of morality in the abstract: good, bad, morally neutral.[71] In the real world of moral activity, according to the received
teaching, no concrete human action can remain neutral; everything we do
either brings us toward God or moves us away from him.

Circumstances

Because actions occur within concrete circumstances, the moral theologian, beyond "object" and "end," must also consider those circumstances which provide the setting for a particular action. For the moral realist,
the moral truth reflects how God knows the world to be, and at the same
time morality concerns what transpires in the real world of human con-
tingency. Therefore, a complete analysis of a moral action requires due
attention to circumstances. In his 1949 edition of the *Vademecum Theologiae Moralis*, a pocket manual commonly used before the Second Vatican
Council by confessors, the Dominican moralist Dominic Prümmer re-
caps the received teaching of the casuists concerning circumstances.

Moral circumstances are those moral conditions which are added to and modify the already existing moral substance of the act, such as the added circumstance of consanguinity in fornication. From the earliest times, it has been
customary to list seven circumstances contained in the following verse: "Quis,
quid, ubi, quibus auxiliis, cur, quomodo, quando."[72]

---

70. See T. S. Eliot, *Murder in the Cathedral*, Part One:

Thomas: Is there no way, in my soul's sickness, / Does not lead to damnation in pride?
/ I well know that these temptations / Mean present vanity and future torment. /
Can sinful pride be driven out / Only by more sinful? / Can I neither act nor suffer
/ Without perdition?

Tempter: You know and do not know, what it is to act or suffer. / You know and do
not know, that acting is suffering, / And suffering action....

Thomas: Now is my way clear, now is the meaning plain: / Temptation shall not come
in this kind again. / The last temptation is the greatest treason: / To do the right
deed for the wrong reason.

71. *Summa theologiae* Ia-IIae, q. 18, a. 8.
72. Dominic M. Prümmer, O.P., *Handbook of Moral Theology*, p. 21.

The questions Who? What? Where? By which means? Why? How? and When? translate the traditional list of circumstances. While circumstances sometimes can alter the moral nature of an act, in a large majority of cases these questions respond to the concrete particulars of a given action, or as one author puts it, they describe "special circumstances that mark the individual lot."[73]

Moral realists, as has been observed above, like to compare a specific moral act to an individual instance of a specific nature. For the adherents of moderate realism, the pure natures of created realities do not enjoy full existence apart from individuals. Similarly, there are no pure types of actions which enjoy full existence outside of an agent who performs them. Concretely, then, human action means individual action. Though each human act transpires only within a given set of historical conditions, these contingencies, no matter how pressing or dramatic they may be, never adequately reveal the full moral meaning of action. Instead, they modify the shape of an action in a way which is analogous to how accidental modifications vary the substantial being of a nature.

According to Aquinas's view on individuation, designated matter, viz., "this flesh and these bones," accounts for the fact that one instance of a universal nature differs ontologically from another instance of the same nature. Something analogous happens in the case of individuating circumstances. For each specific action, circumstances serve as the individuating principles that account for its concrete singularity, which approximates Aristotle's "this of a certain kind" (tóde ti). But paying due attention to the concrete circumstances of an action performed here and now does not translate into situationalism, i.e., the view that circumstances determine the complete morality of an action. Within the practice of Christian realism, prudence alone directs and commands the specific actions of the moment.

Though circumstances of themselves are unable to dictate a prudential course of action, the workings of the virtue of prudence incorporate even the most particular of circumstances into its general determination of how one ought to embrace the good here and now. Prudence affords the Christian believer the opportunity to see beyond the circumstantial qualities of a given human action, and to discover the true nature of a here-and-now action.

73. See George Eliot, *The Mill on the Floss*. For the effect that circumstances have on the moral quality of an action, see *Veritatis splendor*, no. 81, and below, note 75.

Prudence and the moral wisdom that guides its exercise provides the Christian believer with an alternative to looking for moral truth in the findings of the inductive sciences, which are dedicated to gathering, organizing, and interpreting information about the particulars of human actions. *Veritatis splendor* addresses the relationship of moral truth and the experimental sciences directly: "Only Christian faith points out to man the way to return to 'the beginning' (cf. Mt 19:8), a way which is often quite different from that of empirical normality. Hence the behavioral sciences, despite the great value of the information which they provide, cannot be considered decisive indications of moral norms."[74]

Certain theorists have promoted large-scale misunderstandings about the nature of the circumstantial in human activity. Some moral theories advance the view that circumstances form the primary determinant in establishing the morality of a given action. In its more radical form, situationalism tries to make a science out of particulars; and the situation ethics of the 1950s remain an excess to which some moral theologians still succumb. But like exaggerated personalism, situationalism overemphasizes what is unique in each person and overlooks what is common among human beings. A human person subsists in a nature, whose shared or common characteristics mark other human beings. Growth in the good for any individual of the species proceeds within the limits set by common nature. We cannot imagine, for example, any particular circumstance or set of circumstances where lie-telling advances and perfects the good of human communication, nor where an adulterous affair strengthens a marriage bond. To insist that even extraordinary personal circumstances provide the grounds for setting aside the requirements which common human nature imposes on every man and woman leads to frustration, because it compromises the inseparable connection that Tertullian says binds Christian freedom to the virtues.

Circumstances account for the idiosyncratic realizations of an action, but the variety of particulars is never so large that it is impossible to incorporate whatsoever circumstances into a general theory of moral action.[75] No amount of theorizing about circumstances replaces exercising that part of prudence which is called circumspection, that is, giving due attention to circumstances in the formation of a prudential judgment.

74. *Veritatis splendor*, no. 112.

75. See *Summa theologiae* Ia-IIae, q. 18, aa. 3, 10, 11, where Aquinas explains how circumstances can affect, indeed even change, the nature of the moral action.

To make a judgment on the basis of analyzing circumstances provides no substitute for the full and complete exercise of prudence. Only this virtue ensures a true judgment of the practical reason about the order of doing that remains in conformity to the full truth about the moral good.

The importance of distinguishing theorization about circumstances from actual attention to circumstances in a prudential action remains an issue in contemporary debates in moral theology. Certain theories that relied on one or another account of proportionate reason had argued that anticipated consequent circumstances ought to enter directly into the formation of a moral judgment. The practical expediency enshrined in this kind of argument still makes it attractive in certain instances, for example, when offering reasons for non-therapeutic sterilizations. To employ circumstances in this way, however, thwarts the proper exercise of prudence, and so misguides human action. Prudence proceeds as a product of rectified appetite and deliberate reason, and ensures that a person chooses in accord with the goods of excellence. Speculation about what may happen in the future offers no grounds for choosing well here and now, and most likely will persuade a person to choose in accord with whatever seems the most expedient course of action to achieve a desired end.[76]

There are instances, however, where circumstances do affect the moral quality of an action. Consider the example of deliberate theft from a tabernacle of the gold vessels in which the Blessed Sacrament is reserved. In itself, such theft constitutes a complete moral object, but the moral theologian must attend to the complex of circumstances in which such an activity occurs. Excluded from consideration is the person's aim for stealing and whatever good results may follow from the theft. On the other hand, it is easy to recognize that certain circumstances figure so prominently in the performance of an action that they can affect the moral nature of the act. To steal a gold ciborium filled with consecrated hosts is not the same things as to steal a gold watch from my Uncle Louie. The Scholastic theologians acknowledged that certain weighty circumstances may affect the composition of the moral object. A circumstance, they argued, can pass over into the condition of the object (*transit in conditionem obiecti*). In the example cited, the evil of theft is obviously complicated by the additional evil of sacrilege. It is quite another matter, however, to argue for the ster-

76. For a fuller account, see Ralph McInerny, *Ethica Thomistica*, pp. 77–89.

ilization of a psychologically frazzled 35-year-old father of ten living in an over-populated country, on the grounds that the circumstances alter the moral object. Although the man merits whatever relief Christians owe to those in distress, the contingencies of his situation represent nothing more than the "special circumstances that mark the individual lot." The relief offered to him, moreover, must conform to the good and respect the dignity of his person. Mutilating sterilization does neither of these.

The moral theologian is committed to discussion of the issues that open new perspectives about the moral evaluation of human action. *Veritatis splendor* allows for this kind of moral reflection, but it also establishes the limits to the discussion. One clear limit is the encyclical's teaching on intrinsic evil:

> Reason attests that there are objects of the human act which are by their nature "incapable of being ordered" to God, because they radically contradict the good of the person made in his image. These are the acts which, in the Church's moral tradition, have been termed "intrinsically evil" (*intrinsece malum*): they are such *always and per se*, in other words, on account of their very object, and quite apart from the ulterior intentions of the one acting and the circumstances.[77]

Those who offer moral guidance to others should avoid giving the impression that one's personal situation in life authorizes an individual to decide on the basis of historical circumstances and personal intentions about the basic moral goodness or badness of a particular action or course of action. To make this kind of compromise causes true theological scandal, for such bad counsel dissuades people from performing those actions whereby a person cleaves to God as the final perfection and blessedness of human life. To put it otherwise, an error about how circumstances direct moral decision-making shortcircuits the teleology that controls every moment of a Christian's life.

Virtue, Teleology, and Beatitude

The virtue of prudence is one of the four cardinal virtues that shape human actions; it ensures that our activity achieves an end perfective of the human person. The other moral virtues, justice, fortitude, and tem-

77. *Veritatis splendor*, no. 80.

perance, each influences a particular appetite of the human person. As the rounding off of natural law inclinations in us, prudence develops a *recta ratio* for making a complete and happy human life. The teaching reaches back to the earliest centuries of Christian teaching. For example, St. Ambrose observes: "First comes that which I may call the foundation of all, namely, that our passions should obey our reason."[78] In Christian practice, moral truth always coexists with the moral virtues.[79]

In a complete Christian life, all the virtues work toward the perfection of human flourishing and, if we consider the theological and infused virtues, *beatitudo*.[80] To include nature and natural law in Christian ethics does not make life-in-Christ an afterthought for Roman Catholic moral instruction. On the contrary, Jesus stands at the center of every Christian life. To those who remain united in friendship with him, Christ shows the Way, teaches the Truth, and communicates Life itself. These promises cash out into a life of virtue, which in turn gives the virtuous person a fuller comprehension of what the Scriptures teach about the moral life.

Moral virtue forms a good action according to reason in a given circumstance of one's life. Most immediately reason connotes human intelligence as the principle whereby we measure things, i.e., apprehend them according to a certain *ratio*. But is our intelligence, which measures things, itself independent of measure? Plainly not, since it in turn is measured by the reason, or reasons, in things, as when one asks, "What is the reason for the sun's coming up in the morning?" In response one posits some real cause, something in the nature of things, e.g., "The rotation of the earth on its axis is the reason, or cause, why the sun 'rises' daily." So for something to be "according to reason," it must be grasped as being ultimately according to the reason in things, in the nature of things. Conversely, when something is spoken of as against reason, one means, not only against the human capacity of that name, but fundamentally against the

78. See his *De officiis ministrorum* I, XXIV, 106.

79. In addition to the discussion in my *The Moral Virtues and Theological Ethics*, see the overview of the Christian moral virtues in my *Le Virtù*. Volume 19 of Manuali di Teologia Cattolica (AMATECA), Sezione sesta: *La persona umana* (Milan: Editoriale Jaca Book, 1994). English translation: *Virtues* (Münster: Lit Verlag, 2001).

80. For more on the suggested dichotomy between natural end and supernatural finality as it bears on theological ethics, see the essays by Marc Ouellet and Edward Oakes with replies by Russell Hittinger and Angelo Scola in "Discussion: The Foundations of Christian Ethics According to Hans Urs von Balthasar," *Communio* 17 (Fall 1990), pp. 375–438.

reason in nature and reality, i.e., the objective order, or reason, in nature which the mind grasps. Our human reason operates as a "measured measure" not only in speculative matters, but also, and especially, in practical reasoning.

The God-given created order of reality, how God knows the world to be, stands underneath the order that shapes moral reason. Since virtue is called by Aristotle and Aquinas a "*habitus* of acting according to reason,"[81] when something is "against reason," it is, in its most fundamental sense, against virtue too. Whence comes this law or order of nature which is the reason for things that measures the validity and correctness of human reason? It derives from the divine reason, the eternal law, an order set in things by God, their Creator. Hence when something is described as unvirtuous, this is synonymous with saying that it is against reason. To express it more fully, to act unvirtuously goes against the reason of God whose order placed in things constitutes nature, and is the reason or cause of their being and activity, and which reason, cause, or order, in things ultimately measures human reason.

Veritatis splendor provides an extended critique of what it calls teleological ethical views. To avoid confusion, it might have been better to use the English term "teleologistic," since "teleological" theories in fact reject the Church's teleological tradition in morals.[82] These views, the encyclical says, claim to look at the conformity of human acts with the personal objectives pursued by the doer or with the values that he or she intends. In other words, the measure of the moral act falls principally within the agent. The encyclical, on the other hand, points out the totality that exists in a properly defined moral object that both carries and embodies its own intelligibility independent of subjective considerations. A good human act, good according to its object, perfects a human person because it conforms to human nature. When the action is enacted in charity, the person enters, either for the first time or with greater intensity, into a communion of love with God. Here below, this communion subsists in the Church of Christ, whereas hereafter it becomes that beatific sharing in the divine nature which we call the communion of the saints.

Nominalist reductions of moral action can lead to mistakes about the pursuit of the good and of the ultimate good which is God. Certain mo-

---

81. See *Summa theologiae* Ia-IIae, q. 64, a. 1.

82. See especially no. 75; for further critique of "teleologistic" theories, see my "On Bad Actions, Good Intentions, and Loving God," 100–124, esp. at note 34.

ments in the modern period have illuminated the conceptual affinities between casuistry and nominalism. In the Church of seventeenth-century France, Blaise Pascal's *Fourth Provincial Letter* provides a good illustration of what happens when teachers of the moral life neglect its in-built teleology.

During the conflicts which arose between Jansenists and Jesuits, it seems that certain theologians had advanced the theory that for persons to incur guilt from sinful actions required that an extended set of subjective conditions be realized. In order to enlarge the ambit of personal freedom, some authors included among these conditions the requirement that a person consciously advert to the fact that a particular action actually stands directly opposed to God's law. To be held culpable, then, of even the grossest departures from the natural law meant that a person had to be informed completely of the sinful nature of the acts and advert to it. On the one hand, this outlook represents a certain apogee in extrinsicism, not to mention an excessive concern for establishing culpability; on the other hand, the frame of mind reveals a complete lack of appreciation for the intrinsically evil character of certain specific actions. To this obviously obfuscatory way of talking about practical morals, Pascal retorts to an imaginary clerical advocate of the non-advertence theory:

Blessings on your head, Father, for justifying people in this way! Others teach how to cure souls by painful austerities, but you show that the souls which one would have believed to be the most desperately ill are in the best of health. What an excellent path to happiness in this world and the next! I had always thought that the less one thought of God the more sinful one was. But, from what I can see, once one has managed to stop thinking of him altogether the purity of one's future conduct becomes assured. Let us have none of these half-sinners, with some love of virtue; they will all be damned. But as for these avowed sinners, hardened sinners, unadulterated, complete and absolute sinners, hell cannot hold them; they have cheated the devil by surrendering to him.[83]

In his essay, Pascal plays with a *reductio ad absurdum* in order to make the point that something beyond an analysis of personal subjectivity must enter into the moral meaning of a human act. These words from one of France's finest classical authors impress on us the need for objective moral

---

83. Pascal, IV *Provincial Letter*, trans. A. J. Krailsheimer (Baltimore: Penguin Books, 1967), p. 65.

criteria. In our own day, *Veritatis splendor* has outlined the proper criteria for determining moral behavior within a proper teleology.

Because of the truth about the good and the invitation to participate in it that Christ announces, Christian theology is able to include among the goods required for complete human flourishing the beatific vision of God. "Beatitude, in my opinion," writes Gregory of Nyssa, "is a possession of all things held to be good, from which nothing is absent that a good desire may want. Perhaps the meaning of beatitude may become clearer to us if it is compared with its opposite. Now the opposite of beatitude is misery. Misery means being afflicted unwillingly with painful suffering."[84] The face to face beholding of God's goodness alone fulfills the yearnings of human nature. As the Roman liturgy softly reminds us about heaven, "there we hope to enjoy the vision of your glory." And because heaven remains our vocation, every created thing which forms a basic human good requires integration in God in order to achieve its ultimate perfection.

The call to beatific fellowship with God implies that man possesses an openness to communion with God. The sacred Scriptures and the theological tradition of the Church refer to this capacity as man's being created in the image of God (*imago Dei*). Good moral theology must respect the ordering of the *imago Dei* to its God-given ends. Again Gregory of Nyssa: "He who paints our soul in the likeness of the only blessed One describes in words all that produces beatitude; and he says first: 'Blessed are the poor in spirit, because theirs in the Kingdom of Heaven.' "[85] To describe Aquinas's moral theory as teleological means nothing more than to identify it with this sort of Christian eudaimonism. Without due attention to the Sermon on the Mount, it is impossible to elaborate authentic Christian moral theology. Warrant for this assertion comes from the theological traditions of both East and West.

Moral theories which reject the notion that the human person achieves its perfection through freely accomplished virtuous actions are committed to developing models other than a realist teleological one to guide human behavior. Utilitarian consequentialism, to take an example which has its roots in the British moral tradition, judges morality somewhat math-

84. St. Gregory of Nyssa, *The Beatitudes*, Sermon 1, trans. Hilda C. Graef, *The Lord's Prayer. The Beatitudes* (Westminster, Md.: Newman Press, 1954), p. 88.

85. Sermon 1.

ematically on the basis of the overall good accomplished for the largest number. Kantian deontology, which is typical of continental schools of ethics, grounds moral judgments in the duty or obligation to follow a moral imperative which itself usually results from some *a priori* moral reasoning. Whatever contributions to Christian moral theology these schools of ethics can make, experience has shown that Christian moral realism best suits the requirements of the Catholic tradition. As the topics that will be addressed in this series reveal, Catholic moral theology is too much concerned with the concrete existent not to take its form seriously, e.g., the contents of safes, freshwater lake fishes, jewelry in Zurich's Bahnhofstrasse, fine cars like a Rolls Royce, etc.

Because Christian moral theology finds its beginning in God's own knowledge about himself, the eternal law gives a determinate and recognizable shape to the whole of Christian morality. Though Aquinas describes the natural law as a participation in this effective ruling design whereby God governs creation, his natural law theory enunciates a position quite different from the "Book of Nature" theories developed by Enlightenment thinkers. It was characteristic of many *Lumières* either to deny God altogether or to assume that the only trace left of him in the universe was to be found at its origins.

The English Dominican Thomas Gilby benefitted from the critique of modern thought that the nineteenth-century Leonine revival of Thomism introduced into European and other centers of learning. With an eye on the alternative proposals about morality that still dominated especially English intellectual circles, Gilby summarized under four headings what is distinctive about Thomist teaching on the nature of the moral good: First, moral good shares in the nature of the good, which is a transcendental property of being, *bonum*, and as such is described by nonmoral disciplines; second, that the moral good is reserved to a good-to-be-done, *bonum faciendum*; third, that the doing in this case is that of a self-directing agent, *ex voluntate deliberata*, and so concerned with choices; fourth, the moral good is held in the mind with evidence for its existence and nature, and according to a measure, norm, or law.[86] On the ba-

---

86. Thomas Gilby, O.P., *Principles of Morality*, p. 163. For personal and bibliographic information on Father Gilby, and background on the English Dominicans who formed him, see Aidan Nichols, O.P., *Dominican Gallery: Portrait of a Culture* (Leominster: Gracewing, 1997), pp. 184–222.

sis of this summary analysis of moral good, Gilby further observes that the moral law should be reasonable, a human reason reflecting the divine which is common and communicable, and manifest to those who keep it. Aquinas's view on this matter rests admittedly on an epistemological confidence about man's ability to grasp the natures of things. St. Thomas does not share the philosophical agnosticism about human nature common among post-Kantian thinkers.

Aquinas's realist moral theology supposes that human actions possess a specific moral form realized by the correct configuration of object, end, and circumstance, in a given action. These actions, in turn, qualify the acting person by the very fact that he or she deliberately performs them. In the case of evil actions, their minimum effect, in the case of those actions performed out of invincible ignorance or through a non-culpable error of judgment, establishes in the person "a disorder in relation to the truth about the good."[87] No more than a diet of rocks nourishes a healthy individual does a vicious action upbuild a happy person. While impaired voluntary or erroneous judgments of individual conscience may exculpate an individual from responsibility within the framework of an overly juridicized moral theology, neither factor can relieve the deleterious effect of bad actions. To take a practical example, a variety of factors may account for depreciated moral responsibility in the teenager who continually resorts to speaking lies of convenience, yet the impairment of the person's ability to develop mature human communication, not to mention a sense of adult responsibility, abides whether the youth recognizes it or not.

The moral thinking inspired by Aquinas and exemplified in *Veritatis splendor* represents a steady course between the Scylla of transcendental fundamental-option theories, which locate moral evaluation primarily in the subject's personal disposition toward God, and the Charybdis of consequentialist proportionate-reason theories, which measure moral goodness in terms of an overall calculation of a particular action's effects. Both approaches to gaining wisdom move the moral agent away from engagement with the real world. Their outlooks descend more from Platonic than from Aristotelian sources.

What really counts for a Platonist lies beyond the world of the sensible or the world of categorical moral objectives, in a world of pure intelligible forms. Confidence in the ability of the mind to shape reality and

---

87. See *Veritatis splendor*, no. 63.

to give any "meaning" whatsoever to concrete moral goods goes hand in hand with theories that appeal to "fundamental option." It remains a question whether these sorts of mental maneuvers in morality can provide a theoretical basis that supports the Christian call to perfection. The Magisterium warns that "fundamental option" theories can foster self-deception.[88] Even with a healthy confidence in the powers of human intelligence, it is difficult to estimate the projected results of an action that one is about to perform. Consequentialism, however, assumes that a person can make a prognostication about outcomes. The Magisterium, on the other hand, recognizes that an effort to engage in the calculation of foreseeable consequences can easily eclipse the absolute prohibition on mortal sin.[89]

The pragmatic spirit that drives compromise moral theologies should be evident to the person of sound moral experience. It is easy to see the expediency present in the effort to justify bad moral actions on the basis of the alleged beneficial results that may result from this or that action, or on the basis of distinguishing goodness in a person from rightness in human action. But *Veritatis splendor* encourages us in the face of difficult moral alternatives to find another kind of consolation. The encyclical recalls the witness of the Christian martyrs: "The unacceptability of 'teleological,' 'consequentialist' and 'proportionalist' ethical theories, which deny the existence of negative moral norms regarding specific kinds of behavior, norms which are valid without exception, is confirmed in a particularly eloquent way by Christian martyrdom, which has always accompanied and continues to accompany the life of the Church even today."[90]

If the graced development of the *imago Dei* constitutes an intrinsic perfection for the individual, serious questions arise from moral theories which base themselves primarily on such extrinsic factors as an action's likely results. Such speculations easily relativize the effect that a vicious action leaves on the character of the acting person. They also ignore the fundamental truth of Christian moral theology, namely, that the human

88. For example, *Veritatis splendor* warns that "the separation of fundamental option from deliberate choices of particular kinds of behavior, disordered in themselves or in their circumstances, which would not engage that option, thus involves a denial of Catholic doctrine on *mortal sin*" (no. 70).

89. For example, *Veritatis splendor*, see especially nos. 74–75, explains that some forms of consequentialism in present-day Roman Catholic theology deviate from a proper account of the 'sources of morality.'"

90. *Veritatis splendor*, no. 90.

act depends on its object, and on whether that object is capable or not of being ordered to God. The perfection of the person is never achieved outside of a proper ordering to the One who, as Jesus reminds the rich young man, "alone is good" (see Mt 19:17). Moralities of compromise finally betray a certain despair regarding the sanctification of persons, for they are less concerned with genuine human perfection than with conciliating circumstances which may do harm to our deepest personal reality as *imago Dei*.[91]

Actions that embrace good moral objects reflect the providential order within which God heals and elevates human nature. Whatever is healthful and perfective for human persons respects their common human nature and orders them toward its uplifted fulfillment in grace. The power of the Gospel affords the moral theologian good ground for hope that the impediments to truthful living, even when exacerbated by long-standing bad habits, may be overcome through the gradual growth of virtue, and that persons may be enabled through the gift of divine grace to experience a growing union with God. It is this destiny that *Veritatis splendor* envisages when it reminds us of the fundamental dynamics of the Christian life: "Love of God and of one's neighbor cannot be separated from the observance of the commandments of the Covenant renewed in the blood of Jesus Christ and in the gift of the Spirit."[92]

91. For a penetrating analysis of what went wrong in much pre-*Veritatis splendor* moral argument, see Russell Hittinger, "The Pope and the Theorists," *Crisis* (December 1993): 31–36.

92. *Veritatis splendor*, no. 76.

CHAPTER FIVE

The Life of Christian Virtue
and Freedom

Habitus and Virtues: Pattern of a Graced Life

From its earliest days, the Christian Church professed both to teach about a new way of life and to confer it on those who accepted the Gospel in faith.[1] Consider the practice of community life, as recorded in the Acts of the Apostles: "Now the company of those who believed were of one heart and soul, and no one said that any of the things which he possessed was his own, but they had everything in common" (Acts 4:32). An objective as noble and arduous as maintaining a common life tells us something important about the character of "those who believed." In any event, this and other signs of newness of life experienced by the first Christians testify to the efficacy of the salvation that Christ's death and the sending of the Holy Spirit introduced into the world. In short, the person saved by Christ is the person transformed in Christ.

To reveal the mystery of transformation, the New Testament rarely appeals to juridical concepts and language. Such metaphors are not helpful to express the offer of divine intimacy that Christ extends to his disciples. The New Testament instead chooses images such as the Vine and the Branches (Jn 15:1–11) or the Good Shepherd (Jn 10:11–18).[2] These par-

---

1. *Veritatis splendor*, no. 73, makes the point succinctly: "In Jesus Christ and in his Spirit, the Christian is a 'new creation,' a child of God; by his actions he shows his likeness or unlikeness to the image of the Son who is the first-born among many brethren (cf. Rom 8:29), he lives out his fidelity or infidelity to the gift of the Spirit, and he opens or closes himself to eternal life, to the communion of vision, love and happiness with God the Father, Son, and Holy Spirit." For an interesting study of how St. Paul treats the new way of life, see J. Paul Sampley, *Walking between the Times: Paul's Moral Reasoning* (Minneapolis: Fortress Press, 1991). Also, George T. Montague, *Growth in Christ. A Study in Saint Paul's Theology of Progress* (Kirkwood, Mo.: Maryhurst Press, 1961).

2. In the post-synodal Apostolic Exhortation *On Reconciliation and Penance*, the Holy

ables remind us that Christian transformation is a work that depends on the believer's union with the divine person of Jesus himself. At the same time, the text from Acts makes it clear that the Church announces not only a transformation of persons, but also the formation of a communion of persons.

The Example of St. Benedict

In the sixth century, we see the grace of both personal transformation and communion of persons illustrated in the work of Benedict of Nursia, who adapted a form of community life by then already several centuries old in the East to the specific requirements of Western Christianity. His example remains the first in a long history of initiatives in the Western Church that propose a specific rule or way of life aimed at helping men and women achieve evangelical perfection. The moral theologian takes special interest in the language of virtue found in the *Rule* ascribed to the man we now venerate as Saint Benedict. Among other objectives, his use of language confirms that the archetypical spiritual tradition that springs from Benedictine life associates the practice of virtue with the realization of authentic Christian freedom.[3]

In his *Rule*, St. Benedict explains how the development of virtue first requires the practice of humility. He then goes on to affirm that the love of God shapes the character of the monk, making him a kind of "workman" in whom the Holy Spirit can, as it were, move about freely.

Now therefore after ascending all these steps of humility, the monk will quickly arrive at the "perfect love" of God which "casts out fear" (1 Jn 4:18). Through this love all that he once performed with dread he will now begin to observe without effort, as though naturally, from habit, no longer out of fear of hell, but out of love for Christ, good habit and delight in virtue. All this the Lord will by the Holy Spirit graciously manifest in his workman now cleansed of vices and sins.[4]

St. Benedict directs his monks toward the practice of the virtues and away from involvement in vice. He further offers them a description of

---

Father himself reminds us that even the sense of sin itself can disappear as a result of wrongly identifying it with a morbid feeling of guilt or "with the mere transgression of legal norms and precepts" (no. 18).

3. For a thorough technical discussion of the *Rule*, see the six-volume Sources Chrétiennes edition by Adalbert de Vogüé, *La règle de Saint Benoît* (Paris: Cerf, 1971–72).

4. *Rule of St. Benedict*, c. 7, 67–70.

Christian life that can be lived in perfect love and without fear of reprisal for failure caused by weakness, provided of course that a man remain dedicated to the monastic way of life.

As a Christian teacher, St. Benedict instructs about those virtues that come directly from God, but his description of how virtue works would also apply to the acquired or human virtues. The important point that we learn from St. Benedict is that the virtues are the means whereby the Christian believer is transformed and made into an active image of God. This example is of more than just historical interest, for proponents of a realist moral theology still describe the Christian life as a pattern of virtuous habits or dispositions that manifests itself in good works.[5]

By encouraging the practice of virtue, St. Benedict clearly did not intend to exempt his monks from observing the Commandments. On the contrary, by reminding them that the Christian life consists principally in "good habit and delight in virtue," he encouraged them to live in conformity with the law of Christ. At the same time, he reassured them with the promise of good *habitus* and delight in acting. In other words, he pointed immediately to what constitutes the internal state of the virtuous person, not to the norms that direct right conduct.

Obedience should result in joyful conformity, not dour submission. This theme emerges as a dominant one in the Christian moral tradition. For example, in commenting on the psalm verse "Let them exult and rejoice" (Ps 35:27), Aquinas observes that "the fruit of the saints is enjoyment because 'delight' expresses 'dilatation' of the heart and so signifies that joy is interior."[6] Just as action flows from being *(agere sequitur esse)*, Christian justification first creates a joyful heart conformed to God, and from this kind of person flow the works of justice and sanctification. For the Christian believer, the practice of a virtuous life increasingly becomes labor without toil.

---

5. *Veritatis splendor*, no. 73, quotes from St. Cyril of Alexandria, *Tractatus ad Tiberium Diaconum sociosque*, II: "Christ 'forms us according to his image, in such a way that through sanctification and justice and the life which is good and in conformity with virtue.... The beauty of this image shines forth in us who are in Christ, when we show ourselves to be good in our works.'"

6. *Postilla super Psalmos* 34 [35]: 27 (Parma edition, 14:276). In this text, Aquinas sees *laetitia* as expressing the *latitudo* of the heart, a play on words that approximates "delight" and "dilatation." For further discussion of the affective dimensions of Aquinas's writings, see Walter H. Principe, *Thomas Aquinas' Spirituality*, Etienne Gilson Series, no. 7 (Toronto: Pontifical Institute of Mediaeval Studies, 1984).

To put this conception of the Christian life into contemporary categories, one could argue that St. Benedict proposes a moral theology that aims to reveal the "newness of life" that Christ makes available to his members (see Rom 6:4). It is impossible to specify the kind of life this gift produces in the believer without first giving a full account of those interior dispositions of the human person that supply the immediate sources of both doing the good deed and making the right decisions. This preliminary step is required because an adequate moral theology must render an account of what shapes the personal powers from which human behavior flows. To put it otherwise, moral theology must explain what causes a person "to grasp the beauty and attraction of right dispositions toward goodness."[7] This means that the moral theologian cannot rest content with providing only directions for human actions. Recall what St. Benedict in fact promised to those in whom perfect love had cast out all fear. Without an account of what shapes the powers/ capacities/ dispositions from which all human action flows, it would make no sense to promise "good habit and delight in virtue." What is important for our purposes, the Church in her moral catechesis still makes this promise to those who follow the way of Christ.

The patristic and medieval traditions developed St. Benedict's teaching. Although the history of moral theology involves many complexities, it is fair to say that the foundational theologians of Western Christianity present the Christian moral and spiritual life as an exercise of the human and Christian virtues.[8] St. Thomas Aquinas is one of the best guides to show how the virtues and the gifts of the Holy Spirit accord with the life of freedom and grace that leads to beatitude. The following discussion follows the general outline of his presentation of the moral life found in the *Summa theologiae*, and developed afterwards in the commentatorial tradition.

What Is a Virtue?

Since in the *Summa theologiae* he follows a method of discovery, Aquinas takes up the standard definition of virtue handed down in the textbooks of moral theology used in the Middle Ages: "Virtue is a good quality of

7. *Catechism of the Catholic Church*, no. 1967.

8. For one of the few histories of moral theology available in English, see Servais Pinckaers, *The Sources of Christian Ethics*, Part Two, "A Brief History of Moral Theology," pp. 191–323.

mind, by which one lives righteously, of which no one can make bad use, and which God works in us without us."[9] This definition still governs the Church's presentation of virtue, and so several of its elements warrant close attention and further explanation.

To explain these elements, Aquinas relies on the four causes that Aristotle employs when he wants to render a full account of a given reality. A cause is that from which something proceeds with dependence in being. Aquinas adapts the four causes of classic philosophy as a tool to explain what a virtue is. His analysis runs as follows:

First, the formal cause: "Virtue is a good quality of mind." Virtue belongs to the generic category of quality, specifically that quality which we call a *habitus*. As a philosophical notion, *habitus* signifies the perfection or adaptation of a human capacity so that it functions well. The *habitus* of virtue affect the psychological resources for action.[10] Today, the *Catechism of the Catholic Church* sets forth this teaching in the following language: "The virtuous person tends toward the good with all his sensory and spiritual powers; he pursues the good and chooses it in concrete actions."[11] Unfortunately, in modern English the term, "habit," carries connotations of boring routine and uncreative predictability. Virtue, on the other hand, provides a source of intelligently creative activity. In order to avoid creating the wrong impression, sound theological usage retains the Latin *habitus bonus* to describe the internal state of an individual whose actions are maximally conformed to the good of the human person.

Second, the material cause. Since virtues represent a kind of moral or spiritual reality, there is nothing material in them to serve as a cause of their being. Instead, it is customary to designate the capacities that the virtues modify as their "material cause." These are the interior powers of the human person that form the immediate sources of human action. As possible seats for virtue, these capacities are identical with the human powers of the rational soul: intellect, will or rational appetite, and also the sense appetites.[12] Human nature alone does not suffice to cause virtue;

9. See *Summa theologiae* Ia-IIae, q. 55, a. 4.

10. For a long-forgotten but still useful study on the notion of *habitus* in the Christian life, see Placide de Roton, O.S.B., *Les Habitus. Leur Caractère spirituel* (Paris: Labergerie, 1934), pp. 149–63.

11. *Catechism of the Catholic Church*, no. 1803.

12. The sense appetites correspond to what the *Catechism of the Catholic Church* calls the sensory powers. In these pages, the appetites are sometimes referred to as passions and emotions. The sense appetites are distinguished between impulse or concupiscible and

rather, acquired virtue develops by some deliberate exercise of those operative capacities or powers (i.e., intellect, will, sense appetites) that in turn become the seat or subject of different virtues. To cite only the cardinal moral virtues, prudence shapes the intellect, justice the will, and fortitude and temperance the sense appetites.

Third, the efficient cause: "which God works in us without us." Though human actions develop natural *habitus*, there exist virtues that are gifts of divine grace received directly from God, as from an efficient cause. Because their origin and development depend on the divine agency, we call these virtues infused instead of acquired. These are the Christian virtues that cannot exist apart from grace. While moral theology is principally concerned with the workings of divine grace, it also recognizes that even the human virtues dispose the powers of the human being for communion with divine love.

Fourth, the final cause: "by which one lives righteously, of which no one can make bad use." Because the final cause of virtue is the performance of the virtuous action itself, virtue is designated an operative *habitus*. The exercise of virtue results in the virtuous person acting so as always to embrace the true good.[13] It is impossible, however, to include every moral good in the definition of virtue, so a generic formulation, e.g., righteousness, is used to signal that the general character of virtue includes the realization of all moral goodness. This moral goodness concerns the whole universe of moral objects, including that supreme Object of all human pursuit and energy, who is God. As Gregory of Nyssa teaches, the goal of a virtuous life is to become like God.[14]

From this brief analysis, we can see that the moral and theological virtues are defined as good operative *habitus*. This means that each virtue represents a good quality of human character that renders both the person who possesses the *habitus* and his or her actions thoroughly good. The goodness of the action is determined by the fact that the virtues are "in harmony with the true good of the person."[15] In Aquinas's short-

---

contending or irascible, depending on whether they serve to impel the creature toward sense goods or steady the creature against sense dangers.

13. Some philosophers dispute this claim, arguing that fortitude can be put at the service of assault and plundering, but A. Chadwick Ray, "A Fact about the Virtues," *The Thomist* 54 (1990): 429–51, offers a convincing explanation that supports the no-bad-use theory that Aquinas and others held to be the case.

14. See his *De beatitudinibus*, 1 (PG 44, 1200 D).

15. *Veritatis splendor*, nos. 72–73, emphasizes this teleology as well as the "newness"

hand, virtuous actions always move the person *ad finem,* toward the proper ends of the human person. Since we now are concerned mainly with the Christian virtues, this good end is identified with the beatitude of heaven, which sets the standard for discernment about the goods of the present life.

End, not environment, dominates the realist moral life.[16] For the Christian believer, these ends find their perfection only in the vision of God, the Ultimate End of all human activity. Both the ultimate and penultimate ends enter into the constitution of our moral actions. The difference between virtue and vice lies precisely in this ordering to an end.[17] Bad moral *habitus,* or what we call vices, lack conformity with the good and put us in conflict with our ultimate end. On the other hand, good moral *habitus* or virtues respect the proper purpose of a human power or capacity. Virtue ensures the conformity of a concrete action with the human good. This conduces to happiness and at the same time ensures a person's ability to act well with joy, promptness, and facility. The virtues shape all of our spiri-

---

which characterizes the morality of a Christian's actions. In his 1962 article "Virtue Is Not a Habit," *Cross Currents* 12 (1962): 65–81, Servais Pinckaers recalled this important theme in moral theology. Virtue, he remarks, constitutes a constant disposition in the self for choosing the good ends of human flourishing. "The psychological modification in the subject's soul-capacities *(potentiae animae)* accounts for the promptness and facility of action which the virtuous person displays in the performance of the good deed. As a result, virtue also produces a spiritual joy. For these reasons, the individual's creative powers are actually heightened by the development of virtue rather than restricted. On the other hand, vice crimps the soul. There are a thousand ways to do good creatively, but only one way to act viciously, even if it takes a variety of forms." He later developed this insight in his *Sources of Christian Ethics.* For another presentation, see my *The Moral Virtues and Theological Ethics,* esp. chap. 2.

16. See again A. Chadwick Ray, "A Fact about the Virtues," for a good rebuttal to those who claim that the formal characteristics of virtue alone suffice to instantiate an authentic *habitus.* Ray challenges the supposition that the bravery of the rapist or the cunning of the thief constitute real virtues, on the basis of virtue's relation to "end."

17. Aquinas makes this principle the grounds for his insistence on the distinction between the infused and the acquired virtues. In the *De virtutibus in communi,* we find: "Just as our first perfection, which is the rational soul, exceeds the power of corporeal matter, so the ultimate perfection which man can attain, which is the blessedness of eternal life, exceeds the powers of the whole of human nature. And since each thing is ordered to reach its end by some operation, and since the means must be in some manner proportionate to the end, of necessity there must be in man certain perfections whereby he may be ordered to his supernatural end, and these perfections must surpass the power of man's natural principles. Now this cannot be, unless certain supernatural principles of operation be infused into man by God, *over and above man's natural powers of action.*"

tual and sensory powers so that they are ready to embrace those virtuous ends that compose the true human good.

Not every virtue transforms the whole person. In fact, we distinguish the moral virtues from the intellectual virtues on the basis of a virtue's ability to perfect the whole person. Intellectual virtues, such as geometry or culinary arts, enable the one who possesses them to think productively or to make something well, but they do not ensure that the whole person as well as the actions of the person become good. One can encounter a gluttonous geometrician or cheating chef. On the other hand, the moral virtues, organized around the cardinal virtues of prudence, justice, fortitude, and temperance, perfect the whole person, so that he or she possesses a steady and firm disposition to do good in particular circumstances. The moral virtues guide our conduct in accordance with reason and faith.

We also distinguish both the moral and intellectual virtues from the theological virtues of faith, hope, and charity. God alone specifies the theological virtues: He is first Truth for faith; he is my highest Good for hope; he is the highest Good in himself for charity. This means that the theological virtues have the One and triune God for their origin, motive, and end. The theological virtues "dispose Christians to live in a relationship with the Holy Trinity."[18] As such, the theological virtues exist only as a result of God's freely bestowed grace; although prayer disposes us for them, nothing that we ourselves do in fact acquires them. Because the theological virtues inform and give life to all the moral virtues, there is never a question of living the infused virtues apart from faith, hope, and charity.[19]

Infused Virtues

Christian virtue shapes the life of a believer who is set on the path to beatitude. Aquinas explains God's special action in the virtuous life by enumerating the divine benefactions that come to the person with the presence and action of the Holy Spirit:

There is infused into us by God, to enable us to perform acts ordered to eternal life as their end: first grace, which gives the soul a certain spiritual or divine being; and then, faith, hope, and charity. By faith the mind is enlightened concerning supernatural truths, which in their order stand as do principles

18. *Catechism of the Catholic Church*, no. 1812.
19. For a discussion of the seven virtues of the Christian life, see my *Virtues*.

naturally known in the order of natural actions. By hope and charity the will acquires an inclination to the supernatural good to which the human will, by its own natural operations, is not adequately ordered.

Besides the natural principles which a man has, for his perfection in the order natural to him, a man needs virtuous habits.... So also, besides the aforesaid supernatural principles, man is endowed by God with certain infused virtues which perfect him in the ordering of his actions to their end, which is eternal life.[20]

The expression "infused virtue" means that God directly bestows this virtue on us as a free gift of divine grace. Infused virtues afford the moral theologian a way of speaking concretely about divine grace at work in the moral life of the Christian believer, without capitulating to extrinsicism.

The universal call to holiness determines the reason for the existence of the infused virtues. Because we need a special psychological conformity to eternal life, charity and faith by themselves do not suffice to elevate fully our moral life to one set fully upon God. In other words, we must learn to love God with our whole being. As the Letter to the Philippians puts it: "Fill your minds with everything that is true, everything that is noble, everything that is good and pure, everything that we love and honor, and everything that can be thought virtuous or worthy of praise" (Phil 4:8). To help them observe this precept, Saint Ignatius of Loyola taught his followers to make frequently a particular examination of conscience.

The infused virtues describe the kind of life which is proper to the City of God, the heavenly city of grace.[21] In another text, Aquinas further explains what he considers a person's need for both the acquired and infused virtues.

One who is some distance from an end can know the end and desire it; however, he cannot engage in activity which directly concerns the end, but only in that which is connected with the means to the end. Therefore, if we are to reach our supernatural end, we need faith in this life to know the end, for natural knowledge does not go that far. But our natural powers do extend the means to the end, although not precisely as ordained to that end. Therefore,

20. *De virtutibus in communi*, q. 1, a. 10. For a discussion of the virtue of faith, see my *Christian Faith and the Theological Life*.

21. See R. Bernard, O.P., in his Éditions de la Revue des jeunes commentary on *Summa theologiae* Ia-IIae, qq. 61–70, in *La Vertu*, vol. II (Paris: Desclée & Cie, 1935), esp. Appendix II, "La vertu acquise et la vertu infuse," pp. 434ff.

we do not need infused habits for any other activity than that which natural reason dictates, but just for a more perfect performance of the same activity. However, this is not the case with knowledge, for the reason given above.[22]

This means that the infused moral virtues provide a safer and surer performance of the same action, even though acquired and infused virtue produce the same action materially considered, to wit, to moderate the impulse emotions or to bolster the contending emotions.

Theologians have reflected on the difference between the acquired and infused virtues. For example, the Thomist school reduces this difference to three categories: (1) their cause; (2) their relation to an end; (3) their formal object. The difference between the infused and acquired virtues in relation to both their cause and their end is the same for all the virtues. In short, this difference means that God abides as both the origin and the goal of any infused virtue, whereas neither need be the case for the acquired virtues. Christian virtue produces in the believer the unity of faith and knowledge about Jesus Christ, making him or her live according to "the measure of the stature of the fullness of Christ" (Eph 4:13). A formal object expresses the distinguishing constitutive element of the virtue. Because the infused virtue operates according to a higher principle, namely, according to a divine measure—*secundum regulam divinam*—an infused virtue differs formally from its acquired counterpart.[23] The difference in formal object is realized one way in justice. For justice and its allied virtues, a new formal object even changes the very stuff which justice transforms, or as the Second Vatican Council expresses it, "the material of the heavenly Kingdom."[24] The virtues of the passions work differently. When it comes to the virtues of personal discipline, temperance and fortitude, the activity itself of the acquired and infused virtues—the passions tempered or bolstered, sustained or strengthened—remains the same. But the virtuous conduct still differs formally in the same way that the athlete-in-training differs from the Lenten penitent or the martyr differs from the soldier of fortune.[25]

22. *De veritate*, q. 14, a. 10.

23. Special attention should be paid to *Summa theologiae* Ia-IIae, q. 91, a. 4, ad 1, which discusses the relationship between natural law and divine positive law as distinct participations in the *lex aeterna*.

24. See *Gaudium et spes*, no. 38.

25. The infused virtues form part of the supernatural organism which makes up the Christian life. But virtue does not mean determinism. Stanley Hauerwas, *Character and*

As an innovator in moral realism, Aquinas adopted the position that infused virtue shapes even our sense powers of soul, what are known as the irascible or contending appetites and the concupiscible or impulse appetites. His anthropological and psychological suppositions led him both to perceive and to defend this holistic view of the human person as transformed by grace. For according to his conception, the several capacities or powers of the rational soul *(potentiae animae)* all belong to a single subject, which we denominate the acting person. In other terms, Aquinas remained convinced that moral truth can affect every aspect of our personality, "just as it is better for someone both to will the good and to do it by an external act, so it also belongs to perfect moral good that we be moved toward the good not only through our will but also through our sense appetites, according to the saying of Psalm 83:3: 'My heart and my flesh have rejoiced in the living God.'"[26]

St. Bonaventure, on the other hand, hesitated to believe that infused virtue could abide in the same powers or capacities as disordered sense urges, which he identified with human concupiscence. For concupiscence stands as an effect of original sin, the primal alienation of the human person from God, whereas Christian virtue comes only as a free gift from God. Accordingly, St. Bonaventure and the tradition that followed him explained infused temperance and fortitude as dispositions of the will that influence only indirectly the lower passions. Even today, St. Bonaventure could bolster his position by appeal to a wide sampling of human experience that seems to support the view that, in the end, human passions are at best restrained, but never really transformed.

Aristotle remarked on the unruly character of sexual urges in the human person; he opined that they possess a life of their own. And St. Paul, referring to all the movement of our appetites, registered a similar view concerning the power that the "law of the members" exercises in our lives (cf. Rom 7:23, 24). Aquinas had read both Aristotle and Saint Paul. But his deep penetration of the mystery of the Christian life led him nonetheless to affirm that the infused virtues are able actually and directly to affect the sense appetites. In other terms, Aquinas understood that the

---

the Christian Life: A Study in Theological Ethics (San Antonio: Trinity University Press, 1975), for instance, emphasizes virtue-development as a way to counteract various forms of social determinism. In his judgment, virtue underscores the role of freedom as an indispensable quality of the human person within the human community.

26. *Summa theologiae* Ia-IIae, q. 24, a. 3.

infused virtues conform the unruly sense appetites to the law of reason. Sense appetites form a natural part of human life and well-being. For Aquinas both acquired and infused virtues bring about the ordering of the emotions or passions by what he calls the "impression of reason" on the appetites.[27]

This opinion about the place of the infused virtues in the sense powers of the soul reflects Aquinas's profoundly meditative understanding of the Incarnation, and his application of Christology to the moral life. One discovers the infused virtues preeminently in the human nature of Christ, who, though he had full, strong, human passions or emotions, always acted virtuously. Because his human powers remained rightly ordered by an internal principle, Christ lived virtues of moderation and strengthening that were perfect in their formation.[28] The capital grace of Christ explains how the created graces that Christ himself possesses flow into those who are united with him in the Church.[29] Aquinas defended a strong version of the theory of infused virtues so that he would have a theological medium to explain the influence that the person of Jesus Christ exercises on Christian believers.

The infused virtues of temperance and fortitude are not the same thing as dispositions of continence and perseverance. Christian virtue promises more than enabling a person to enact a willed enforcement of moderation in face of attractive things and strengthening in the face of harmful ones. Virtue accomplishes more than effecting a simple truce between unruly passions and the imperatives of a duly informed will. The voluntarist opinion that the human will alone achieves all virtuous behavior possesses a distinctive disadvantage inasmuch as it holds out grim prospects for achieving harmony between reason and the affective life. Moreover, if we view the infused virtues as heroic exercises of will power, we ignore a fundamental truth concerning human sense appetite, namely, that the lower appetites are born to obey reason.[30]

Just as the bad angels lost by their sin nothing of their superior natural

---

27. *Summa theologiae* Ia-IIae, q. 60, a. 1.

28. See *Summa theologiae* IIIa, q. 15, a. 2.

29. For further discussion, see *Summa theologiae* IIIa, q. 8, "The Grace of Christ as Head of the Church."

30. See *Summa theologiae* IIIa, q. 15, a. 2, ad 1. For an interesting study of some contemporary questions raised by this teaching, see John R. Bowlin, "Psychology and Theodicy in Aquinas," *Medieval Philosophy and Theology* 7 (1998): 129–56.

abilities, so vicious *habitus* lose nothing of their psychological force simply because their energies are directed toward disordered ends. The vices, then, exemplify disordered *habitus*, i.e., *habitus malus*, which incorporate patterns of behavior that go against the good of the human person, and so disfigure the image of God. There is a difference, however, between how virtue builds up and vice tears down. The practice of virtue develops a sound and integrated human character, whereas the steady pursuit of vices reduces the self to a disorganized state of potential. But for the Christian believer, even a state of habitual vice does not invite despair. The promise of the Gospel still holds true that where sin abounds, grace abounds the more (see Rom 5:20).

The infused virtues belong to a Christ-centered life of faith, hope, and charity. For the Christian believer, this desire to embrace a virtuous life is realized only within the context of living by faith in Christ. "He is not weak in dealing with you, but is powerful in you" (2 Cor 13:3). In one who believes in him, Christ supplies the full measure of virtue, "for he was crucified in weakness, but lives by the power of God" (2 Cor 13:4). The renewal that Christian virtue accomplishes in a person never represses sense urges, but rather orders them according to the mind of Christ. This ordering occurs as a promised work of grace that overcomes whatsoever indisposition may exist in a person. The power of Christ sent into our lives by the Holy Spirit means that no human limitation, including those rooted in the emotions, is able to frustrate definitively a Christian's growth in holiness.

A life of virtue results in full and perfect accomplishment of the moral law. Because virtue moves us from within, it establishes a harmony between ourselves and the true human goods that compose an authentic moral life. In the Christian believer, we can properly ascribe this harmonization to the work of the Holy Spirit. The old law restrained only the hand, but the new law changes hearts. Aquinas emphasizes this point when he affirms that the whole power of the new law lies in the grace of the Holy Spirit. Those whom the Holy Spirit empowers to unite themselves with Christ in the face of any moral crisis—for example, by repeating his holy name, Jesus—receive a sweeter anointing from on high than what Moses received on Mount Sinai. This brief summary of the virtues leads us to consider their companion graces, the gifts of the Holy Spirit.

The Gifts of the Holy Spirit:
Guides for the Moral Life

Warrant for including the gifts of the Holy Spirit in an account of the Christian moral life is found within the pages of the New Testament itself.[31] For example, in taking leave of his disciples, Jesus told them, "It is good for you that I go away; for if I do not go away, the Paraclete will not come to you; but if I go, I will send him to you" (Jn 16:7). Theological reflection concerning the status, function, and purpose of the gifts of the Holy Spirit articulates the precise nature of this promised divine aid. According to a standard account, these gifts shape the personal psychology of Christian believers so that they can respond positively to those *instinctus* or inspirations that the theological tradition customarily ascribes to the Holy Spirit.[32] In other terms, the gifts round out the exercise of the moral and theological virtues in the daily experiences of the Christian life, making the moral agent more and more amenable to learn and receive moral truth. Since the gifts proceed from the Holy Spirit, the Person of love, as an active principle, they introduce a note of receptivity and even passivity into the rhythms of Christian life. The Christian Gospel requires attention to the most particular circumstances of human life, and so these gifts attend the ordinary living out of the Christian moral life.

Although moral theology in general develops under the guidance of the Holy Spirit, the Christian tradition additionally specifies certain gifts of the Spirit that concretely guide the Christian believer. To borrow Aquinas's lapidary formula, these gifts complete and perfect the virtuous life.[33] That is, they represent seven distinct ways in which the individual believer receives divine impulses or movements that assist him or her to perform specific kinds of virtuous activity. According to their traditional enumeration, the seven gifts of the Holy Spirit are wisdom, understanding, counsel, fortitude, knowledge, piety, and fear of the Lord.[34]

31. Servais Pinckaers explains this kind of scriptural reading in "The Use of Scripture and the Renewal of Moral Theology: The *Catechism* and *Veritatis splendor*," *The Thomist* 59 (1995): 1–19.

32. For a discussion of this central notion in the theology of the gifts, see Servais Pinckaers, "L'instinct et l'Esprit au coeur de l'éthique chrétienne," in *Novitas et Veritas Vitae. Aux Sources du Renouveau de la Morale Chrétienne. Mélanges offerts au Professeur Servais Pinckaers à l'occasion de son 65e anniversaire*, ed. Carlos-Josaphat Pinto de Olivera (Paris: Editions du Cerf, 1991), pp. 213–23, as well as *Sources of Christian Ethics*, esp. 151–55.

33. See *Summa theologiae* Ia-IIae, q. 68, a. 8.

34. See *Catechism of the Catholic Church*, no. 1831.

To grasp what role they play, it will be useful to review Aquinas's general teaching on the gifts.[35] Taking his cue from Scripture's own way of speaking, Aquinas observes that the sacred texts use the term "spirit" to designate what the theologians call a gift. By underscoring the inherent connection between *spiritus* and *motus*, Aquinas is able to define the gifts as habitual dispositions in the believer to receive special divine inspirations or promptings that surpass the basically human mode of activity established by the virtues.

Based on patristic exegesis of the qualities that Isaiah the prophet ascribed to the Messiah (see Is 11:1–2), the early medieval theologians developed a general theology of the gifts of the Holy Spirit. These same theologians held differing views both about how to distinguish a gift from a virtue and about how to distinguish the seven gifts among themselves. Aquinas defines the gifts as those dispositions in believers that dispose them to receive divine inspirations by which they can act beyond the mode of virtue.[36] By "mode of virtue," is understood the human mode of right reasoning that prudence institutes for each virtuous action. One sentence from Aquinas summarizes his teaching about the difference between a virtue and gift: "The gifts perfect the powers of the soul in regard to the Holy Spirit as moving principle, whereas the virtues perfect either reason itself, or the other capacities as subordinate to reason."[37] In other words, the doctrine of the gifts confirms that believers possess immediate sources of inspiration that allow them to surpass the ordinary mode of human reasoning in moral matters.

According to the seventeenth-century Thomist commentator known as John of St. Thomas, the new mode of gift-activity produces some startling outcomes in the Christian life.[38] For example, he argues that once a virtuous act comes under the influence of the gifts, the action acquires an entirely new moral character or species. In other words, we are talking about a new kind of action. Such a startling evaluation depends on the

---

35. A foundational text is found in *Summa theologiae* Ia-IIae, q. 68. A version of this overview of the Thomist teaching on the gifts also appears in my *Christian Faith*, pp. 159–69.

36. See *Summa theologiae* Ia-IIae, q. 68, a. 1.

37. *Summa theologiae* Ia-IIae, q. 68, a. 8.

38. John Poinsot (1589–1644), better known as John of St. Thomas, represents the best theological traditions of seventeenth-century Spain. Thomas Merton expresses an appreciation of this Dominican's spiritual theology in *The Ascent to Truth* (New York: Harcourt Brace Jovanovich, 1951), pp. 208–16.

unique regulatory principle that governs the working of the gifts. In order to illustrate how diverse modes of activity can work on the same material action, one can imagine a boat moved both by the rowing of oarsmen and by the force of the wind:

This interior illumination, this experiential taste of divine things and of other mysteries of the faith, excites our affections so that they tend to the object of virtue by a higher mode than these very same ordinary virtues do themselves. This happens to the extent that our affections obey a rule and measure dependent upon higher realities, viz., that interior prompting (*instinctus*) of the Holy Spirit—according to the rule of faith—and his illumination. As a result, the gifts effect a different kind of moral action, that is, they establish a distinctive moral specification; indeed we are led to a divine and supernatural end by a mode that differs from the rule formed by our own efforts and labors (even in the case of infused virtue), that is, one formed and founded upon the rule of the Holy Spirit. In a similar way, the work of oarsmen moves a ship differently than the wind does, even if the waves waft it toward the same port.[39]

The illustration employs the example of two categorical causes, viz., oarsmen and wind, to explain two *modes* of a single divine activity in the person: a human mode, when the infused and theological virtues remain under the direction of our own ingenuity and resources, and a supra-human mode, when the same virtues come under the influence of the gifts. Because the gifts, by definition, do not figure in the case of one who only exercises the acquired virtues in a strictly human way, the text does not envisage two competing causal agents, one from human agency and the other from divine.[40]

Common experience supports the distinction between wind and oars.

39. *Cursus Theologicus*, Disp. XVIII, a. 2, n. 29: "Ex ista autem interiori illustratione, et experimentali gustu divinorum, et aliorum mysteriorum fidei, inflammatur affectus ad hoc ut altiori modo tendat ad objecta virtutum, quam per ipsasmet ordinarias virtutes, quatenus sequitur regulationem, et mensurationem altiorem, scilicet ipsum instinctum interiorem Spiritus sancti juxta regulas fidei, et illustrationum [sic] ejus. Et sic diversam moralitatem ponit, et diversam specificationem, diverso quippe modo ducimur ad finem divinum, et supernaturalem ex regulatione formata nostro studio, et labore, etiam si virtus infusa sit, vel formata, et fundata in regulatione, et mensuratione Spiritus sancti, sicut diverso modo ducitur navis labore remigantium, vel a vento implente vela, licet ad eumdem terminum per undas tendat."

40. Some may find the example reminiscent of Luis de Molina (1535–1600) and his memorable, though misleading, metaphor for the concurrence of divine and human causality in a work of grace.

As the evident contrasts in fervor among the members of the Church makes clear, each justified believer retains the capacity to direct the progress even of his or her supernatural life. In some persons, human reason remains the dominant directive rule or measure for the virtues, even for the infused moral and theological virtues. However in other persons, the Holy Spirit, like a prompter on a theatrical set, inspires a virtuous action in accord with a measure that surpasses that of human reason. A good example may be found in the different ways that people devote themselves to prayer: some fulfill what is required by the commandments, whereas others are prompted to give themselves over with greater intensity and for longer periods to the practice of divine communication. No human explanation explains fully why one person prays more than another. The only answer lies in the divine beneficence and the inscrutable designs of divine providence.

Because Christ promises the Paraclete to every believer, each one of us requires the gifts of the Holy Spirit in order that the virtuous Christian life might achieve its full flourishing.[41] In order wholly to appreciate the role of the gifts, we must recall that no adequate proportion exists between human nature and the goal of beatific fellowship with God. As we learn from everyday experience, even Christians engage in the pursuit of created goods that are proportionate to them more easily than they aspire to divine realities. "And so the moving of reason is not sufficient," affirms Aquinas, "to direct us to our ultimate and supernatural end without the prompting and moving of the Holy Spirit from above."[42] To put it differently, we cannot take heaven for granted, as if a life of communication with the Blessed Trinity were something as akin to us as eating, drinking, or playing.

The case made for the necessity of the gifts may strike the one who hears it for the first time as far-fetched. Indeed, it is bold to assert that faith and grace itself do not ensure that Christians will use these divine gifts in a way that moves them evenly toward beatitude. Only the magnitude of heavenly bliss makes sense out of the need for additional divine aids to reach it. Aquinas further explains that the gifts of the Holy Spirit

41. For a brief, but comprehensive, treatment of how Aquinas understands the importance of the Holy Spirit in the Christian life, see Luc-Thomas Somme, O.P., "La rôle du Saint-Esprit dans la vie chrétienne, selon saint Thomas d'Aquin," *Sedes Sapientiae* 26 (1988), pp. 11–29, and his developed work, *Fils adoptifs de Dieu par Jésus Christ* (Paris: Librarie Philosophique J. Vrin, 1997).

42. *Summa theologiae* Ia-IIae, q. 68, a. 2.

subject our everyday human activity to the promptings of divine inspiration. The gifts conform our human thoughts to the "supra-rational" or "supra-sensible" mode of operation that God alone can inspire. As Advocate and Comforter, the Holy Spirit pushes the believer beyond the restrictions of human inclination and judgment in matters which pertain to eternal life. St. Paul corroborates this theological truth when he speaks about those who are led by the Spirit of God as "heirs" to the Kingdom (cf. Rom 8:14–17). And the First Letter of John also points to this divine action: "... but the anointing which you received from him abides in you, and you have no need that any one should teach you; as his anointing teaches you about everything (1 Jn 2:27).

The gifts are permanent spiritual endowments, even though Aquinas's Vulgate term *spiritus* suggests something transient, even charismatic, in nature. The gifts render an individual continually receptive to the divine promptings that conduce toward Christian perfection, and so it is argued that they become part of one's moral character. John of St. Thomas reflects on the gifts as permanent not transient endowments. His explanation refers back to the elements of Christology: "The reason and foundation is, first of all that in the Scriptures themselves it is indicated that these gifts are given in a permanent way, when it is said in Isaiah 11: 'The Spirit of the Lord will rest upon him, the spirit of wisdom, and of knowledge, etc.' ... therefore these gifts have a permanent status."[43] The Gospel of John further recounts that Jesus reassures his disciples with the promise that the Counselor "dwells with you, and abides with you" (Jn 14:17). As formed *habitus* in the believer, the gifts shape the moral character of the Christian in determined ways.[44] Aquinas offers an instructive example, comparing the Holy Spirit to a teacher who gradually leads his pupil to a knowledge of higher things by providing moments of insight that help the one being instructed escape the limitations of ignorance imposed by a fallen world.

Even though the gift renders us highly receptive to a divine prompting,

43. See his *Cursus*, Disp. XVIII, a. 2, n. 8.

44. The following chart displays the definitive relationship which Aquinas establishes between the gifts and the virtues:

Intellectual Gifts	Affective Gifts
Wisdom (Charity)	Fortitude (Fortitude)
Understanding & Knowledge (Faith)	Piety (Justice)
Counsel (Prudence)	Fear of the Lord (Hope/Temperance)

this special grace of the Holy Spirit does not destroy human freedom. Rather, the gifts infallibly produce in the believer that sort of ordered spiritual liberty that characterizes New Testament existence.[45] The gift-*habitus* illuminates the paradoxical quality of Christian life; we learn from the saints that from the time they seek nothing because of what they themselves want, everything is given to them by God, even though they did not ask for it. The gifts perfect Christian freedom inasmuch as it accompanies the achieving of excellence in human behavior.

The Thomist teaching on the gifts rests on the central place that the virtue of charity holds in the Christian life. "The gifts of the Holy Spirit," Aquinas explains, "are connected with one another in charity, in such wise that one who has charity has all the gifts of the Holy Spirit, while none of the gifts can be had without charity."[46] In the Preface for the Christmas Mass at Midnight, the Church proclaims: "In the wonder of the Incarnation your eternal Word has brought to the eyes of faith a new and radiant vision of your glory. In him we see our God made visible and so are caught up in the love of the God we cannot see."[47] The gifts of the Holy Spirit complete the practice of Christian moral theology, for they ensure that each virtuous action of the believer conforms perfectly to the will of God. Moral realism is able to explain in terms of the exercise of the gifts the profound personalization that informs Christian moral action, without recourse to a false subjectivism that separates a person from the Law of the Lord. To meet our human limitations, the Spirit comes not only as Comforter but also Guide. The invisible action of the Holy Spirit makes itself visible in the good works of the saints, and assures that the divine plan for the salvation of the world continues to be realized fully in the lives of those redeemed by Christ.

A Christian life lived freely under the movement of the Holy Spirit accords entirely with the confession that Jesus is Lord and the Holy

45. In more technical terms, theology understands the gifts as instances of a *gratia operans*, i.e., graces in which the divine initiative accounts for the direction of the human will.

46. *Summa theologiae* Ia-IIae, q. 68, a. 5. The tradition correctly emphasizes that the gifts of the Holy Spirit work their effect on the moral life through the theological virtues, so that everything the Christian believes and hopes for plays an active role in the faithful exercise of Christian virtue.

47. *Missale Romanum*, editio typica altera (Vatican, 1975), Preface for Christmas I: "Quia per incarnati Verbi mysterium nova mentis nostrae oculis lux tuae claritatis infulsit: ut, dum visibiliter Deum cognoscimus, per hunc in invisibilium amorem rapiamur."

Spirit is sent into the world for our sanctification. A life lived according to the Spirit initially entails the will's conscious but passive consent to the dominance of divine grace and, in turn, enables the individual's own self-determinations that such a divine movement renders possible. Within this context of moved freedom, the gifts perfect the life of the theological, moral, and intellectual virtues—they are said, according to standard teaching, to serve as helps to the virtues. Because no one other than God himself can ensure that a creature freely embraces the ultimate good of beatific fellowship, authentic Christian liberty cannot exist without the gifts of the Holy Spirit. "Do not quench the Spirit ..." warns 1 Thessalonians 5:19. This serves as the biblical warrant for Aquinas's doctrine of the gifts insofar as they infallibly produce what the tradition describes as "a spiritual liberty."

The New Law of Freedom: Christ's Gift to His Church

Christian doctrine instructs us that *beatitudo* shapes and orders human freedom. To seek a warrant for this claim leads one back to the central message that Christ came to reveal to the world. It is the incarnate Son who announces that the Blessed Trinity exists as both the final cause of all human activity and the true perfection of the human person. Only one of the divine Persons authoritatively could make such an extraordinary declaration. We know, moreover, that from the beginning God has placed in man a longing for truth and goodness that only God can satisfy.[48] The nature of the longing remains a matter of theological disputation, but there is no dispute about the fact that we experience restless hearts until we attain God. Because the beatitude of heaven has become in Christ the destiny of man, human freedom is governed by the law of the Lord. Thomas Gilby has observed that freedom (like morality) rises from and aspires to conditions beyond its control.[49] The overall picture of the Christian life that this view of freedom suggests is imposing, and

48. For a contemporary catechetical formulation of this fundamental Christian truth, see *Catechism of the Catholic Church*, no. 2002: "God's free initiative demands man's free response, for God has created man in his image by conferring on him, along with freedom, the power to know him and to love him.... The promises of 'eternal life' respond, beyond all hope, to this desire...."

49. Thomas Gilby, O.P., *Psychology of Human Acts*, p. 218.

does not accord easily with those interpretations that make human freedom the equivalent of personal autonomy, even an autonomy that the person agrees to limit by self-imposed imperatives.[50]

We have already seen the basic outlines of the teaching. The Christian tradition first of all understands human freedom as a quality of action that finds its roots in the human voluntary. As the standard expression *natura ut voluntas* ("nature as will") suggests, human nature itself is identified with the movement toward freedom. The fact is explained theologically by our likeness to the divine nature. The biblical doctrine of the *imago Dei* further entails that human nature is born to move toward the free accomplishment of its own perfection. This anthropological given explains why the Church holds that "the rational ordering of the human act to the good in its truth and the voluntary pursuit of that good, known by reason, constitute morality."[51] Not whatsoever choice guarantees Christian freedom. Deliberate or free choice (*liberum arbitrium*) captures true freedom only when the object of choice remains in conformity with the true good of the human person. The dynamism of the *image of God* moves in only one direction.

In order to account for two basic meanings of freedom, namely, *natura ut voluntas* (the radical capacity for freedom in the human person) and *liberum arbitrium* (the actual choosing of means to an end) the Scholastic theologians distinguished between freedom with respect to exercise (*quoad exercitium*) and freedom with respect to a sort of action (*quoad specificationem*). Freedom with respect to exercise, sometimes called "philosophical freedom," refers to the radical ability of the will to choose or not to choose; in other words, freedom of exercise posits the basic condition for human freedom. Freedom with respect to a sort of action, sometimes called "psychological freedom," refers to the person's ability to choose among options, that is, from among a clash of positives. As St. Thomas tells us:

Free will stands to the choice between means to an end as the mind stands with regard to conclusions reached by reasoning. Now clearly, it belongs to the mind's power to be able to reason to different conclusions according to given principles; but if it argues to a conclusion without taking account of the principles relevant to the case, then it fails precisely as a mind. And the case of the will is similar. That it can choose between alternative means while respect-

---

50. For further study about the true nature of Christian freedom, one may usefully begin reading the treatise on the new law of grace in *Summa theologiae* Ia-IIae, qq. 106–14.

51. *Veritatis splendor*, no. 72.

ing the order imposed by ends, that is what its freedom—the fulness of freedom—signifies. But should it make a choice at variance with that order—that
is to say, commit a sin—it would fall short of its own capacity for freedom.[52]

Moralists contend that "psychological freedom" is what contributes to
the development of personal character. Persons are more remarkable on
account of the kinds of choices that they in fact make than on account of
the fact that they are free to make a choice or not.[53]

The American savant Mortimer Adler once prepared a brief survey of
some basic models of freedom that he discovered in the course of an encyclopedic survey of religious, philosophical, and psychological writings
that deal with freedom.[54] Because these patterns influence the way people interpret theological accounts of freedom, Adler's categories provide
helpful background for defining the proper Christian model for freedom. The first of these basic models of freedom is that of self-realization:
S-R freedom consists primarily in the ability of the person to achieve
some sort of subjective fulfillment. The second of these models is self-
determination: S-D freedom consists primarily in the ability of the person to make choices, without direct reference to the usefulness or fruitfulness of the choice measured against an objective norm or standard, for
example, the greatest good for the greatest number. The third model of
freedom identified by Adler is that of self-perfection. On his account, S-P
freedom consists primarily in achieving some perfection for the subject
which is measured by its purpose (telos) and activity.

While elements of self-realization and self-determination also figure
in freedom as self-perfection, Gaudium et spes stipulates that the latter conception of freedom best accords with the Christian ideal. "Human dignity requires man to act through conscious and free choice, as motivated
and prompted personally from within, and not through blind internal
impulse or merely external pressure. Man achieves such dignity when he
frees himself from all subservience to his feelings, and in a free choice of
the good, pursues his own end by effectively and assiduously marshaling

52. *Summa theologiae* Ia, q. 62, a. 8, ad 3.
53. The Christian Gospel does not equate freedom with a multiplication of choices
or unrestricted access to options. "With respect to the sort of action," our blessed Lady
had no freedom in uttering her "Fiat." But this state of being settled on the good did
not reduce at all the value of her positive reply to the Angel Gabriel; on the contrary, the
fact that she was full of grace made that response efficacious for the whole world.
54. See his *Freedom*, published in Overview Studies (Albany: Magi Books, 1968).

the appropriate means."[55] In other words, the Christian ideal of freedom situates freedom within the larger schema of what constitutes the good for man. To return again to the phrase that Father Gilby coined, freedom aspires to conditions that remain outside of its control.

Some theologians identify S-P freedom with freedom for excellence, and so distinguish it from the freedom of indifference, which is a kind of radical autonomy that exists outside of any framework of ends or purposes.[56] The Pauline Letters repeatedly affirm that Christ made each of his members free so that they could find their perfection in him. "For you were called to freedom, brethren, but do not use your freedom as an opportunity for the flesh, but through love be servants of one another.... And those who belong to Christ Jesus have crucified the flesh with its passions and desires" (Gal 5:13, 24). On the basis of biblical warrants such as this, *Veritatis splendor* makes the bold assertion that human freedom and divine instruction are called to intersect.

Theonomy

In order to make the connection between human freedom and divine order clear, *Veritatis splendor* speaks about true freedom in terms of theonomy. This term means that our "free obedience to God's law effectively implies that human reason and human will participate in God's wisdom and providence."[57] Although the term "theonomy" is introduced into Christian ethics only in the nineteenth century, Aquinas had set the stage for this development when he taught that divine guidance need not subtract from free will. His argument is based on the New Testament assertion that the children of God are led by the Holy Spirit not as slaves, but as free people (see Gal 5:13ff.). Aquinas goes on to explain:

The Holy Spirit so inclines us to act as to make us act voluntarily, inasmuch as he makes us love, and not slavishly.... Since the Holy Spirit inclines the will, through love, toward the true good toward which the will is inclined by nature, he takes away both the slavery whereby the person having been made a slave of passion and sin, acts against the [natural tendency] of the will; and also the slavery whereby, contrary to the movement of his will, a person acts according to the law like a slave of the law, not a friend. That is why the Apos-

55. *Gaudium et spes*, no. 17, as cited in *Veritatis splendor*, no. 42.
56. See Pinckaers, *Sources of Christian Ethics*, esp. pp. 374–78.
57. *Veritatis splendor*, no. 41. For further clarification, see Rhonheimer, *Natural Law*, pp. 234–56.

tle says in 2 Corinthians 3:17, "Where the Spirit of the Lord is, there is freedom," and in Galatians 5:18, "If you are led by the Spirit, you are not under
the law."[58]

True Christian freedom flourishes within the limits set by divine love and
manifested in the order of nature and grace. To make the point even clearer, *Veritatis splendor* asserts that "by submitting to the law, freedom submits
to the truth of creation."[59] Secular assertions that promote a maximally
unrestricted self-autonomy compare more favorably with the original presumption and rebellion of our First Parents than with the freedom that
we receive in Christ.

Christian freedom remains situated within the overall structure of the
eternal law. It comes as no surprise, then, that in a Christian view of civil
order every legitimate expression of human law also must express the designs of divine wisdom and providence. When, however, Aquinas inquires
whether the new law should concern itself with enjoining or forbidding
external actions, he makes a point of insisting that Christ leaves many
things to the determination of individuals and lawgivers who participate
in the communion of grace. It is instructive to note that Saint Thomas
is chiefly concerned to emphasize the place that the sacramental system,
and the moral obligations that ensure its continuance—for example, pro-
hibitions against sacrilege—hold within the new dispensation.[60] In other
words, the full flourishing of Christian freedom does not require theo-
cratic structures to sustain it.

To insist that the human person is free only when he or she observes
the commandments of God is not to instrumentalize human freedom to
the point that it no longer makes sense to speak about a free human creature. The key to understanding this basic Christian doctrine lies in the
recognition that God cannot enter into competition with his own creature. The freedom that Christ introduces into the world is first realized
in that conformity to the Father's will expressed through his own human

58. *Summa contra gentiles* IV, c. 22.

59. *Veritatis splendor*, no. 41.

60. See *Summa theologiae* Ia-IIae, q. 108, a. 1. Aquinas holds that the new law imposes
only the sacramental system and those grace-inspired *(ex instinctu gratiae)* external deeds
that are required to preserve the presence of divine grace in the world, for example, the
confession of faith. See also *Catechism of the Catholic Church*, no. 2003: "Grace is first and
foremost the gift of the Spirit who justifies and sanctifies us. But grace also includes the
gifts that the Spirit grants us to associate us with his work, to enable us to collaborate
in the salvation of others and in the growth of the Body of Christ, the Church."

will: "Father, if thou art willing, remove this cup from me; nevertheless not my will, but thine, be done" (Lk 22:42). As a Dominican friar, Aquinas modeled his own life on these words of Christ. Personal experiences of the divine friendship, confirmed toward the end of his life by words from Christ himself, undoubtedly influence the way that Aquinas teaches about Christian freedom lived out under the new law of grace.

As Aquinas explains, beatitude governs the range of Gospel freedom: "The New Law is called the law of freedom in two senses. Firstly, because it does not constrain us to do or to avoid anything apart from what of it-self is necessary or contrary to salvation, falling under the precept or the prohibition of the law. Secondly, because even such precepts or prohibi-tions it makes us fulfil freely, as much as we fulfil them by an inner stir-ring of grace (ex interiori instinctu). For these two reasons the New Law is called the 'law of perfect freedom.' "⁶¹ Christ of course receives this in-terior grace by reason of the mystery of the hypostatic union, whereas all those who belong to Christ receive their inner stirring through the be-stowal of created grace. As Saint Thomas learned from his own encoun-ter with the crucified Lord, this grace is nothing other than the gift of Christ himself: "Non nisi te, Domine."

The freedom that is revealed in the New Testament and promised in the Church of faith and sacraments originates in "an inner stirring of grace" and terminates with the accomplishment of the divine commands. God himself moves the believer to accomplish freely those good actions that make up the Christian way of life. Ours, then is a situated freedom that operates according to the interaction of a principal cause and a sec-ondary cause. Aquinas applies this philosophical intuition to his theo-logical purposes: "Since the grace of the Holy Spirit is a kind of interi-or habitus infused into us which inclines us to act rightly, it makes us do whatever is in accordance with grace, and avoid whatever is contrary to it."⁶² The Church continues to make this teaching her own; for example, Veritatis splendor insists that "human freedom and God's law meet and are called to intersect."

61. The text from Summa theologiae Ia-IIae, q. 108, a. 1, ad 2, is part of a reply to the ob-jection that there is no freedom when a person is obliged to perform or to refrain from external works.
62. Ibid.

Freedom and the Reconciling Christ

The rich young man who appears in the nineteenth chapter of Saint Matthew's Gospel represents a kind of theological Everyman. Pope John Paul II uses this biblical text effectively to introduce his teaching on Christian morality. As a means to achieving the perfection of what it means to be human, every man and woman must pose and answer the question, "What good must I do ... ?" The young man asks Christ, "Teacher, what good must I do to have eternal life?" (Mt 19:16). Answering this question continues to supply work for moral theologians. However, the differences that arise among professional theologians should not discourage us from discovering for ourselves the correct answer to the rich young man's question. Aquinas provides sound direction. He first points to the seven sacraments of the new law, which are the actions that mediate in a specific way the divine love that Christ's death has restored uniquely to the world. Christian moral law obliges us to celebrate, according to our vocation in the Church, the seven sacraments. Aquinas next indicates "those moral precepts which of themselves are formally implied in virtuous action." The virtues of the Christian life, which come to the baptized as free gifts of grace, provide to those who both profess the Christian religion and remain united with Christ whatever is needed, both intellectually and emotionally, to sanctify their personal comportment.[63]

The proposal that Christ himself provides the norms for the new dispensation makes sense only to those who have learned that the infused virtues and gifts of the Holy Spirit actively animate the Christian moral life. The highly specific and even meticulous legislation of old law Torah surrenders to a reign of grace that "is rightly exercised by works of charity."[64] When Aquinas insists on charity as the virtue that adequately specifies the Christian moral life, he repeats what the long Christian tradition had taught about conformity to Christ establishing the foundation of the moral life. In her liturgy, the Church prays that God will see and love in us what he sees and loves in Christ. It has been argued that this gift of

---

63. For further discussion of this perspective, see *Summa theologiae* Ia-IIae, q. 108, a. 2, as well as the biblical commentary on this theme by Benedict Ashley, O.P., *Living the Truth in Love. A Biblical Introduction to Moral Theology* (Staten Island: Alba House, 1996), esp. pp. 3–38.

64. *Summa theologiae* Ia-IIae, q. 108, a. 2.

grace makes the soul beautiful and brings about in the Christian man and woman a recognizable form of moral beauty.[65]

Charity does not provide a cover for vagueness or ambiguity in the moral life, as if one could remain satisfied with the intention to achieve charity but forget about specific moral truths. Aquinas makes an important clarification on this point: He says that "so far as [the works of charity] are a necessary part of virtuous action, they fall under the moral precepts, which were provided even in the old law."[66] The text refers to those human goods safeguarded by the Ten Commandments, which, on Aquinas's account, contain the whole of the natural law. In order to emphasize that the freedom we receive in Christ provides no warrant for neglect of the Commandments, *Veritatis splendor* reaffirms an important point about the relationship that exists between freedom and love: "Love of God and of one's neighbor cannot be separated from the observance of the commandments of the Covenant renewed in the blood of Jesus Christ and in the gift of the Holy Spirit."[67]

The general teaching on freedom and charity assumes that the redemptive Incarnation restores a true connaturality between the human person and the human good. This connaturality is the fruit of a heart converted to the Lord and to the love of what is good.[68] Connaturality is associated with the development and exercise of virtue, and explains why a human person can fulfill the law without putting too much strain on his or her psychological equilibrium. Connaturality also explains why Aquinas expresses a hearty confidence in the moral life lived under the new law of grace.[69] He finds it sufficient to affirm "that the new law did not have to prescribe any external works by way of precept or prohibition apart from the sacraments and those moral precepts which of themselves are formally implied in virtuous action, such as the prohibition of mur-

---

65. For example, see the essay by Thomas Hibbs, *"Imitatio Christi* and the Foundation of Aquinas's Ethics," *Communio* 18 (1991): 556–73. He argues that the *Summa theologiae* exhibits its own kind of theological aesthetics and that it is "undeniably christocentric." For a fuller account of Pope John Paul II's views on the relationship of Christ and the moral life, see Lorenzo Albacete, "The Relevance of Christ or the *sequela Christi?" Communio* 21 (1994): 252–64.

66. In *Summa theologiae* Ia-IIae, q. 108, a. 2.

67. *Veritatis splendor,* no. 76.

68. This teaching is spelled out in *Veritatis splendor,* no. 64.

69. See *Summa contra gentiles* IV, c. 22. For a longer discussion, see Ceslaus Spicq, O.P., *Charity and Liberty in the New Testament,* pp. 75–109.

der or theft and the like."[70] This kind of confidence would make no sense at all apart from what we know about the power of the grace of Christ. What is specific in the new law flows from the grace of Christ the Head, his capital grace, which supplies each of his members everything that is required for a perfect life. "Following Christ," proclaims Pope John Paul II, "is thus the essential and primordial foundation of Christian morality."[71] When Christian believers hold fast in faith to the person of Jesus, this union accounts for the existence in them of the infused virtues, and ensures that they always act in fulfillment of the law of love.

How does the new law of grace compare with other written codes that prescribe ethical conduct?[72] Essentially, it does not correspond with any of these. Aquinas underscores that "before all else the New Law is the very grace of the Holy Spirit, given to those who believe in Christ."[73] He supports his view by direct reference to the teaching of the New Testament—especially that found in the Letter to the Romans—and of St. Augustine. And so Aquinas resolutely concludes: "Now it is the grace of the Holy Spirit, given through faith in Christ, which is predominant in the law of the New Covenant, and that in which its whole power consists."[74] This teaching forms the heart of Aquinas's interpretation of New Testament morality. For from the moment that the Holy Spirit dwells in the believer, the Christian possesses the capacity to make those moral decisions that are required to sustain a holy life. This gift of grace appears primarily in the exercise of the virtue of prudence. Likewise the Holy Spirit provides the rectitude of emotion and appetite—especially in the infused moral virtues and the allied gifts of the Holy Spirit—that sets the believer in motion toward the authentic goods of human flourishing and *beatitudo*. Rectitude of appetite ensures that disordered emotions and desires—the penalty of original sin—do not obstruct prudence and its work of making right choices about the means to develop the virtue.

The assurance that Christ gives to the Church provides the necessary

---

70. *Summa theologiae* Ia-IIae, q. 108, a. 2.

71. *Veritatis splendor*, no. 19.

72. The objections considered in the first article of *Summa theologiae* Ia-IIae, q. 106, consider some alternatives to recognizing the uniqueness of the new law: Is it rather something written (arg. 1), or identical with the natural law (arg. 2), or one with the wisdom possessed by the saints of the old dispensation (arg. 3)?

73. *Summa theologiae* Ia-IIae, q. 106, a. 1.

74. *Summa theologiae* Ia-IIae, q. 106, a. 1.

guarantee that those who are united to him not only are able to know God's will for them but also will possess the grace required to fulfill it. "When the Advocate comes, whom I will send to you from the Father, the Spirit of truth who comes from the Father, he will testify on my behalf" (Jn 15:26). Because of the indwelling of the Holy Spirit, the Christian believer abides in what Aquinas calls the "truth of life." He describes this virtuous state as "the kind of truth by which something exists as true." And he goes on to explain, "Like everything else, one's life is called 'true' on the basis of its reaching its rule and norm, namely divine law, that is, the eternal law; by measuring up to this, a life has uprightness. This is the kind of truth, i.e. rectitude, common to every virtue."[75] The Holy Spirit provides both the law of virtuous living and the virtue itself to those who attend to his promptings. Neither the many complexities of daily life nor the sometimes unruly power of human emotion constitute obstacles to making the divine power effective in the life of the believer. The whole of the Christian dispensation, especially the sacramental life of the Church, finds its ultimate purpose in the creation of a new people who, by their holy lives, offer a pleasing sacrifice to the Lord.

Since it mediates to those who honestly acknowledge their sins and disordered inclinations to sin the graces required for an honest and upright life, the sacrament of reconciliation retains an essential place in the Christian life. The example of the saints illustrate this truth. St. Jane Frances de Chantal gave testimony at the canonization process of her friend St. Francis de Sales. Her remarks about the bishop of Geneva's popularity as a confessor provide inspiring evidence concerning the saint's determination to root up the evil of sin and to provide sound instruction on how to seek God's mercy. Francis de Sales' exemplification of pastoral charity toward those caught in a sinful condition makes him a worthy model for every minister of reconciliation:

When he realized that people found it difficult to speak out in confession and were inhibited by shame or fear, he tried every way of opening their hearts and giving them more confidence: "I'm your Father, don't you see?" he would say, and go on asking till one said yes; and then, "Now don't you want to tell me the whole story? God is waiting for you to open out to him, he's holding out his arms to you...." He liked you to be clear, simple and straightforward in confession, and taught his penitents to explain clearly what led them into sin;

75. *Summa theologiae* IIa-IIae, q. 109, a. 2, ad 3.

they were not to treat confession lightly but to show him what made them go wrong, and he used to say that if you were not clear in your own mind about this you couldn't ever get really straight. By taking the trouble to insist on a clear confession to purify the heart, he uprooted evil inclinations which others who did not use his methods might well have left untouched.[76]

The example of Saint Francis de Sales remains a model for the Church. In fact, on the basis of the harm that it causes the Christian believer, the Church warns against an accommodating moral relativism, and *Veritatis splendor* includes a special exhortation on the discipline that the truth of life imposes on each member of the Church.[77]

Rationalizations and excuses for sinful behavior obstruct a person's growth in Christian holiness. Moreover, they are needless. The Church always supplies to the contrite person both the forgiveness of sins in the sacraments and the healing of sin's effects through charity and penance. The Letter of James encourages us: "But he who looks into the perfect law, the law of liberty, and perseveres, being no hearer that forgets but a doer that acts, he shall be blessed in his doing" (Jas 1:25). Christ makes it possible for each person to become a "doer" of the new law of grace.

The disordered effects of sin remain even in the baptized. There is only one grace of the Immaculate Conception. This privilege belongs by divine decree to the virgin Mother of God. Christian moral theology should provide both instruction for a holy life and consolation for times of failure and temptation. Sin causes God no embarrassment. In fact, the principal purpose of a redemptive Incarnation and sending of the Holy Spirit originates in God's desire to accomplish in those whom he calls to holiness both the restoration of the Godly image, which heals the effects of sin, and the perfection of the same image, which enables the life of merit, grace, and glory.

Christian moral theology instructs us to appreciate the reason God allowed sin to gain entrance into the world. Although the notion seems paradoxical to unaided human reason, the words *"O felix culpa!"* "O happy fault!" sung at the Easter vigil, explain best the divine permission for sin. From the vantage point of having been redeemed by Christ, the believer can look back at the original sin and recognize that it has become

---

76. From the *processus* for the canonization of St. Francis de Sales.

77. See the 1984 Post-Synodal Apostolic Exhortation *On Reconciliation and Penance in the Mission of the Church Today*, esp. no. 19, and *Veritatis splendor*, no. 104.

a happy fault. Ancient Christian wisdom avows that it is better for the human race to have been redeemed by Christ than to have persevered in innocence. St. Ambrose captures the encouragement that this profound Christian wisdom imparts to the individual Christian, when he writes: "My guilt became for me the cause of redemption, through which Christ came to me."[78] The Christian must accept this wisdom, or otherwise learn to deal with depression.

Early Christian literature records the dynamic interplay between sin and forgiveness that shapes the Christian moral life. For example, St. Augustine's *De doctrina christiana* clearly indicates that the Christian life moves from involvement with sin to participation in grace. The Doctor of Grace describes the circle of conversion that begins with the exercise of the moral conscience and leads to "the new nature, created after the likeness of God in true righteousness and holiness" (Eph 4:24). In this catechetical summary, he says: "From the law comes knowledge of sin, by faith the reception of grace against sin, by grace the soul is healed of the imperfection of sin; a healthy soul possesses freedom of choice; freedom of choice is ordered to love of righteousness; love of righteousness is the accomplishment of the law."[79] The passage exhibits the dynamics of Christian conversion that unfolds within the context of the Church and her sacraments.

Augustine formulated this synopsis of orthodox teaching as a reply to the position of Pelagius. According to Augustine's account, Pelagius taught that the grace of God means that, from its establishment, our nature receives the possibility of not sinning simply by reason of the fact that it was established with the ability to choose freely.[80] Pelagius thought that Adam's sin left in the world only a bad example instead of a wounded nature. This view, however, would have encouraged in the believer a self-reliance that is difficult to reconcile with the Gospel injunction that each one remain united with Christ.

Saint Augustine saw the fatal error in the Pelagian argument. By way

---

78. *De Jacob et vita beata*, Bk. I, chap. 6, no. 21.

79. *De doctrina christiana* 30, 52: "Sed per legem cognitio peccati, per fidem inpetratio gratiae contra peccatum, per gratiam sanatio animae a vitio peccati, per animae sanitatem libertas arbitrii, per liberum arbitrium justitiae dilectio, per justitiae dilectionem legis operatio."

80. *De gestis Pelagii* 10:22: "Hanc esse Dei gratiam quod possibilitatem non peccandi natura nostra, cum conderetur, accepit, quoniam condita est cum libero arbitrio."

of rebuttal, he insisted that human nature by itself remains inefficacious with respect to fulfilling the requirements of the moral law. In an actually existing state of sin, human freedom without the help of divine grace is more likely to fail than to succeed. The Church still stands by Saint Augustine's conviction.[81] And although interpretations of his texts differ even among Catholic scholars, the basic lines of his account have been incorporated by the Church into her official teaching on the necessity of divine grace.

It is impossible to overestimate how much the human creature requires the gift of divine grace.[82] Even with the help of grace, human freedom remains fragile. Saint Augustine offers sound pastoral advice when he reminds us that, "while he is in the flesh, man cannot help but have at least some light sins." This circumstance provides reason for neither presumption nor despair. Instead, as he further points out, even the everyday experiences of wounded nature return us to Christ, his Church and the sacraments: "But do not despise these sins which we call 'light': if you take them for light when you weigh them, tremble when you count them. A number of light objects makes a great mass; a number of drops fills a river; a number of grains makes a heap. What then is our hope? Above all, Confession...."[83] For St. Augustine, the moral life leads back to the sacramental life, and conversely the sacraments strengthen the moral life. Were it not for the grace freely given in Christ, the human predicament would become a source of profound discouragement.

The truth of the Catholic religion provides a refreshing alternative both to the claims of a narrow legalism and to the uncertainties of the various kinds of teleologisms that *Veritatis splendor* describes. The great teachers of the Catholic faith instruct us that the overarching concern of the Christian moral life is union with God. In this present life, such godly union finds its highest realization in the personal presence of the blessed Trinity to the souls of the just. We attribute this transforming presence to the Holy Spirit who unites us in charity to God and gathers us togeth-

---

81. The Church has incorporated St. Augustine's teaching into her official teaching (see *Catechism of the Catholic Church*, no. 406).

82. One of the best modern studies of the human person's need for grace comes from the pen of Bernard Lonergan, S.J., *Grace and Freedom: Operative Grace in the Thought of St. Thomas Aquinas*, ed. J. Patout Burns (New York: Herder & Herder, 1971).

83. The text comes from his *In epistulam Johannis ad Parthos tractatus*, 1, 6 (PL 35, col. 1982) and is cited in the *Catechism of the Catholic Church*, no. 1863.

er in the *communicatio* or fellowship of divine love. In the Church of Christ we listen together to the sacred Scriptures. These dispose the believer's mind toward understanding and accepting the mystery of Christ, even as they instruct about that authentic "contempt for the world" which attends the exercise of a spiritual life.

Growth in the moral life cannot happen apart from an effective, personal union with Christ in the Church of faith and sacraments. Those who provide good moral teaching recognize this truth, and so refrain from imposing moral obligations without giving a clear explanation about how these demands may be suitably met. The Pelagian mentality neglects the importance that the mystery of personal union with Christ holds for the successful living out of the Christian moral life. Some have observed the historical affinities between Pelagians and Nestorians, whose explanation of the unity in the Incarnation the Church later judged insufficient. To first emphasize determined human willing rather than affective union with the person of Christ only provokes frustration. Whenever the Pelagian mentality prevails, however, the believer confronted by the reality of his or her personal sin faces one of three options: a denial of the sin's objective character, depression based on the perception of one's utter helplessness, or despair born from the fear that God either will not give the means for living a holy life or will not forgive the sins of the past. None of these options is reconcilable with Gospel of Christ. On the contrary, Christ's promises overflow with hope. We can only conclude that Pelagian optimism is doomed to disappoint, and that its spirit will keep people from absorbing the authentic Gospel message.

According to the teaching of Christ, the whole efficacy of the new law results in the restoration and perfection of the *imago Dei*. We call this achievement the grace of justification. Some persons suppose that grace is weak and inefficacious. One phenomenon that persuades to such a view is the widespread evidence of sin that continues to exist in the world even millennia after Christ's salvific death. Without a proper understanding of the Gospel message, personal sin—whether our own or that of others—can easily promote what might be called the "devil's blackmail." By insisting on the hopeless state of the sinner, the tactic urges believers to give up on believing in Christ's love and forgiveness. When this blackmail works, these people look for a remedy for their sins that moves them away from the holiness of Christ. But as Jesus himself instructs us, there is no moment in our lives when sin provides a reason for turning away from

God. Remember that when one of the criminals who was crucified with Jesus, turned to him and said, " 'Jesus, remember me when you come into your kingdom.' He replied, 'Truly I tell you, today you will be with me in Paradise' " (Lk 23:42–43). The truth about God's love for the sinner and the transformation that occurs in the lives of all those who seek to do God's will must accompany every instruction about morality. Failure to pay heed to these truths results in a gross perversion of the basic New Testament teaching about the divine love, namely, that God loves us, not because we are good, but because He is Goodness Itself.

Only the grace of the Holy Spirit given inwardly to those who are united with Christ saves. Nothing else can directly and immediately bring about the divine, saving action in the creature. Whatever forms part of the Christian religion remains instrumental to our justification: the Creed, the Decalogue, all other truths of divine and Catholic faith. Indeed, these elements in themselves are considered subordinate elements of the new law. They of course serve an important and irreplaceable purpose in the Christian life, but none of them possess the ability in themselves of transforming the human person into a son or daughter of God. Aquinas even makes the very strong affirmation: "Thus even the Gospel letter kills unless the healing grace of faith is present within." The assertion leaves no room for ambiguity about how to interpret this central point of his moral theology.[84] But Aquinas is only repeating what he himself learned from divine wisdom. Consider the teaching of the First Letter of John: "And this is his commandment, that we should believe in the name of his Son Jesus Christ and love one another, just as he has commanded us. All who keep his commandments abide in him, and he in them. And by this we know that God abides in us, by the Spirit which he has given us" (1 Jn 3:23–24). The love of Christ opens up the way for the final perfection of each man and woman created in the image of God.

---

84. *Summa theologiae* Ia-IIae, q. 106, a. 2.

Flight from Virtue

The Outlook of the Casuist Systems

The Casuistic Conception of Morality

In the course of this study, it has been made apparent that Servais Pinck-aers, O.P., has contributed a great deal to our understanding of the nature and origins of post-Reformation casuistry.[1] The title of the first casuist manual, *Enchiridion Confessariorum et Poenitentium*, published by Martin Azpilcueta (Na-varrus) in 1556, suggests that the concerns and necessities of pastoral theology, especially of confessors, explains, at least from the historical point of view, the commencement and evolution of casuistry.[2] From the Council of Trent until the Second Vatican Council, the casuist systems, which we may provisionally define as a morality based on the formulation of precepts, the formation of conscience, and the obligation to obey duly established norms, largely eclipsed the virtue tradition of moral theology that had guided Roman Catholic moral theology since its beginning in the patristic era.

In his study of the philosophical antecedents of casuistry, Pinckaers points out that the view of human freedom which the casuist authors adopted derived from the view developed by fourteenth-century nominalists such as William of Ockham (c. 1285–1347). Hence, even though there existed a variety of methods among the schools of casuistry, each of the schools in fact shared the same basic philosophical conception about the nature of human freedom. This conception holds that human freedom amounts to freedom from constraint. Accord-

---

1. For a discussion of the theological and historical aspects of casuistry, see Pinck-aers, *Sources of Christian Ethics*, pp. 327–53.

2. Martin Azpilcueta (1493–1586), known as Navarrus because of his native region, distinguished himself as both a canonist and a moralist. He served several popes, in-cluding St. Pius V, Gregory XIII, and Sixtus V, as a penitentiary and advisor in morals. His *Manuale sive Enchridion Confessarum et poenitentium* (Rome, 1588) represents a significant example of classical casuistry.

ingly, the casuists advanced the thesis that each person possesses the ability to remain radically indifferent or undetermined when confronted with a judgment of reason about a good to be pursued. The casuists designated this sort of human freedom the "liberty of indifference." The liberty of indifference is not to be identified with *natura ut voluntas* and the distinctive ordering to an end ("velle, intendere, frui") that governs the realist view of the moral life. On the contrary, the liberty of indifference expresses a sort of pure willing (*voluntas ut voluntas*) that remains inherently unrelated to the goods of excellence that perfect the human person.

Casuist moral theologians conceived of human freedom in a way that gravely affected subsequent developments in moral theology. It especially suited the promotion of a legalistic conception of morality. The liberty of indifference means that human freedom embodies a power to choose between contraries, that is, between what the mind presents as reasonable and its contrary or between what the law requires and its contrary. Furthermore, because such a notion of freedom supposes a divorce between our cognitive and volitional powers, the casuists necessarily understood free choice as specified entirely by the will or the rational appetite. They paid very little attention to the deliberative and judgmental acts of the practical intellect that shape human choosing. In other words, the casuists' notion of freedom downplays the influence that right reason—*recta ratio*—exercises on human choosing. On their account, neither reasoned appetition nor appetitive reasoning accounts for why a person acts in such and such a way; rather, human activity is explained solely by appeal to naked free will.

The historical roots of this conception of human freedom as a liberty of indifference lie in the *via moderna* and, especially, as has been said, in the work of William of Ockham. Much of Ockham's theological thinking is determined by his resolute attempt to eliminate anything that would limit the divine omnipotence and God's freedom. Significantly, Ockham considered the doctrine of the eternal law, that is, how God knows the world to be, as an overly restrictive one, for it appeared to place constraints on God's freedom to do as he pleases in the world. The casuist conception of freedom as unfettered self-determination owes much to how the nominalist thinkers envisioned the divine freedom.

Certain epistemological suppositions affect the nominalist view of freedom. The liberty of indifference conforms to nominalist misgivings concerning the intellect's ability to possess universal moral knowledge. To offer a broad generalization of Ockham's philosophical outlook: only individual things exist, and the human mind is able directly to apprehend these singulars. But when human reason cognizes only the particular, then it is difficult to explain how *recta ratio*, or a universal moral truth based on the knowability of moral forms, points the way toward moral good. As we have noted, moral realism offers a more optimistic view about that which *recta ratio* can communicate to the moral agent. Since natural law represents a created human nature's participation in the eternal law, moral realism argues that the person can know moral truths, even as these concretely and specifically apply to life situations.

Nominalism's false sense of moral neutrality derives from the lack of a teleological framework in which to locate the moral life. Nominalism offers a person little to consider about final causality. And because it possesses no way to analyze the final end of human flourishing, casuistry replaces the notion of moral natures—first of all constituted by reference to an action's "object"—with a tally sheet of sins, both mortal and venial. In brief, for the casuists, moral commands replace moral objects as the way in which one comes to identify right from wrong. The classical casuist model was built upon three foundational pillars: law, liberty, and conscience. Moreover, in order to ensure that something would prompt an individual's moral conscience to follow the law, the casuists developed and enforced a highly refined notion of personal obligation.

Any overly juridical construal of the moral life possesses its own set of built-in tensions. Since casuistry imposes an extrinsic morality on the individual, it remains ill-equipped to satisfy the authentic desires—*velle*—of human nature. One tension which the casuist system engendered resulted from misunderstanding the New Testament contrasts between law and liberty, interpreting them as dramatic conflicts, rather than as complementary expressions of God's saving providence.[3] Because in their system neither *recta ratio* nor the good ends of human flourishing shape human freedom, the casuist moralists were forced to rely on the effective use of moral law as a way of preaching morality. On their account, human freedom requires divine commands (imparted either directly, as in the Decalogue, or mediately, through ecclesiastical and other positive legislation) in order to develop the proper constraints on its powerful dynamism. This view of the moral law led the casuistic moral theologians to divide human actions between two categories: actions that the law controlled (as either enjoined or forbidden) and those that went unregulated (the so-called "free" actions). The latter category includes those actions for which no law applies.

It was left to the casuist moral theologians themselves to establish the

---

3. See Graham Greene, *Monsignor Quixote* (New York: Simon and Shuster, 1982), pp. 74–77, for a good literary representation of this tension.

bounds within which the human person may operate without moral fault. For instance, consider the casuist adage, "Possidet lex, possidet libertas," that is, the one who obeys the law, possesses true liberty. This adage, along with many others that were commonplace, indicates the important role that a correct appropriation of the moral law plays in classical casuistry. Since authentic liberty is achieved only as a result of "possessing" the law, a central task that the casuists assigned to an individual's conscience involves the interpretation of a law's applicability in a given circumstance.

The role of obligation in the moral life receives unprecedented emphasis in casuistry. Some interpreters point out that in the casuist way of looking at morality, obligation itself gained such an importance that simply to fulfill an obligation even took on a value in itself. In other words, if some action were obliged by law, the pursual of the good deed becomes more praiseworthy than if it were not so enjoined. To take one example, spiritual authors of the casuist period regarded religious life as a better form of Christian life simply because its members freely chose to bind themselves by obligation through the vows.

The plan adopted by the moral theology textbooks of the era reflects the casuist conception of morality. The basic plan usually proceeded according to the following standard outline: (1) free, i.e., human, acts; (2) the moral law; (3) conscience and sins. However, when the juridical liability to punishment (either temporal or eternal) no longer psychologically enforces this kind of legalism, conscience quickly ceases to function effectively as part of the practical judgment about the pertinence of moral laws in particular circumstances.

Another tension which exists within the casuist system pertains to the relationship of human action to human flourishing and *beatitudo*. In general, casuist theology did not pose questions such as whether this particular action conduces to happiness or how it stands in relation to human flourishing. The casuists only enquired as to how this action conformed to an existing prescription, and whether on that basis its performance would merit either reward or punishment.

Aquinas places his treatise on beatitude at the very start of his moral theology, and so it shapes everything that follows. In many casuists's manuals, however, this introductory treatise disappears altogether.[4] When an author did make mention of heaven, the reference was found usually in the final chapter, where

---

4. Some casuist authors who include a discussion of the last end include B. H. Merkelbach, *Tractatus de ultimo actuum humanorum fine seu de beatitudine*; Noldin-Heinzel, *Liber Primus, De fine hominis ultimo*; and Regatillo-Zalba, *Pars Prima, Tractatus I, De fine ultimo*.

eschatological considerations brought closure to the argument of the moral textbook. This practice only enforced the view that beatific union with God supplies a reward for having lived a morally good life, whereas the Christian tradition holds that beatitude constitutes a principle from which moral action takes its beginning and from which it receives its definitive shape. A deflated teleology, however, suits the perspectives of casuistry. Since the casuist authors presented virtue mainly in terms of moral obligation, they accordingly presented beatitude as the reward due those who had successfully fulfilled the duty to be virtuous.

The casuists also discarded the doctrines of the *imago Dei* and of the natural desire for God, or at least emptied these of their meaning for moral theology. This happened because casuistry, as a form of moral positivism, failed to discover in sound theological interpretations of anthropology and psychology anything that would contribute significantly to advancing the grounds for moral obligation. Furthermore, according to casuist opinion, collective human experience amply illustrates that men and women desire all kinds of things which they judge, sometimes incorrectly, will make them happy. For similar reasons, casuistry displaced the patristic doctrine of divinization in favor of a moral legalism that describes the moral life in terms of blameworthiness and praiseworthiness. Why? Just as the casuist authors distrusted theological anthropology to support the juridical claims of casuistry, so they distrusted divinization to provide a sure foundation for moral argumentation.

Casuistry also fosters subjectivism. This feature of casuistry generated one of the least commendable features found in some pre-conciliar schools of Catholic moral theology, namely, excessive concern for private morality. We discover one sign of this imbalance in the excessive consideration that the casuists expended on determining the state of the unsure or doubtful conscience. Doubtful conscience meant that a person experiences uncertainty about what the moral law requires in a particular circumstance. Such uncertainty was all too common within the context of the casuist systems in which moralists held such a great diversity of opinions about serious issues of the moral life and which stressed the attention that the faithful were required to give to these "approved authors." Consonant with a legalistic mode of moral theology, casuistry promoted the practice of "consulting approved authors" as a necessary step in the process of accurately informing one's conscience.[5]

---

5. Sometimes persons received bad advice. For an overview of some contemporary authors' views on the erroneous conscience, see James F. Keenan, S.J., "Can a Wrong

Persons were accustomed to consult experts when a moral dilemma arose. A perplexed individual had to consider how various authors "solved" the particular "case"—from which the name "casuistry" derives. Then, depending on the school to which such an individual—or, in the ordinary run of events, to which his or her confessor ascribed—the person would apply that school's approved solution according to the specific circumstances of the "case." In this way, however, the casuist system turns the new law of grace into something which looks very much like the old law of written precepts and commentary. Moral realism, on the other hand, insists that one can know the truth about moral matters, and that a well-developed conscience is found in a person whose prudence is informed by divine wisdom mediated through the Church's Magisterium.

As casuistry involves the weighing of collected moral opinions in order to arrive at a course of action, a certain mathematical approach to morality emerges in this approach to the moral life. In fact, the various schools of casuistry arose because of the different opinions scholars held concerning how to settle the case of the perplexed conscience.[6] Historians of the period usually enumerate the main schools of casuistry as follows: Laxism, Probabilism, Probabiliorism, Aequiprobabilism, Rigorism/Tutiorism.

Laxism

As the most permissive school of casuistry, laxists held that as long as the perplexus could ferret out at least one approved authority to support a moral action, the course could be followed as morally justifiable. Highly permissive laxists even mooted exceptions to the natural law, for example, during the carnival season. Although sometimes unfairly associated with the Jesuits as a result of Pascal's *Lettres provinciales* (1656), many diverse authors in fact contributed to the flow of laxist opinions. Laxism embodies the first modern attempt in Roman Catholic moral theology to turn an individual's opinion into a universal rule for everyone. Because of the patent abuses which this approach may easily generate, the Holy See issued condemnations of Laxism between 1659 and 1679.

Action Be Good? The Development of Theological Opinion on Erroneous Conscience," *Église et Théologie* 24 (1993): 205–19.

6. Historians of theology note that the development of the casuistic mode of moral theology gained considerable impetus from the directives of the Council of Trent for priestly formation. This reflected the concern of the Council that the faithful receive suitable instruction in matters that pertained to Christian doctrine and the moral life.

Probabilism

The Spanish Dominican Bartholomew Medina gave this theory its classical expression in his sixteenth-century commentary on the *Summa theologiae* (1577). Contrary to common opinion, both Dominicans and members of the Society of Jesus developed this school during the course of the sixteenth century. Probabilism adopted the principle that, if the probity or impropriety of an action is in question, it is lawful to follow a solidly probable opinion favoring liberty, even though the opposing opinion, favoring the law, remains more probable. Probabilism allowed its adherents to follow a course of action that did not enjoy the support of a majority of approved authors.

One could imagine that the probabilists were the proponents of a "new morality" in the sixteenth century.[7] To grant them the most favorable interpretation, the probabilist authors most likely wanted to ease the burden of a moral jurisprudence that may have become too restrictive. Such restrictiveness constituted a special burden for certain classes of people who were obliged to deal with an increasingly secular society. For example, recall that the *raison d'etat*, as a convention that provides diplomats in certain circumstances with an expedient alternative to telling the truth, comes into prominence during the casuist epoch. Towards the middle of the seventeenth century (c. 1656), however, the Dominicans had begun to react to some interpretations of Probabilism as expressed by the noted Jesuit moralists Gabriel Vázquez (1549–1604) and Francisco de Suarez (1548–1617).

Probabiliorism

Why seek a more probable opinion? The Dominicans recognized the danger inherent in moral guidance which depends too much on human autonomy, and which may even become susceptible to personal whimsy. In order to promote moral decisions based on sound and universal doctrine, they sought to correct the potential deficiencies of this system by promoting another method for determining right conduct. Probabiliorism encouraged a *perplexus* to develop his or her prudence on the basis of a *consensus* of approved authors, instead of relying on the restricted and partial consensus that probabilism allowed. This "more probable" way guaranteed, so they argued, a surer and safer form of moral guid-

---

7. For a late-nineteenth-century example of how the Dominicans reacted to probabilism, see Marie Ambroise Potton, O.P., *De Theoria Probabilitatis. Dissertatio Theologica* (Paris: Poussielgue, 1874).

ance—one that found its value in the combined wisdom of many prudent and experienced authors.

The conflict between the Dominicans and the Jesuits on the question of Probabilism withered by the mid-eighteenth century. St. Alphonsus Ligouri tried to overcome the difficulty by promoting a compromise position called Aequiprobabilism. Although a different name was employed to avoid recapitulating worn-out polemics, this system resulted in essentially the same practice as that promoted by Dominican moralists. In brief, Aequiprobabilism disallowed appeal to marginal opinions about important moral questions. Nonetheless, the Dominican Inquisitor forbade the saint's works to enter the Kingdom of Naples. Acting on a solidly probable opinion, however, St. Alphonsus overcame this obstacle by crossing the Bay of Naples stealthily and under the cover of darkness in a dinghy, and his pastoral work in the Church earned him the title of heavenly patron for all moral theologians.[8]

Rigorism or Tutiorism

At the other end of the spectrum of casuist systems lies Rigorism or Tutiorism. This position allowed no room for independent maneuver, but obliged its unhappy and misguided adherents always to follow the strictest course of moral action. Personal initiative enjoyed no place among the rigorists—outright submission formed the only model for the Christian life. Rigorism/Tutiorism developed principally in reaction to certain extravagances of those casuist systems that allowed intelligent people to manipulate the legal categories to the extent that sanction for any sort of moral behavior came easily. This pattern lead to a depreciation of Gospel fervor, and the backlash quickly produced its own extravagance.

But neither the lack of personal creativity among the tutiorists nor the risk of uncontrolled autonomy among the laxists constitutes casuistry's most significant defect. Above all, casuistry lacks a theological foundation. For only with difficulty did moral deontologies succeed in relating their structure intrinsically to the good of the human person and the mysteries of faith. It remains one of the most interesting phenomena in the history of theology that a practice that had generated so much debate and literature, and which had dominated the lives of Catholic, and even non-Catholic, faithful vanished almost completely within a decade after the Second Vatican Council.

---

8. See *Veritatis splendor*, no. 78.

Eight Features of Casuist Moral Theology

Servais Pinckaers identifies eight distinct features of casuist moral theology.[9] Compared to the perspectives adopted by the 1993 encyclical *Veritatis splendor*, it is possible now to recognize in these emphases of casuistic moral theology certain theoretical deficiencies. The renewal of moral instruction and theology in the Church should proceed without a repristination of the following errors promoted in the casuist manuals.

1. *The atomization of the moral action.* When one conceives human action in accord with the liberty of indifference, there occurs an atomization or splintering of moral activity. In the casuist system, acting in order to respect a law replaces acting for a purpose, or for an end. In other words, since there unfolds no prudential movement through the *ea quae sunt ad finem* toward an ultimate and specifying good end, there is no hierarchy of divine things that provides structure for or gives context to the moral life.[10] Instead, casuistry views each discreet action as an independent and isolated moment within the moral life. Moreover, since the liberty of indifference does not directly envision man as set between God as first principle and God as our beatitude, casuistry does not adequately cognize or explain the dynamism of the moral life. The chief dynamism in casuistry coincides with its moralistic spirit and arises from whatever psychological strictures the concepts of duty and obligation are able to impose on a given person.

2. *Final Cause.* Like nominalism, casuistry practically eschews the notion of final causality. The absence of any reference to final cause, exemplified by the omission of an adequate account of the New Testament Beatitudes and our final beatitude, implies that no effective final end exists for the human person, and, therefore, no end draws him or her. To fill the place of final causality, the casuists stressed obedience, which becomes the fundamental virtue of the casuist systems. Building on a natural sense of duty, this virtue compensates for the missing elan which "tending toward the good" (*intendere*) provides in teleological systems. Whereas a teleological account of the moral life, such as *Veritatis splendor* endorses, contextualizes obedience in the light of the graced perfection of the human person, casuistic accounts wrench obedience from its place in the

---

9. This analysis first appeared in his essay "La nature de la moralité: morale casuistique et morale thomiste," in *Somme théologique. Les actes humains*, vol. 2, trans. S. Pinckaers (Paris: Desclée & Cie, 1966), pp. 215–76.

10. For an interesting account of order in the moral life, see Thomas S. Hibbs, "The Hierarchy of Moral Discourses in Aquinas," *American Catholic Philosophical Quarterly* 64 (1990): 199–214.

constellation of human virtues, rendering it virtually the sole denominator of
the good. Consider some examples from mid-twentieth-century religious life.
When obedience serves as the architectonic virtue, it easily occasions the exercise of an autocratic spirit by those in authority and a correlative servile spirit in
those who serve under them.

3. *Disappearance of virtuous disposition.* Because the casuists confined their analysis of human freedom to the actual moment of free choice, these authors were
unable to find a place for the virtuous dispositions that shape the character of
the free person. The temptation to relegate the virtues to the field of spirituality
still manifests itself among some moralists. On the other hand, moral realism
describes virtue as a constant disposition or *habitus* for acting well. And classical
moral theology considers these good qualities as stable dispositions of character
which make the moral activity of the individual prompt, easy, and joyful. In the
casuist systems, moral calculation replaced moral virtues, and obligation supplied for inclination. Also, because of the emphasis put on the "moment" of free
choice, the abiding gifts of the Holy Spirit that assist the enactment of virtuous
deeds fell out of active consideration in the casuist systems.

4. *The punctual character of human autonomy.* Casuistry fostered a view of the human person in which the role of the will predominates to the exclusion of other human powers such as the intellect and the sense appetites. Classical ethical
teaching considered the whole person, and affirmed that all of the soul's powers, or capacities, were as suitable subjects from which virtuous, free activity
may originate. Therefore, genuine virtuous activity does not simply result from
the will's commanding other human powers to act in a certain way or to refrain
from acting. It is important to recall that moral dispositions such as continence
and perseverance fail to measure up to the complete definition of virtue. Casuistry overlooked the fact that the formation of virtuous character involves a synergy of activities in which the intellect, will, and sense appetites reciprocally affect one another.

The liberty of indifference favors a dualist anthropology insofar as the theory envisions the will as set over and against the rest of the powers of the human
person. This may explain why casuist moral theology took a disproportionate
interest in regulating sexual morality. No greater threat to the liberty of indifference could be imagined than the sudden upsurge of bad lust. So every precau-
tion had to be taken to maintain the serene "indifference" of the will in the face
of some *de facto*, especially unexpected, compelling good. Recall that, according
to the casuist theorists, no factor outside of the will itself could set human willing effectively upon a particular course of action.

5. *Extrinsicist view of law and liberty.* Classical Christian moral theology assumed that the natural law is an imprint (*participatio*) of the eternal law in the rational creature. This profoundly interior conception of the wellspring of morality finds no equivalent explanation in the casuist plan. Rather, all law represents something extrinsic to the human person and constitutes a limitation on the person's God-given autonomy. Perhaps the critical juncture concerns the mode of promulgation of the natural law, as well as the mode of this law's efficacy. Rather than discerning that creation itself, in its very inwardness, participates the eternal law and groans for its completion in grace, the casuist account confines its treatment of law to the fonts of its promulgation. Thus divine precepts are voluntaristically taken as first expressing the "will" of God, of the Church, of civil authority, or of some other legitimate power, with the result that any constellation of rightful commands usurps the contextualizing role of providence and virtue in the moral life. What is most pernicious about this view of law is that it easily fosters, on the one hand, an attitude of suspicion toward the law and, on the other, the kind of libertarianism that makes each one master of himself. The classical view that law—whether it be the natural law or the new law of grace—moves the human person from within, forms no part of the casuists' conception.

This fatal abstraction from the inward attraction and intrinsic efficacy of natural and divine law produces a Christian morality that approximates more the spirit of the old dispensation than the teaching of the New Testament. It is also interesting to note that this extrinsicist view of law[11] promotes a heavy reliance in moral theology on the distinction between so-called "subjective" morality and "objective" morality. This happens because human subjectivity needs some arena in which to take shelter from the stern objectivism of the law and its claim to universality. Once we accept this distinction, however, a great deal has been lost both to the Church and to authentic moral theory. It belongs to the moral theologian to employ some means to safeguard and to represent the requirements of a common nature and of our common life together. Curiously, al-

---

11. Of course, there are respects in which the natural law is rightly described as extrinsic, in that it is promulgated by God in the creation of nature and is not simply identical with nature, of which it is the eternal norm. But the mode of its promulgation via creation renders our awareness of it, and its moving power in our lives, to be inward and not merely externalized. A highly refined analogical metaphysic of participation is the root of St. Thomas's account, safeguarding both the divine transcendence of the eternal law and its inward natural impress whereby it guides our lives. See Chapter Two, pp. 77–83.

though situation ethics sought to alleviate the burdensome objectivity and universality of this view of the moral law, it succumbed to the same extrinsic and particular account.

6. *The juridicism of casuistry.* According to the casuists, the practice of moral theology is best suited to those trained in the legal profession. In their view, secular jurisprudence provides the best model for a properly theological science. As a matter of fact, canon lawyers exercised great influence in the development of moral theology during the casuist epoch, even with regard to regulating the dispensation of the sacraments. Casuistic moral theology resolved moral difficulties in much the same way as the competing claims of two clients are arbitrated by a judge. The Council of Trent in fact had described the confessor as a judge.[12] Although we can suitably incorporate this description into a broader sacramentalist notion of reconciliation, the metaphor by itself risks a distorted image of the purpose of the sacrament in the Christian moral life.

7. *Individualism.* Casuistry fostered individualism and, therefore, failed to stress the social character of Christian life. The casuist conception of the individual's relationship with God practically excluded the place that love of neighbor holds in the Gospel. And this personal relationship with God transformed the sacrament of Penance almost wholly into a personal experience of purification, occluding its character as an ecclesial action of reconciliation. As the Church reflects in the post-synodal exhortation *Reconciliatio et paenitentia*, the sacrament of Penance and Reconciliation is still recovering from the reaction to this casuist exaggeration.[13]

Individualism also promotes an exaggerated view of the role of conscience in the moral decision-making process. The casuist view of individual conscience and responsibility seems to encourage a line of demarcation between maximal exercise of free will and adherence to the divine will. Casuistry forgets that the movement of authentic human freedom and the just demands of the moral law both are ordered toward the same ultimate end. Conscience comes to be preoccupied with arbitrating human freedom and establishing the frontiers of human autonomy. The emergence of dissent in the Church probably owes, paradoxically, a great deal to the casuists' perspective on the role of the individual in the moral life.[14]

---

12. The Council of Trent, Session 14 (25 November 1551), chapter 6 (DS 1685): "... sed ad instar actus iudicialis, quo ab ipso velut a iudice sententia pronunciatur."

13. See especially no. 16 and its analysis of the proper use of the expression "social sin."

14. See Congregation for the Doctrine of the Faith, "Instruction on the Ecclesial

8. *Minimalism.* Although the more uplifted authors of the casuist tradition may not appear to promote a niggardly spirit, minimalism is built into the casuist model. Emphasis on observance of norms and precepts risks communicating to those who are unable to situate these directives in a larger context a narrow view of Christian life and perfection. Such emphasis also makes it difficult to associate the goal of the Christian life with the fullness of life described in the Sermon on the Mount. The New Testament rejects straining out the gnat and swallowing the camel (see Mt 23:24). The human person created as *imago Dei* is destined to participate in the fullness of divine life, and should not be reduced to a puny lawyer constantly looking to satisfy the claims law has made against him. In the casuist scheme of things, sometimes he wins the case, and at other times he loses it. In any event, the anthropology of the imago Dei frequently is submerged in and distorted by the process of moral calculations that casuistry requires of the Christian.

Given its preference for the moral minimum, it is small wonder that casuistry effected a divorce between spiritual or ascetic theology and moral theology. Elaborations on the mystical life, such as those that draw upon what the Greek Fathers taught about divinization, are absent from both the casuist manuals and mentality. What promoted this dissociation of law from life? The important features of the moral life that the mystical tradition emphasizes ostensibly impose no clear-cut obligation. Because they place no concrete and specific demands on conscience-although some positive demands do result from the theological virtues, e.g., to profess the faith—spiritual goods such as prayer, asceticism, benevolence, grace, faith, hope, and even the practice of charity escape the everyday interest of a moral theology which relies predominantly on juridically formulated obligation.

This casuistic emphasis on doing the minimum produces a certain irony. Since the fullness of the divine life and the energies which it supplies for the creature fall out of their proper place in moral theology, casuistry actually loses its driving-power. For the New Testament asserts only one primary obligation in the Christian life, namely, that the member of Christ remain united with him. According to the witness of the Johannine Gospel, it is Jesus himself who teaches his disciples that "apart from me you can do nothing"(Jn 15:5).

Vocation of the Theologian," nos. 32–41, especially, "Finally, argumentation appealing to the obligation to follow one's conscience cannot legitimate dissent.... Conscience is not an independent and infallible faculty. It is an act of moral judgment regarding a responsible choice. A right conscience is one duly illumined by faith and by the objective moral law and it presupposes, as well, the uprightness of the will in the pursuit of the true good" (no. 38).

Conclusion

After the Second Vatican Council, casuistry suffered a serious reverse. This eclipse of the casuist model is one of the most remarkable signs of renewal effected by the Second Vatican Council. However, the rebuilding of moral theology requires that we bear in mind the excesses and misdirections of the casuist authors. Certain features of casuistry may reappear in modern dress.[15] Foremost among these undesirable marks of casuistry are the appeal to conscience as a way to escape observance of the moral law and the tendency to evaluate moral acts only with reference to their immediate context.

A casuistic mentality generates problems for the proper exercise of authority in the Church. The teaching authority of the Church, the Magisterium, suffers to the extent that it is assimilated into a casuist schema of authorities. It constitutes poor pastoral practice to explain only "what the Church teaches" to people who are not properly prepared to appreciate how any particular norm promotes human and spiritual well-being. When due consideration is given to the way that the Church presents the moral life, especially in the *Catechism of the Catholic Church* and *Veritatis splendor*, we see that all forms of ecclesiastical moral positivism fall short of communicating the full dimensions of what the Church in fact teaches about the Christian life.

The moral life is coincident with the Christian believer's relationship to God in Christ and through the power of the Holy Spirit. No other *locus* than the indwelling of the blessed Trinity, lived in a context of ecclesial communion and liturgical prayer, can provide the "setting" for living the Christian life. No explanation for moral activity separated from the life of divine grace, celebrated worthily within the Church's sacraments, is adequate to the believer's following of that vocation. Yet these are the very factors that many contemporary theorists, including some Catholic theologians, habitually leave out of their lessons on moral theology.

15. For instance, see my review of Albert R. Jonsen and Stephen Toulmin, *The Abuse of Casuistry* in *The Thomist* 54 (1990): 151–54.

Select Bibliography

This bibliography includes mostly recent literature in English, including a few works not mentioned in the footnotes. Other items, including the documents of ecumenical councils, pontifical and ecclesiastical documents, citations from ecclesiastical writers, including the works of St. Thomas Aquinas, and references to ancient classical authors are cited fully in the appropriate notes.

Adler, Mortimer. "A Question about Law." In *Essays in Thomism*, edited by R. E. Brennan, pp. 207–36. New York: The Thomist Press, 1942.

Aertson, Jan. *Nature and Creature: Thomas Aquinas's Way of Thought*. Translated by H. D. Morton. Leiden: E. J. Brill, 1988.

Albacete, Lorenzo. "The Relevance of Christ or the *sequela Christi?*" *Communio* 21 (1994): 252–64.

Anscombe, G. E. M. "Modern Moral Philosophy." *Philosophy* 33 (1958). Reprinted in *Ethics, Religion and Politics*. Minneapolis: University of Minnesota Press, 1982.

Armstrong, Ross A. *Primary and Secondary Precepts in Thomistic Natural Law Teaching*. The Hague: Martinus Nijhoff, 1966.

Ashley, Benedict M., O.P. *Choosing a World-View and Value-System*. New York: Alba House, 2000.

———. *Living the Truth in Love. A Biblical Introduction to Moral Theology*. Staten Island, N.Y.: Alba House, 1996.

———. "What Is the End of the Human Person? The Vision of God and Integral Human Fulfillment." In *Moral Truth and Moral Tradition. Essays in Honour of Peter Geach and Elizabeth Anscombe*, edited by Luke Gormally, pp. 68–96. Dublin: Four Courts Press, 1994.

———. "Thomism and the Transition from the Classical World View to Historical Mindedness." In *The Future of Thomism*, edited by Deal W. Hudson and Dennis William Moran, pp. 109–21. South Bend, Ind.: American Maritain Association, 1992.

———. "The River Forest School and the Philosophy of Nature Today." In *Philosophy and the God of Abraham*, edited by R. James Long, pp. 1–16. Toronto: Pontifical Institute of Mediaeval Studies, 1991.

———. *Theologies of the Body: Humanist and Christian*. Brighton, Mass.: Pope John XXIII Center, 1985.

Balthasar, Hans Urs von. "Nine Theses in Christian Ethics." In *International Theological Commission: Texts and Documents 1969–1985*, edited by Michael Sharkey, pp. 105–20. San Francisco: Ignatius Press, 1989.

Beards, Andrew. "Christianity, 'Interculturality,' and Salvation: Some Perspectives from Lonergan." *The Thomist* 64 (2000): 161–210.

———. *Objectivity and Historical Understanding.* Brookfield, Vt.: Avebury, 1997.

Bedouelle, Guy, Romanus Cessario, and Kevin White, eds. *Jean Capreolus en son temps (1380–1444). Mémoire Dominicaine,* numéro spécial, 1. Paris: Les Éditions du Cerf, 1997.

Bertone, Tarcisio, S.D.B. "The Magisterium of the Church and the Professio Fidei." In *Proclaiming the Truth of Jesus Christ: Papers from the Vallombrosa Meeting,* pp. 31–48. Washington, D.C.: United States Catholic Conference, 2000.

Blackburn, S. W. "Moral Realism." In *Morality and Moral Reasoning,* edited by John Casey, pp. 101–24. London: Methuen, 1971.

Blanchette, Oliva. *The Perfection of the Universe According to Aquinas: A Teleological Cosmology.* University Park, Pa.: Pennsylvania State University Press, 1992.

Boler, John. "Aquinas on Exceptions in Natural Law." In *Aquinas's Moral Theory. Essays in Honor of Norman Kretzmann,* edited by Scott MacDonald and Eleonore Stump, pp. 161–204. Ithaca, N.Y.: Cornell University Press, 1999.

Bourke, Vernon J. "The Background of Aquinas' Synderesis Principle." In *Graceful Reason,* edited by Lloyd P. Gerson, pp. 345–60. Toronto: Pontifical Institute of Mediaeval Studies, 1983.

———. "Is Thomas Aquinas a Natural Law Ethicist?" *The Monist* 58 (1974): 52–66.

Bowlin, John R. "Psychology and Theodicy in Aquinas." *Medieval Philosophy and Theology* 7 (1998): 129–56.

Boyle, Leonard, O.P. "The Setting of the *Summa theologiae* of Saint Thomas." Etienne Gilson Lecture Series, no. 5. Toronto: Pontifical Institute of Mediaeval Studies, 1982.

Brock, Stephen L. *Action and Conduct: Thomas Aquinas and the Theory of Action.* Edinburgh: T&T Clark, 1998.

Brocklehurst, Mark, O.P. "The *Summa theologiae* and Modern Ethical Thought." *Dominican Studies* 1 (1948): 195–208.

Brown, Oscar J. *Natural Rectitude and Divine Law in Aquinas.* Toronto: Pontifical Institute of Mediaeval Studies, 1981.

Cahill, J., O.P. "The Sapiential Character of Moral Theology." *Irish Theological Quarterly* 27 (1960): 132–45.

Cahill, Lisa Sowle. "Teleology, Utilitarianism, and Christian Ethics." *Theological Studies* 42 (1981): 601–29.

Carré, Ambroise-Marie. *Le Christ de Saint Thomas d'Aquin.* Paris: Revue des jeunes, 1944.

Cessario, Romanus, O.P. "The Trinitarian Imprint on the Moral Life." In *The Oxford Handbook of the Trinity,* edited by Gilles Emery and Matthew Levering, pp. 487–92. Oxford: Oxford University Press, 2011.

———. *The Moral Virtues and Theological Ethics.* Notre Dame, Ind.: University of Notre Dame Press, 1991, 2008.

———. *Virtues.* Münster: Lit Verlag, 2001.

———. "What the Angels See at Twilight." *Communio* 26 (1999): 583–94.

———. *Le thomisme et les thomistes.* Paris: Les Éditions du Cerf, 1999.

———. "On Bad Actions, Good Intentions, and Loving God: Three Much-Misunderstood Issues about the Happy Life That St. Thomas Clarifies for Us." *Logos* 1.2 (1997): 100–124.

———. "Epieikeia and the Accomplishment of the Just." In *Aquinas and Empowerment: Classical Ethics for Ordinary Lives,* edited by G. Simon Harak, pp. 170–205. Washington, D.C.: Georgetown University Press, 1996.

———. *Christian Faith and the Theological Life.* Washington, D.C.: The Catholic University of America Press, 1996.

———. "Moral Absolutes in the Civilization of Love." *Crisis* 13 (May 1995): 18–23.

———. "Boethius, Christ, and the New Order." *Carmina Philosophiae* 1 (1992): 53–64.

———. *The Godly Image.* Petersham, Mass.: St. Bede's Publications, 1990.

Chenu, M.-D., O.P. *Towards Understanding St. Thomas.* Translated by A.-M. Landry, O.P., and D. Hughes, O.P. Chicago: Henry Regnery Company, 1964.

Connery, John R., S.J. "The Non-Infallible Moral Teaching of the Church." *The Thomist* 51 (1987): 1–16.

Corbett, John Dominic, O.P. *Sacra Doctrina and the Discernment of Human Action.* Washington, D.C., n.p., 1999.

Cranston, Maurice. *The Noble Savage: Jean-Jacques Rousseau 1754–1762.* Chicago: University of Chicago Press, 1991.

Crowe, Michael Bertram. *The Changing Profile of the Natural Law.* The Hague: Martinus Nijhoff, 1977.

———. "Natural Law Theory Today." In *The Future of Ethics and Moral Theology,* edited by D. Brezine and J. McGlynn, S.J., pp. 78–105. Chicago: Argus, 1968.

———. "Human Nature—Immutable or Mutable?" *Irish Theological Quarterly* 30 (1963): 204–31.

Damich, Edward. "The Essence of Law according to Thomas Aquinas." *American Journal of Jurisprudence* 30 (1985): 79–96.

Dauphinais, Michael A. "Loving the Lord Your God: The *Imago Dei* in Saint Thomas Aquinas." *The Thomist* 63 (1999): 241–67.

DiNoia, J. A., O.P. "Communion and Magisterium: Teaching Theology and the Culture of Grace." Modern Theology 9 (1993): 403–18.

DiNoia, J. A., O.P., and Romanus Cessario, O.P. *Veritatis Splendor and the Renewal of Moral Theology.* Chicago: Midwest Theological Forum, 1999.

Donohoo, Lawrence J., O.P. "The Nature and Grace of *Sacra Doctrina* in St. Thomas's *Super Boetium De Trinitate.*" *The Thomist* 63 (1999): 343–401.

Dougherty, Jude P. "Thomism," in *Encyclopedia of Applied Ethics.* Volume 4, pp. 365–72. Academic Press, 1998.

Dulles, Avery., S.J. "Criteria of Catholic Theology." *Communio* 22 (1995): 303–15.

Dwyer, John C. *Foundations of Christian Ethics.* New York: Paulist Press, 1987.

Edwards, Steven Anthony. "Structure and Change in Aquinas's Religious Ethics." *Journal of the American Academy of Religion* 54 (1986): 281–302.

Emonet, Pierre-Marie. *God Seen in the Mirror of the World. An Introduction to the Philosophy of God.* New York: Herder & Herder, 2000.

Ernst, Cornelius., O.P. "Metaphor and Ontology in Sacra Doctrina." *The Thomist* 38 (1974): 403–25.

Eschmann, Ignatius. "The Ethics of the Image of God." In *The Ethics of Saint Thomas Aquinas. Two Courses,* edited by Edward A. Synan, pp. 159–231. Toronto: Pontifical Institute of Mediaeval Studies, 1997.

Evans, Illtud, O.P., ed. *New Light on the Natural Law.* London: Burns & Oates, 1965.

Fabro, Cornelio. *Participation et causalité selon s. Thomas d' Aquin.* Louvain: Publications Universitaires, 1961.

Farley, Edward. *Theologia.* Philadelphia: Fortress Press, 1983.

Farrell, Walter. *The Natural Moral Law according to St. Thomas and Suarez.* Ditchling: Saint Dominic's Press, 1930.

de Finance, Joseph. *Etre et agir dans la philosophie de saint Thomas.* Paris: Beauchesne, 1945.

Finnis, John. *Aquinas: Moral, Political, and Legal Theory.* Oxford: Oxford University Press, 1998.

––––––. *"Historical Consciousness" and Theological Foundations.* Etienne Gilson Lecture Series, no. 15. Toronto: Pontifical Institute of Mediaeval Studies, 1992.

––––––. "Object and Intention in Aquinas." *The Thomist* 55 (1991): 3–10.

––––––. *Fundamentals of Ethics.* Washington, D.C.: Georgetown University Press, 1983.

––––––. "Natural Law and the Is-Ought Question: An Invitation to Professor Veatch." *The Catholic Lawyer* 26 (1980–81): 266–77.

––––––. *Natural Law and Natural Rights.* Oxford: Clarendon Press, 1980.

Flynn, Thomas V., O.P. "The Cogitative Power." *The Thomist* 16 (1953): 542–63.

Ford, John, S.J., and Germain Grisez. "Contraception and the Infallibility of the Ordinary Magisterium." *Theological Studies* 39 (1978): 258–312.

Fortin, Ernest. "On the Presumed Medieval Origin of Individual Rights." In Ernest L. Fortin, *Collected Essays, Classical Christianity and the Political Order. Reflections on the Theologico-Political Problem,* edited by J. Brian Benestad, pp. 243–64. New York: Rowman & Littlefield, 1996.

Frankena, William F. *Ethics.* Englewood Cliffs, N.J.: Prentice-Hall, Inc., 1973.

Fuchs, Josef. *Natural Law: A Theological Investigation.* New York: Sheed & Ward, 1965.

––––––. *Theologia Moralis Generalis.* Rome: Gregorian University, 1954.

Gamwell, Franklin I. "Moral Realism and Religion." *Journal of Religion* 73 (1993): 475–95.

Garcia de Haro, Ramón. *Cristo, Fundamento de la Moral.* Barcelona: Ediciones Internacionales Universitarias, 1990.

Gardeil, Ambroise. *Le donné révélé et la théologie.* Paris: Éditions du Cerf, 1932.

Gauthier, R.-A. "Quelques questions à propos du commentaire de S. Thomas sur le De anima." *Angelicum* 51 (1974): 419–72.

Geenen, Gottfried, O.P. "The Council of Chalcedon in the Theology of Saint Thomas." In *From an Abundant Spring,* pp. 172–217. New York: P. J. Kenedy & Sons, 1952.

Geiger, Louis-Bertrand, O.P. *La participation dans la philosophie de S. Thomas d'Aquin.* Paris: J. Vrin, 1942.

George, Robert P. "Recent Criticism of Natural Law Theory." *University of Chicago Law Review* 55 (1988): 1371–1429.

George, Robert P., and Christopher Wolfe, eds. *Natural Law and Public Reason.* Washington, D.C.: Georgetown University Press, 2000.

Gilby, Thomas, O.P. *Psychology of Human Acts.* Volume 17 of the Blackfriars *Summa.* New York: McGraw-Hill Book Company, 1970.

———. *Purpose and Happiness.* Volume 16 of the Blackfriars *Summa.* New York: McGraw-Hill Book Company, 1969.

———. *Law and Political Theory.* Volume 28 of the Blackfriars *Summa.* New York: McGraw-Hill Book Company, 1966.

———. *Principles of Morality.* Volume 18 of the Blackfriars *Summa.* New York: McGraw-Hill Book Company, 1966.

Glendon, Mary Ann. "Rousseau and the Revolt against Reason." *First Things* 96 (1999): 42–47.

Grisez, Germain. "A Critique of Russell Hittinger's Book, *A Critique of the New Natural Law Theory.*" *New Scholasticism* 42 (1988): 438–65.

———. *The Way of the Lord Jesus.* Vol. 1, *Christian Moral Principles,* with the help of Joseph M. Boyle, Jr., Basil Cole, O.P., John Finnis, John A. Geinzer, Robert G. Kennedy, Patrick Lee, William E. May, and Russell Shaw. Chicago: Franciscan Herald Press, 1983.

———. *Contraception and Natural Law.* Milwaukee: Bruce Publishing Company, 1964.

Gustafson, James M. *Ethics from a Theocentric Perspective.* Volume 1, *Theology and Ethics.* Volume 2, *Ethics and Theology.* Chicago: University of Chicago Press, 1981, 1984.

Hauerwas, Stanley. *Character and the Christian Life: A Study in Theological Ethics.* San Antonio: Trinity University Press, 1975.

Hayen, André. *Saint Thomas d'Aquin et la vie de l'Eglise.* Essais philosophiques 6. Louvain and Paris: Publications universitaires, 1952.

Hayes, Zachary, O.F.M. *The Hidden Center: Spirituality and Speculative Christology in St. Bonaventure.* New York: Paulist Press, 1981.

Hibbs, Thomas S. "Aquinas, Virtue, and Recent Epistemology." *Review of Metaphysics* 52 (1999): 573–94.

———. "Imitatio Christi and the Foundation of Aquinas's Ethics." *Communio* 18 (1991): 556–73.

———. "The Hierarchy of Moral Discourses in Aquinas." *American Catholic Philosophical Quarterly* 64 (1990): 199–214.

———. "A Rhetoric of Motives: Thomas on Obligation as Rational Persuasion." *The Thomist* 54 (1990): 293–309.

Hill, John. "The Debate between McCormick and Frankena." *Irish Theological Quarterly* 49 (1982): 121–33.

Hill, William J. *The Three-Personed God.* Washington, D.C: The Catholic University of America Press, 1982.

Hislop, Ian. "Man, the Image of the Trinity, according to St. Thomas." *Dominican Studies* 3 (1950): 1–9.

Hittinger, Russell. "The Pope and the Theorists." *Crisis* (December 1993): 31–36.

———. "Theology and Natural Law Theory." *Communio* 17 (1990): 402–8.

———. *A Critique of the New Natural Law Theory.* Notre Dame, Ind.: University of Notre Dame Press, 1987.

Hoffmann, Tobias. "The Distinction between Nature and Will in Duns Scotus." *Archives d'Histoire Doctrinale et Littéraire du Moyen Age* 66 (1999): 189–224.

Hoose, Bernard. *Proportionalism: The American Debate and Its European Roots.* Washington, D.C.: Georgetown University Press, 1987.

Hütter, Reinhard. "The Twofold Center of Lutheran Ethics: Christian Freedom and God's Commandments." In *The Promise of Lutheran Ethics*, edited by Karen Bloomquist and John Stumme, 33–38. Minneapolis: Augsburg-Fortress, 1998.

Hume, David. *Treatise of Human Nature.* Edited by L. A. Selby-Bigge. Oxford: Clarendon Press, 1896.

Ingham, Mary Elizabeth. "Practical Wisdom: Scotus's Presentation of Prudence." In *John Duns Scotus: Metaphysics and Ethics*, edited by L. Honnefelder et al., pp. 551–71. Leiden: E. J. Brill, 1996.

Johnson, Mark. "Proportionalism and a Text of the Young Aquinas: Quodlibetum IX, Q. 7, A. 2." *Theological Studies* 53 (1992): 683–99.

Jonsen, Albert R. "Casuistry, Situationism, and Laxism." In *Joseph Fletcher: Memoir of an Ex-Radical*, edited by Kenneth Vaux, pp. 10–24. Louisville, Ky.: John Knox Press, 1993.

Jónsson, Gunnlaugur A. *The Image of God: Genesis 1:26–28 in a Century of Old Testament Research.* Stockholm: Almqvist & Wiksell, 1988.

Johnstone, Brian, C.Ss.R. "The Meaning of Proportional Reason in Contemporary Moral Theology." *The Thomist* 49 (1985): 223–47.

Keenan, James F., S.J. "Can a Wrong Action Be Good? The Development of Theological Opinion on Erroneous Conscience." *Église et Théologie* 24 (1993): 205–19.

———. *Goodness and Rightness in Thomas Aquinas's Summa Theologiae.* Washington, D.C.: Georgetown University Press, 1992.

Kent, Bonnie. *Virtues of the Will: The Transformation of Ethics in the Late Thirteenth Century.* Washington, D.C.: The Catholic University of America Press, 1995.

Koch, Kurt. "Recent Ecumenical Progress and Future Prospects." *Origins* 41 (November 2011).

Kupczak, Jaroslaw, O.P. *Destined for Liberty: The Human Person in the Philosophy of Karol Wojtyla/John Paul II.* Washington, D.C.: The Catholic University of America Press, 2000.

Lamb, Matthew. "The Notion of the Transcultural in Bernard Lonergan's Theology" *Method: Journal of Lonergan Studies* 8 (1990): 48–73.

Langan, John, S.J. "Beatitude and Moral Law in St. Thomas." *Journal of Religious Ethics* 5 (1977): 183–95.

Lee, Patrick. "Permanence of the Ten Commandments: St. Thomas and His Modern Commentators." *Theological Studies* 42 (1981): 422–43.

Levering, Matthew. "Israel and the Shape of Thomas Aquinas's Soteriology." *The Thomist* 63 (1999): 65–82.

Lisska, Anthony J. *Aquinas's Theory of Natural Law: An Analytic Reconstruction.* Oxford: Clarendon Press, 1996.

Lonergan, Bernard, S.J. "The Transition from a Classicist World-View to Historical Mindedness." In *A Second Collection*, edited by William Ryan and Bernard Tyrrell, pp. 1–9. Philadelphia: The Westminster Press, 1974.

———. *Grace and Freedom: Operative Grace in the Thought of St. Thomas Aquinas.* Edited by J. Patout Burns. New York: Herder & Herder, 1971.

Long, Stephen A. *The Teleological Grammar of the Moral Act.* Naples, Fla.: Sapientia Press, 2007.

———. "On the Possibility of a Purely Natural End for Man." *The Thomist* 64 (2000): 211–37.

McDonagh, Enda. *Invitation and Response.* New York: Sheed & Ward, 1972.

McInerny, Daniel. "Deliberation about Final Ends: Thomistic Considerations." In *Recovering Nature: Essays in Natural Philosophy, Ethics, and Metaphysics in Honor of Ralph McInerny*, edited by Thomas Hibbs and John O'Callaghan, pp. 105–25. Notre Dame, Ind.: University of Notre Dame Press, 1999.

McInerny, Ralph. *Aquinas on Human Action. A Theory of Practice.* Washington, D.C.: The Catholic University of America Press, 1992.

———. *Art and Prudence. Studies in the Thought of Jacques Maritain.* Notre Dame, Ind.: University of Notre Dame Press, 1988.

———. *Ethica Thomistica: The Moral Philosophy of Thomas Aquinas.* Washington, D.C.: The Catholic University of America Press, 1982.

MacIntyre, Alasdair. *Dependent Rational Animals. Why Human Beings Need the Virtues.* Chicago and La Salle, Ill.: Open Court, 1998.

———. "Natural Law As Subversive: The Case of Aquinas." *Journal of Medieval and Early Modern Studies* 26 (1996): 61–83.

———. *Three Rival Versions of Moral Enquiry: Encyclopaedia, Genealogy, and Tradition.* Notre Dame, Ind.: University of Notre Dame Press, 1990.

———. *A Short History of Ethics.* New York: Macmillan Publishing Co., Inc., 1966.

McNicholl, Ambrose, O.P. "Person, Sex, and Marriage and Actual Trends of Thought." In *Human Sexuality and Personhood*, pp. 142–52. St. Louis: Pope John Center, 1981.

Mahoney, Edward P. "Albert the Great on Christ and Hierarchy." In *Christ among the Medieval Dominicans: Representations of Christ in the Texts and Images of the Order of Preachers*, edited by Kent Emery Jr., and Joseph Wawrykow, pp. 364–92. Notre Dame, Ind.: University of Notre Dame Press, 1998.

Maritain, Jacques. *La loi naturelle or loi non écrite.* Edited by Georges Brazzola. Fribourg: Editions Universitaires, 1986.

———. *The Person and the Common Good.* Translated by John J. Fitzgerald. New York: Scribner's, 1947.

Mauri, M. "Aristotle on Moral Knowledge." *Studia Moralia* 30 (1992): 227–46.

May, William E. "The Natural Law and Moral Life." In *An Introduction to Moral The-*

ology, rev. ed., pp. 43–105. Huntington, Ind.: Our Sunday Visitor Publishing Division, 1994.

————. "Aquinas and Janssens on the Moral Meaning of Human Acts." *The Thomist* 48 (1984): 566–606.

Melina, Livio. *Sharing in Christ's Virtues. For the Renewal of Moral Theology in Light of Veritatis Splendor.* Translated by William E. May. Washington, D.C.: The Catholic University of America Press, 2001.

Merriell, D. Juvenal. *To the Image of the Trinity: A Study in the Development of Aquinas' Teaching.* Toronto: Pontifical Institute of Mediaeval Studies, 1990.

Monden, Louis. *Sin, Liberty and Law.* New York: Sheed & Ward, 1965.

Muniz, Francisco, O.P. *The Work of Theology.* Translated by John P. Reid, O.P. Washington, D.C.: Thomist Press, 1953.

Murdoch, Iris. *Metaphysics as a Guide to Morals.* New York, N.Y.: Allen Lane, Penguin Press, 1993.

————. *The Sovereignty of Good.* London: Routledge & Kegan Paul, 1971.

Nicolas, Jean-Hervé, O.P. *Synthèse dogmatique.* Fribourg: Editions Universitaires, 1986.

Nichols, Aidan, O.P. *Dominican Gallery: Portrait of a Culture.* Leominster: Gracewing, 1997.

Norton, David Fate. *David Hume: Common-Sense Moralist, Skeptical Metaphysician.* Princeton: Princeton University Press, 1982.

Nussbaum, Martha C. *The Fragility of Goodness. Luck and Ethics in Greek Tragedy and Philosophy.* Cambridge: Cambridge University Press, 1986.

Oberman, Heiko. *The Harvest of Medieval Theology. Gabriel Biel and Late Medieval Nominalism.* Cambridge: Harvard University Press, 1963.

O'Brien, T. C. *Faith.* Volume 31 of the Blackfriars *Summa.* New York: McGraw-Hill Book Company, 1974.

O'Neill, Colman E., O.P. "The Rule Theory of Doctrine and Propositional Truth." *The Thomist* 49 (1985): 417–42.

————. "Analogy, Dialectic and Inter-Confessional Theology." *The Thomist* 47 (1983): 43–65.

Pelikan, Jaroslav. *Confessor between East and West: A Portrait of Ukranian Cardinal Josyf Slipyj.* Grand Rapids, Mich.: Eerdmans, 1990.

Pieper, Josef. *Reality and the Good.* Chicago: H. Regnery, 1967.

Pinckaers, Servais, O.P. *Morality: The Catholic View.* Translated by Michael Sherwin, O.P. South Bend, Ind.: St. Augustine's Press, 2001.

————. *The Pursuit of Happiness—God's Way.* Translated by Sr. Mary Thomas Noble, O.P. New York: Alba House, 1998.

————. *The Sources of Christian Ethics.* Translated by Sr. Mary Thomas Noble, O.P. Washington, D.C.: The Catholic University of America Press, 1995.

————. "The Use of Scripture and the Renewal of Moral Theology: The *Catechism* and *Veritatis splendor.*" *The Thomist* 59 (1995): 1–19.

————. "Virtue Is Not a Habit." *Cross Currents* 12 (1962): 65–81.

Porter, Jean. *The Recovery of Virtue: The Relevance of Aquinas for Christian Ethics.* Louisville, Ky.: Westminster/John Knox Press, 1990.

————. "Desire for God: Ground of the Moral Life in Aquinas." *Theological Studies* 47 (1986): 48–68.

Principe, Walter, C.S.B. "Affectivity and the Heart in Thomas Aquinas' Spirituality." In *Spiritualities of the Heart: Approaches to Personal Wholeness*, edited by Annice Callahan, R.S.C.J., pp. 45–63. New York: Paulist Press, 1990.

Prümmer, Dominicus. *Handbook of Moral Theology*. Translated by Gerald W. Shelton. New York: P. J. Kenedy & Sons, 1957.

Ratzinger, Joseph. "Deus locutus est nobis in Filio: Some Reflections on Subjectivity, Christology, and the Church." In *Proclaiming the Truth of Jesus Christ. Papers from the Vallombrosa Meeting*, pp. 13–30. Washington, D.C.: United States Catholic Conference, 2000.

Ray, A. Chadwick. "A Fact about the Virtues." *The Thomist* 54 (1990): 429–51.

Reilly, James P., Jr. *Saint Thomas on Law*. Etienne Gilson Series, no. 12. Toronto: Pontifical Institute of Medieval Studies, 1990.

Rhonheimer, Martin. *Natural Law and Practical Reason. A Thomist View of Moral Autonomy*. Translated by Gerald Malsbary. New York: Fordham University Press, 2000.

————. "Intentional Actions and the Meaning of Object: A Reply to Richard McCormick." *The Thomist* 59 (1995): 279–311.

————. "'Intrinsically Evil Acts' and the Moral Viewpoint: Clarifying a Central Teaching of Veritatis Splendor." *The Thomist* 58 (1994): 1–39.

Rorem, Paul. *Pseudo-Dionysius. A Commentary on the Texts and an Introduction to Their Influence*. New York: Oxford University Press, 1993.

Ross, James F. "Justice Is Reasonableness: Aquinas on Human Law and Morality." *The Monist* 58 (1974): 86–103.

Sampley, J. Paul. *Walking between the Times: Paul's Moral Reasoning*. Minneapolis: Fortress Press, 1991.

Santamaria, Anthony. "The Parameters of Being and Acting Human: The True Case for Moral Science in the Philosophy of Saint Thomas Aquinas." Ph.D. diss., University of Toronto, 1999.

Schindler, David L. *Heart of the World, Center of the Church. Communio Ecclesiology, Liberalism, and Liberation*. Grand Rapids, Mich.: William B. Eerdman Publishing Company, 1996.

Schmitz, Kenneth L. "The Idealism of the German Romantics." In *The Emergence of German Idealism*, edited by Michael Baur and Daniel O. Dahlstrom, pp. 176–97. Studies in Philosophy and the History of Philosophy, volume 34. Washington, D.C.: The Catholic University of America Press, 1999.

————. *The Gift: Creation*. Milwaukee: Marquette University Press, 1982.

Schüller, Bruno. *Wholly Human. Essays on the Theory and Language of Morality*. Translated by Peter Heinegg. Washington, D.C.: Georgetown University Press, 1986.

Simon, Yves R. *The Tradition of Natural Law. A Philosopher's Reflections*. Edited by Vukan Kuic. Introduction by Russell Hittinger. New York: Fordham University Press, 1992.

Simpson, Peter. *Goodness and Nature. A Defence of Ethical Naturalism*. Dordrecht: Martinus Nijhoff Publishers, 1987.

Smith, Ignatius, O.P. "Aquinas and Some American Freedoms." *The New Scholasticism* 21 (1947): 105–53.

Spicq, Ceslaus, O.P. *Charity and Liberty in the New Testament.* Translated by Francis V. Manning. New York: Alba House, 1965.

Squires, Aelred. "The Doctrine of the Image in the *De Veritate* of St. Thomas." *Dominican Studies* 4 (1951): 165–77.

Sullivan, John Edward. *The Image of God: The Doctrine of St. Augustine and Its Influence.* Dubuque, Iowa: Priory Press, 1963.

Torrell, Jean-Pierre, O.P. *Saint Thomas Aquinas.* Vol. 1, *The Person and His Work.* Translated by Robert Royal. Washington, D.C.: The Catholic University of America Press, 1996.

Vacek, Edward Collins. "Divine-Command, Natural-Law, and Mutual-Love Ethics." *Theological Studies* 57 (1996): 633–53.

Veatch, Henry, and Joseph Rautenberg. "Does the Grisez-Finnis-Boyle Moral Philosophy Rest on a Mistake?" *Review of Metaphysics* 44 (1991): 807–30.

Wadell, Paul J. *The Primacy of Love. An Introduction to the Ethics of Thomas Aquinas.* New York: Paulist Press, 1991.

Weisheipl, James A., O.P. *Friar Thomas D'Aquino. His Life, Thought, and Works.* Washington, D.C.: The Catholic University of America Press, 1983.

Westerman, Pauline C. *The Disintegration of Natural Law Theory.* Leiden: Brill, 1998.

White, Victor, O.P. "Holy Teaching, the Idea of Theology according to St. Thomas Aquinas." *Aquinas Papers* 33. London: Blackfriars Publications, 1958.

Wolfe, Alan. "The Pursuit of Autonomy." *The New York Times Magazine*, May 7, 2000, pp. 53–56.

Index

propositions, 6, 12n
Protestant Reform/Protestantism, 63, 66, 67
Providence, divine, xix, 15, 23, 50–65, 76, 82,
    88, 89, 94, 98, 100, 119, 183, 200, 206, 221,
    229; and freedom, 138–42, 206–7. *See also*
    eternal law
prudence, xxiii, 6, 32, 41, 57n, 83n, 89, 90,
    96n, 111, 116, 123–38, 147, 149, 157, 175, 189,
    201n, 211, 224, 225; and charity, 128; and
    circumstances, 172–74; forms of, 137;
    integral parts of, 136n; sham, 135, 138
Prümmer, Dominic, 74, 109n, 171
Psalms, 84, 136, 186, 194
Pseudo-Dionysius the Areopagite, 4n
psychological freedom, 204–5
Pufendorf, Samuel, 87n
punishment, 19, 63, 92, 93, 101, 132, 163–64,
    222
pure act, 26, 75
purification, 4, 60, 106n, 230
purpose(s), xx, 29, 35, 38, 100, 112, 148, 151, 161,
    162, 167–68, 190, 205, 227. *See also* end(s);
    motive(s)

quality, virtue as. *See habitus*

ratio, 12, 54n, 56, 60, 129, 176
Ratzinger, Joseph, xiv, xvin
Rautenberg, Joseph, 45n
Ray, A. Chadwick, 189n, 190n
reason, xvii, 6–8, 17–18, 38n, 64n, 100, 130,
    162, 195, 200, 206, 213; faith and, 11, 69n,
    117, 120, 191; ordinations of, 149; practical,
    32, 57n, 61, 78, 83, 86n, 90, 96, 110–11,
    124–30, 131, 133–34, 154, 174, 177, 220 (*see
    also* prudence); right (*recta ratio*), 73, 93,
    116, 124, 129, 157, 165, 170–71, 176, 220–21;
    speculative, 60, 83. *See also* intellect;
    knowledge
reasons, eternal, 147. *See also* eternal law
Reconciliatio et paenitentia, 184–85n, 213n, 230
reconciliation, xxiv–xxv, 9, 212–17; sacrament
    of, 145, 212–13, 215, 230
recta ratio. See reason, right
rectitude, 129, 133, 163, 211. *See also* reason, right
redemption, order of, 9, 214
Reformation. *See* Protestant Reform/
    Protestantism

Reilly, James P., Jr., 76n
relations, Trinitarian, 53
"remainder concept," 76
representation, image of, 27
responsibility, xvii, 45, 80, 98, 101–2, 119, 145,
    181, 230
rest (*quies*), 117
revelation: xiii, xx, 7, 15, 19, 22, 23, 47, 52,
    110, 111–12, 117, 119, 121, 137; as adapted to
    human knowing, 5, 17; basis of faith, 5,
    10; in Christ, xiv, 5, 10, 13–14, 28, 50, 55,
    60, 120, 203; reason and, 10–12 (*see also*
    faith, and reason)
Revelation, Book of, 33n
revisionist moral theologians, 67–71, 74, 103
Rhonheimer, Martin, 72n, 110n, 162n, 206n
right, notion of, 39, 45n, 58, 91n
righteousness, 189
right to life, 89
Rigorism, 224, 226
Robinson, J. D., 81n
Roland of Cremona, 88
Roland-Gosselin, M.-D., 150n
Romans, Letter to the, xxiin, 18, 52, 60, 65,
    88, 144, 145, 158, 184, 187, 194, 196, 201, 211
romanticism, 101, 119
Rome, apostolic See of, 2, 13, 224
Romiti, Joseph, 113n
Rommen, Heinrich A., 72n
Rorem, Paul, 4n
Ross, James F., 73n
Roton, Placide de, 188n
Rousseau, Jean-Jacques, 156
Rule of St. Benedict, 185–87

sacra doctrina, xiii, xxn, 1–21, 45, 105, 112, 147
sacraments, xv, xxv, 11, 15, 134, 145, 164, 207n,
    209, 210, 212–15, 230, 232
sacrilege, 174, 207
saints, 16, 17, 26, 50, 63, 118, 131, 138, 144, 202,
    211n, 212; communion of, 121, 177. *See also*
    blessed
Sala, Giovanni B., 65n
Sales, St. Francis de, 212–13
salvation, 5, 6, 10, 14, 15, 51, 59, 65n, 184, 202,
    207; economy of, 13, 52, 77, 164; and
    eternal law, 60–65, 75; history, 46, 52; and
    the moral life, xvii, 112, 143, 164

Introduction to Moral Theology was designed and composed in Centaur by
Kachergis Book Design, Pittsboro, North Carolina, and printed
on 60-pound Nature's Recycled and bound by
McNaughton & Gunn, Saline, Michigan.